Lecture Notes in Computer Science 5471

Commenced Publication in 1973
Founding and Former Series Editors:
Gerhard Goos, Juris Hartmanis, and Jan van Leeuwen

Editorial Board

David Hutchison
Lancaster University, UK

Takeo Kanade
Carnegie Mellon University, Pittsburgh, PA, USA

Josef Kittler
University of Surrey, Guildford, UK

Jon M. Kleinberg
Cornell University, Ithaca, NY, USA

Alfred Kobsa
University of California, Irvine, CA, USA

Friedemann Mattern
ETH Zurich, Switzerland

John C. Mitchell
Stanford University, CA, USA

Moni Naor
Weizmann Institute of Science, Rehovot, Israel

Oscar Nierstrasz
University of Bern, Switzerland

C. Pandu Rangan
Indian Institute of Technology, Madras, India

Bernhard Steffen
University of Dortmund, Germany

Madhu Sudan
Massachusetts Institute of Technology, MA, USA

Demetri Terzopoulos
University of California, Los Angeles, CA, USA

Doug Tygar
University of California, Berkeley, CA, USA

Gerhard Weikum
Max-Planck Institute of Computer Science, Saarbruecken, Germany

Liqun Chen   Chris J. Mitchell
Andrew Martin (Eds.)

Trusted Computing

Second International Conference, Trust 2009
Oxford, UK, April 6-8, 2009
Proceedings

 Springer

Volume Editors

Liqun Chen
Hewlett-Packard Laboratories
Filton Road, Stoke Gifford, Bristol BS34 8QZ, UK
E-mail: liqun.chen@hp.com

Chris J. Mitchell
Royal Holloway, University of London
Information Security Group
Egham, Surrey TW20 0EX,UK
E-mail: c.mitchell@rhul.ac.uk

Andrew Martin
Oxford University
Computing Laboratory
Wolfson Building, Parks Road, Oxford OX1 3QD, UK
E-mail: andrew.martin@comlab.ox.ac.uk

Library of Congress Control Number: 2009921804

CR Subject Classification (1998): D.4.6, K.6.5, E.3, C.2, C.3, D.2, H.4, H.5, K.4

LNCS Sublibrary: SL 4 – Security and Cryptology

ISSN   0302-9743
ISBN-10   3-642-00586-1 Springer Berlin Heidelberg New York
ISBN-13   978-3-642-00586-2 Springer Berlin Heidelberg New York

This work is subject to copyright. All rights are reserved, whether the whole or part of the material is concerned, specifically the rights of translation, reprinting, re-use of illustrations, recitation, broadcasting, reproduction on microfilms or in any other way, and storage in data banks. Duplication of this publication or parts thereof is permitted only under the provisions of the German Copyright Law of September 9, 1965, in its current version, and permission for use must always be obtained from Springer. Violations are liable to prosecution under the German Copyright Law.

springer.com

© Springer-Verlag Berlin Heidelberg 2009
Printed in Germany

Typesetting: Camera-ready by author, data conversion by Scientific Publishing Services, Chennai, India
Printed on acid-free paper   SPIN: 12634439   06/3180   5 4 3 2 1 0

Preface

This volume contains the 15 papers presented in the technical strand of the Trust 2009 conference, held in Oxford, UK in April 2009. Trust 2009 was the second international conference devoted to the technical and socio-economic aspects of trusted computing. The conference had two main strands, one devoted to technical aspects of trusted computing (addressed by these proceedings), and the other devoted to socio-economic aspects.

Trust 2009 built on the successful Trust 2008 conference, held in Villach, Austria in March 2008. The proceedings of Trust 2008, containing 14 papers, were published in volume 4968 of the *Lecture Notes in Computer Science* series.

The technical strand of Trust 2009 contained 15 original papers on the design and application of trusted computing. For these proceedings the papers have been divided into four main categories, namely:

- Implementation of trusted computing
- Attestation
- PKI for trusted computing
- Applications of trusted computing

The 15 papers included here were selected from a total of 33 submissions. The refereeing process was rigorous, involving at least three (and mostly more) independent reports being prepared for each submission. We are very grateful to our hard-working and distinguished Program Committee for doing such an excellent job in a timely fashion. We believe that the result is a high-quality set of papers, some of which have been significantly improved as a result of the refereeing process.

We would also like to thank all the authors who submitted their papers to the technical strand of the Trust 2009 conference, all external referees, and all the attendees of the conference.

It is intended that this conference is the second in an annual series of conferences devoted to trusted computing, and we look forward to Trust 2010.

January 2009

Liqun Chen
Chris Mitchell

Organization

Trust 2009

The Second International Conference on Trusted Computing
(Technical Strand) was held at St. Hugh's College, Oxford, UK during
April 6–8, 2009

General Chair

Andrew Martin   University of Oxford, UK

Program Chairs

Liqun Chen   Hewlett-Packard Laboratories, UK
Chris Mitchell   Royal Holloway, University of London, UK

Program Committee

Endre Bangerter   Bern University of Applied Sciences, Switzerland
David Challener   Lenovo, USA
James Davenport   University of Bath, UK
Robert Deng   Singapore Management University, Singapore
Loïc Duflot   SGDN/DCSSI, France
Paul England   Microsoft, USA
Sigrid Guergens   Fraunhofer, Germany
Dirk Kuhlmann   HP Laboratories, UK
Peter Lipp   IAIK, TU Graz, Austria
Javier Lopez   University of Malaga, Spain
Andrew Martin   University of Oxford, UK
Yi Mu   University of Wollongong, Australia
David Naccache   ENS, France
Heike Neumann   NXP Semiconductors, Germany
Elisabeth Oswald   University of Bristol, UK
Kenny Paterson   RHUL, UK
Raphael Phan   University of Loughborough, UK
Bart Preneel   KU Leuven, Belgium
Graeme Proudler   HP Laboratories, UK
Sihan Qing   Chinese Academy of Sciences, China
Carsten Rudolph   Fraunhofer, Germany
Mark Ryan   University of Birmingham, UK
Ahmad-Reza Sadeghi   Ruhr University Bochum, Germany

Jean-Pierre Seifert	Samsung Research, USA
Ari Singer	NTRU, USA
Sean Smith	Dartmouth College, USA
Christian Stüeble	Sirrix, Germany
Leendert van Doorn	AMD, USA
Vijay Varadharajan	Macquarie University, Australia

Steering Committee

Boris Balacheff	Hewlett-Packard Laboratories, UK
Ian Brown	University of Oxford, UK
Andrew Martin	University of Oxford, UK
Chris Mitchell	Royal Holloway, University of London, UK
Ahmad-Reza Sadeghi	Ruhr University Bochum, Germany

External Reviewers

Tien Tuan Anh Dinh	Sandra Marcello
Kurt Dietrich	Aybek Mukhamedov
Jim Grimmett	Aarthi Nagarajan
Xinyi Huang	Dan Page
Jun Ho Huh	Dries Schellekens
Qingguang Ji	Qingni Shen
Markulf Kohlweiss	Nigel Smart
Stephan Krenn	Ben Smyth
GaiCheng Li	Udaya Kiran Tupakula
Hans Löhr	Bogdan Warinschi
John Lyle	Marcel Winandy

Table of Contents

Implementation of Trusted Computing

Attestation

PKI for Trusted Computing

Applications I

Applications II

Towards a Programmable TPM

Paul England and Talha Tariq

Microsoft Corporation, 1 Microsoft Way,
Redmond WA 98052, USA
{paul.england,talhat}@microsoft.com

Abstract. We explore a new model for trusted computing in which an existing fixed-function Trusted Platform Module (TPM) is coupled with user application code running on a programmable smart card. We will show that with appropriate coupling the resulting system approximates a "field-programmable TPM." A true field-programmable TPM would provide higher levels of security for user-functions that would otherwise need to execute in host software. Our coupling architecture supports many (but not all) of the security requirements and applications scenarios that you would expect of a programmable TPM, but has the advantage that it can be deployed using existing technology.

This paper describes our TPM-smart card coupling architecture and the services that we have prototyped. The services include: (1) An implementation of count-limited objects in which keys can only be used a preset number of times. (2) More flexible versions of the TPM *Unseal* and *Unbind* primitives that allow sealing to groups of equivalent configurations. And (3) a version of *Quote* that uses alternative signature formats and cryptography available within smart cards but not in the TPM itself.

We also describe the limitations of the coupling architecture and how some of the limitations could be overcome with a true programmable TPM.

Keywords: Trusted Platforms, Trusted Platform Module, Smart Cards, Secure Execution.

1   Introduction

Trusted Platform Modules (TPMs) are fixed-function security processors built into many computer platforms [1]. When combined with Core- and Dynamic-Root-of-Trust-Measurement facilities (CRTM & DRTM) for reporting platform state, the TPM provides a basis for a secure and attestable execution environment for system software and applications.

The TPM provides a variety of services [2] that depend on the platform state. These include:

> *Attestation*: Cryptographic reporting of platform state to a remote challenger.

> *Sealing*: Protected storage / encryption of data that will only be released / decrypted when the platform is in a particular configuration and state.

When these services are combined with a secure software stack, the small set of TPM-provided functions can bootstrap rich and powerful execution environments running on the main processors.

L. Chen, C.J. Mitchell, and A. Martin (Eds.): Trust 2009, LNCS 5471, pp. 1–13, 2009.
© Springer-Verlag Berlin Heidelberg 2009

Using the TPM to bootstrap trust into an execution environment like a platform hypervisor or operating system is adequate for many purposes, however data and application programs running on the main processors are much less protected from physical attack than programs and data held inside the TPM. This problem is evident from the recent hardware attacks on applications utilizing TPMs [3], [4], [5]. The problems of software robustness are even more challenging: mainstream operating systems have an ill-defined Trusted Computing Base (TCB) that is generally not secure enough for attestation to be meaningful [6].

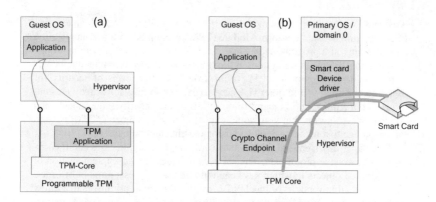

Fig. 1. (a) Schematic illustration of a programmable TPM and its use in a hypervisor setting. We assume that the TPM can load and run applications and the services implemented can be exposed to the hypervisor and guest operating systems. (b) Schematic of one instantiation of our coupled TPM smart card architecture: The TCB and TPM are coupled to the smart card using an out-of-band cryptographic marrying step. The cryptographic channels (thick lines) represent authenticated and secure connections from the smart card to the TPM and the smart card to the channel end-point.

If the host-platform-based secure environment is not secure enough, we might consider building a secure execution environment *inside* a TPM such as that illustrated in Fig 1(a). Such a system should provide much better robustness to hardware and software attack than that offered by platform macrocode. And indeed, such devices have been studied by researchers, but unfortunately they do not yet exist [7].

In this paper we propose an alternative architecture for providing high-assurance extended TPM services. Instead of making changes to the TPM hardware design, we describe and evaluate an architecture in which we *couple* a programmable smart card to a TPM to provide programmable services that are not possible with either alone. See Fig. 1 (b). This architecture has many interesting characteristics: First it is a practical way of providing enhanced security functionality for existing TPMs. Second, it provides a way of prototyping new TPM functions to assess their usefulness before committing them to silicon, and finally it allows us to explore the design and assess the usefulness of a true "programmable TPM."

We have built several advanced security services to help us understand this architecture and demonstrate its capabilities. The services described in this paper are:

Count-Limited Objects: An implementation of TPM keys that can only be used to perform cryptographic operations a preset number of times. This capability is designed to simplify some aspects of key revocation and support rights-management.

Flexible *Seal* and *Unseal*: An implementation of the *Seal*, *Unseal*, and *Unbind* primitives that allow more complex policy expressions than the simple Platform Configuration Register (PCR) equality checks supported by the current TPM specifications[1]. One policy expression allows sealing to a software publisher or other authority identified by a public key. In this case the publisher may later authorize any PCR configuration using a certificate signed using the associated private key. Another policy expression allows more complex logical expressions of authorized configurations (*e.g.* PCR configuration 1 *or* PCR configuration 2). Both of these enhancements are designed to make software updates and grouping of equivalent programs easier to manage.

Attestation Translation: A smart card service that provides attestation using cryptography and signature formats unavailable within a TPM. This is a proof of concept of attestation translation: a more sophisticated implementation could provide platform attestation in more widely used signature and certificate formats like X.509. This facility should simplify the deployment of attestation because existing servers and protocols can be used.

The paper is organized as follows. In section 2 we describe the coupling architecture. In section 3 we describe the security primitives that we have prototyped, and in sections 4 and 5 we describe the limitations of the coupling architecture and possible further work.

2 TPM to Smart Card Coupling

We seek to approximate a field-programmable TPM in which the secure execution environment for user extensible application programs is *part of* the host platform TPM. However when emulating a programmable TPM using a conventional fixed-function TPM and an external smart card, the secure execution environment is external to the TPM, is independent of the host state, and can be freely roamed between machines. This creates several challenges that we need to address: First, the execution environments provided by the host system and a smart card are relatively independent. For example, smart card applications can still run if the smart card is moved between different host machines. Second, TPM-to-host-TCB communications are relatively well protected (for example TPM communications are on a motherboard internal bus) whereas in coupling with an external smart card, the smart card bus is exposed, and communications are sometimes managed by drivers running outside the TCB (Fig. 1(b)).

2.1 Coupling Security Requirements

If the smart card is to provide TPM-enhanced platform services we need to couple the smart card and the host platform more tightly.

---

[1] At the time of this writing the current TPM specifications is version 1.2.

In particular we identify the following security requirements:

1) Smart card applications should be able to determine the host hardware and the host TCB (*e.g.* to support a smart card enhanced version of *Unseal* or *Quote*.)
2) The host TCB should be able determine the identity of the smart card and its applications (*e.g.* to ensure that TCB confidential data is not improperly released to an un-trusted smart.)
3) The smart card applications should have a bi-directional confidential channel to the host. (*e.g.* to support confidential communication of data passed to a smart card enhanced version of *Seal* or confidential communication of data returned from a smart card enhanced version of *Unseal*).

Our solution to these requirements is described in the next section.

2.2 Cryptographic Marrying (Smart Card to TPM Binding)

We assume that a trusted authority determines the TPM-to-smart card binding policy. In the case of an enterprise this might involve an IT department coupling an employee's smart card with the TPM on her PC (either under conditions of physical security, or remotely given knowledge of keys in the devices to be coupled). In the case of an OEM this might involve shipping a pre-coupled TPM and smart card together with an associated platform certificate.

We have implemented a system in which a unique TPM is coupled with a single smart card, but generalizations are straightforward. During this platform binding step we generate and store the following cryptographic keys to identify the smart card and associated TPM:

- The TPM generates an Attestation Identity Key (AIK) which is used to identify the TPM and the host. The public portion of this key is communicated to the smart card under conditions of physical security in the marrying step, and is stored in smart card non-volatile storage as shown in Fig. 2.
- The smart card generates an RSA key pair which is used to identify the card. The public portion of the key is communicated to the platform TCB under conditions of physical security and is secured in host platform secure storage.

The binding and initialization step need only be performed once. At run time code in the TCB and in the smart card builds a secure authenticated channel based on these authentication keys.

The explicit software-constructed secure channel is sufficient to support secure communication between smart card applications and the trusted computing base. Some of our smart card applications additionally employ cryptographic properties of the TPM itself without need for further channel security (beyond boot-strapping with the married AIK). First, the attestation translation and enhanced seal operations need to determine the current platform configuration. We provide this proof using the *TPM_Quote* operation (using the married AIK). This cryptographic primitive is already designed to work securely in the face of untrustworthy host software. Second, the count-limited key function uses the TPMs HMAC-based

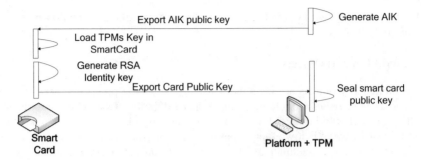

Fig 2. Cryptographic Binding of the TPM and Smart Card

proof-of-password-possession protocols. Finally, the count-limited key function uses the TPM capability for remote creation and encryption of keys using the TPM key-storage hierarchy.

In our implementation two more smart card keys are created as part of the marrying step. A symmetric AES key is created for off-card storage of smart card created sealed data blobs, and an RSA signing key is created for the attestation translation function. If a new binding is performed all previous bound data becomes inaccessible and the quote translation key is destroyed (just like installing a new owner in a TPM).

We also need integrity protected host storage for the host TCB to store the married smart card public key. Since the security model for trusted computing does not generally assume storage is trustworthy unless protected by cryptography, we use the host *TPM_Seal* primitive to integrity protect the married smart card public key. The smart card has genuine access-protected storage so no cryptographic measures are needed.

Our current implementation assumes that the smart card applications are loaded prior to the marrying step. A more sophisticated version would provide a user-accessible smart card execution environment and services that let the smart card applications authenticate themselves (see section 5).

Our architecture is generic and independent of the nature of host software: it can be applied to systems that employ a hypervisor, an operating system without a hypervisor, or applications running directly on the computer hardware. From our perspective all that differs is the nature of the TCB and the PCRs that are used to identify the platform state. Of course the choice of trusted computing base has practical implications for the comprehensibility and relevance of host PCR values [6].

3 Smart Card Enhanced TPM Security Primitives

In this section we describe the implementation of three security primitives that demonstrate the possibilities of the TPM to smart card coupling architecture.[2] Note that the smart card functions appear somewhat hard to use. This is because we generally favor performing only essential security functions in the smart card (which is slow

---

[2] These experiments used a Dell Optiplex 745 running Vista SP1 and containing an Atmel TPM version 1.2 with firmware version 13.9. The smart card was a Gemalto.NET v2 card with 80Kbyte of memory for code and data.

and hard to debug) with other logic and complex data structure creation being performed by host software.

3.1 Count Limited Objects

Count-limited key objects are keys that can only be used a preset number of times [9]. The TPM provides monotonic counters that external software can use to decide whether a key should be used, but - as we have already observed - the attack resistance of host software is low. Our implementation of count-limited keys uses a key on the TPM and a use-counter on the smart card and no external software is involved in authorizing the use of the key.

The design is as follows: The smart card creates a TPM key and sets the key use authorization (the *useAuth*) to a random value (the TPM will not use the key for cryptographic operations unless the requestor proves knowledge of the *useAuth* value). The smart card exports the key as a blob encrypted so that it can only be decrypted by the married TPM. The smart card associates the (secret) *useAuth*-value with an internal counter, and will only authorize use of the key a preset number of times. When the count is exceeded the key can no longer be used.

TPM key use is authorized by means of an HMAC-based protocol that does not reveal the *useAuth* authorization data in plain-text and is replay resistant (with some assumptions – see [8]). This means that host software cannot use keys without the cooperation of the smart card.

In more detail, the smart card exposes a pair of functions to support this functionality. *CreateCountLimitedKey* creates a key with a random *useAuth* value and exports it encrypted so that it can only be loaded into the married TPM. This function also creates a counter set to the maximum number of uses and associates it with the freshly created secret *useAuth*. Later, host software can load the key into the TPM and ask the smart card to provide authorization for its use through *GetCountLimitedUseAuth*. In this function the smart card decrements and then checks that the counter limit has not been exceeded. If not, the requested command is authorized.

The command pseudo-code is as follows:

> ### *CreateCountLimitedKey*
> > **Input**:
> > > A TPM parent storage public key p,
> > > Algorithm parameters for the key to be created a,
> > > The number of times the key can be used n
> > **Output**:
> > > An encrypted key that can be loaded into a TPM, an identifier for the counter c
> > **Actions**:
> > > 1) Create a new RSA key with parameters supplied
> > > 2) Create a new counter set to value n
> > > 3) Create a new random useAuth value a for the key and associate it with the counter
> > > 4) Encode the RSA key and useAuth into a TPM key structure then encrypt with the provided TPM parent public key
> > > 5) Return the key blob and an identifier for the counter

GetCountLimitedUseAuth
> **Input:**
>> The TPM command string to be authorized s,
>> The counter identifier c
>
> **Output:**
>> 20 byte authorization value for the supplied command string or an error
>
> **Actions:**
>> 1) Decrement the counter c. If the counter does not exist or the count value is less than zero return an error
>> 2) Return the HMAC of the command string s using the authorization secret associated with the counter

Some scenarios demand that it be proven that count-limited keys are created under conditions of physical security. For instance in our simple implementation it is not possible to prove to an outside party that the key is indeed count-limited. There are many variations of the simple design that overcome this shortcoming: E.g. rather than creating the key inside the smart card it could be created on a secure server (or a Host Security Module) and the count limit and *useAuth* data could be separately communicated to the smart card. Alternatively the smart card could certify the key that it created.

Our counters share some of the features of the implementation of TPM-supported monotonic counters proposed by *Sarmenta et al.* [9]. In particular our counters can be used as part of the authorization policy for key or other object use.

3.2 Flexible *Sealing* and *Binding*

Sealing encrypts data together with a tag indicating some expected future platform state encoded in PCR values. The related *Unseal* function will only decrypt and reveal the data if the platform is in the pre-authorized state. *Sealing* is a powerful feature of the TPM, but unfortunately it is often hard to predict future configurations because of unexpected changes in the platform configuration and state. The *sealing* capability (and related capabilities for associating keys with PCR states, *Unbinding*, etc.) would be easier to use if the TPM had more flexibility in the expression of authorized configurations.

We have extended the simple TCG binding model to provide more powerful sealing policy specifications using code implemented on the smart card. The cases we have implemented are:

- Sealing and binding to any one of a list of PCR configurations.
- Sealing and binding to a public key so that the key owner can later authorize any PCR configuration with a signed certificate.

In the latter case, when an *Unseal* or *Unbind* operation is attempted, the caller must also provide a valid digital certificate authorizing the current configuration from the policy-associated signature authority.

In both cases the smart card must check that the current married TPM PCR values represent a state authorized by the sealer. In our implementation the smart card performs this check in the same way that any other remote entity would determine the platform configuration: *i.e.* the smart card demands that host software provide evidence for the current state by means of the output of a *Quote* operation using the married AIK and a smart card provided nonce (to prevent replay). If host software can respond with evidence of an authorized configuration, the smart card will release the sealed data to the TCB.

We describe the smart card operations that support the *Seal* and *Unseal* implementations; *Unbind* is similar to *Unseal*.

Sealing to a List of PCR Configurations

The following smart card functions support *sealing* to a list of configurations. *SealToConfigurationList* is the smart card function that protects the data. The sealer need only specify the hash of the list of authorized configurations at this stage. *UnsealConfigurationList* is the corresponding unseal function. Here the caller must specify the whole configuration list (which the smart card will hash to ensure it matches the specified policy) and the policy element number that the smart card should attempt to satisfy. The smart card must also be given proof of the current platform configuration by means of the output of a *TPM_Quote* operation over the relevant PCRs. Replay resistance for the quoted configuration is provided by a smart card provided nonce, which must be obtained using the smart card *GetNonce* function.

In more detail, the pseudo-code for the commands follows:

SealToConfigurationList
> **Input**:
>> A secret s,
>> the hash of a list of authorized configurations l
> **Output**:
>> A sealed encrypted blob
> **Actions**:
>> Integrity-protect and encrypt the concatenation of s, and l

GetNonce
> **Input:**
>> None
> **Output:**
>> A 20 byte random nonce
> **Actions:**
>> Create and return a random nonce

UnsealConfigurationList
> **Inputs:**
>> A sealed blob, b
>> The expected configuration list, l
>> The list element number that we expect to satisfy, i
>> The output of a TPM *Quote* on the current configuration, q
> **Outputs:**
>> The previously sealed data or an error

Actions:
1) Decrypt the sealed blob b returning the secret s and the policy list hash h
2) Check that the hash of l matches the policy hash h
3) Check that the TPM signature q is formed signature using the married AIK over the $l[i]$ (the configuration element that we expect to match) and the previously supplied nonce
4) Return the secret data s if all of the above checks succeed, else return an error

Sealing to a Configuration Authorized by a Public Key

The following smart card functions support *sealing* to PCR configurations authorized by a public key. *SealToPublicKey* encrypts a secret and the public key of an entity trusted to authorize future platform configurations. *UnsealPublicKey* is the corresponding unseal function. *UnsealPublicKey* must be provided with the original sealed blob and a signed statement from policy key holder authorizing a PCR configuration. The caller must also provide the result of a *TPM_Quote* operation that proves compliance with the specified configuration. If policy compliance is proven the sealed data is released. As before, the caller must obtain a fresh nonce from the smart card and have it incorporated into the Quoted data structure.

In pseudo code:

SealToPublicKey
  Input:
    A secret s,
    A public key k
  Output:
    An encrypted blob
  Actions:
    Integrity-protect and encrypt the concatenation of s, and k
GetNonce
  See above

UnsealPublicKey
  Inputs:
    A bound blob b,
    An authorized PCR configuration from the server c,
    A signature over the authorized PCR configuration from the server S,
    The output of a TPM Quote operation q
  Outputs:
    The sealed data or an error
  Actions:
    1) Decrypt the sealed blob b returning the secret s and the public key k
    2) Validate that the signature S is valid for the configuration c using the public key k

3) Validate that q is a TPM signature over the configuration c using the married TPM AIK and the expected nonce
4) Return the secret s if the above checks succeed, else return an error

One detail is omitted from the description above. The TPM implementation of *Seal* records PCR values at the time of *sealing* for the purposes of source platform and configuration authentication. Our implementation of *Seal* also takes the output of a *Quote* operation over a smart card provided nonce to provide similar capabilities.

All data communicated between the TCB and the smart card is passed over the secure channel described in section 2. The channel endpoints are authenticated using the married TPM and smart card keys.

3.3 Enhanced *Quotes*

The *TPM_Quote* operation creates a signature using an AIK over a data structure that includes TPM internal state as reflected in PCR values, and externally provided data (for freshness, or to associate the configuration with some other cryptographic object). This building block is designed to be used in cryptographic protocols that prove knowledge of the AIK *and* prove the current platform state. Unfortunately the TPM signature format is non-standard, and this is one of the things that has made it difficult to adopt TPM attestation technology.

We have prototyped a smart card function that translates the platform configuration provided by the TPM into another format. Our proof of concept also uses non-standard data structures, but a more sophisticated implementation would use a certificate format like X.509. Such certificates could be used for network access control, or in an email or document signing scenario to prove the machine and machine configuration when the document was signed [11],[12].

Our configuration rewriting function is called *TranslateQuote*. It must be called with fresh evidence of the current configuration by means of the output of the *TPM_Quote* operation over a smart card nonce. *TranslateQuote* checks the quote signature is properly formed and is issued by the married AIK. If both conditions hold, the smart card generates a signature over the TPM-specified state, and an external nonce.

In pseudo code:

GetNonce
    See above

TranslateQuote
    Inputs:
        The data structure supplied to the *TPM_Quote* operation q,
        The TPM-quoted signature s over this data structure and the previously obtained nonce,
        External data to sign d
    Outputs:
        A smart card created signature or an error

Actions:
1) Check that s is a valid signature over the data q and the nonce using the married AIK
2) If the check succeeds return a smart card signature over a translation of q and the external data d, else return an error

4 Programmable TPMs

Our coupling architecture strikes a useful balance between flexibility and deployability using today's generally available commodity hardware since it requires no modification to the current specifications of the TPM[3] and uses general purpose programmable smart cards, but it is interesting to speculate on the design and improved functionality of a future programmable TPM.

There are many possible models for a programmable TPM. Useful starting places include multi-application programmable Java or .Net smart cards, or the Trusted Execution Model (TEM) described by *Costan et al.* [13]. Perhaps the simplest conceptual design for a programmable TPM is to replicate the security model for code executing *outside* the TPM but applied to user-code running *inside* the TPM. The TPM already has a model for authenticating security modules executing outside, which is the notion of locality coupled with the DRTM launch procedure [14]. This secure late-launch procedure has been used by the Oslo project [15] and Flicker [16]. Applying this idea to an execution environment *inside* the TPM would involve the definition of a new locality for access by TPM applications, and new PCR-registers dedicated to their measurements. See Fig. 3. However, beyond privileges associated with access locality, internal TPM applications would have the same access to other TPM functions and keys as applications running outside the TPM.

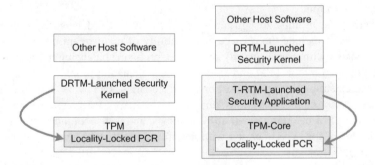

Fig. 3. Left: A TPM supporting a DRTM-launched security kernel. The DRTM procedure and platform hardware and firmware ensures that a special PCR contains a reliable measurement of the external security kernel, and that the TPM can authenticate commands originating from the security kernel. Right: Applying this model to a programmable TPM would define a new locality and associated "TPM-Root-of-Trust-of-Measurement" (T-RTM) to hold measurement of the TPM internal programmable security functions.

---

[3] As of this writing the current version of TPM Specifications is 1.2.

Unfortunately there are limits to the types of functions that can be supported using this sort of programmable TPM because TPM protected data is not accessible to the user applications. So while it would be possible to create a new class of storage key with sophisticated migration features with this design, it would not be possible to provide this migration capability to the storage root key (SRK) because the SRK private data is inaccessible. Allowing third party code access to TPM private keys and other protected data changes the TPM security model profoundly, so we generally prefer designs that supplement existing functionality rather than replacing or modifying it.

5 Conclusions and Future Work

We currently only support applications that are pre-loaded onto the card prior to TPM card marrying. This is probably adequate for most enterprise use (the enterprise will load line-of-business applications onto the smart card prior to issuance) but does not exercise the full potential of the coupling architecture.

To go beyond pre-loaded applications we must provide an isolated execution environment for applications in the smart card, *and* provide a means for these applications to authenticate themselves to the host computer. The isolation and authentication primitives are necessary because we can no longer necessarily trust the applications running on the card. This seems most straightforwardly solved by re-applying the principles of authenticated operation *but within the smart card.* In particular we would need to modify the smart card application loader to measure and record the application digest (or other authentication data) and provide the smart card application with sealing and attestation services. Smart card applications could use these primitives to prove to the platform TCB that it is communicating with a trustworthy card *and* card application.

Delivering the promise of Trusted Computing has been delayed by a number of problems. These include the relative unavailability of mainstream operating systems and hypervisors with useful security properties, problems balancing the high levels of security provided by the TPM and ease of management, and problems using the TPM to enhance existing security applications and scenarios. Our work demonstrates that logic and cryptographic operations running on a smart card coupled with the host platform and TPM can mitigate all of these issues, and is also an interesting prototyping environment for experimenting with new functionality that could be incorporated into future TPM designs.

The three applications we implemented were chosen to exercise local- and remote-trust verification, and to mitigate some of the problems that the authors have experienced in trying to apply trusted computing to real problems. Other candidate applications included keys with more sophisticated key management and migration functions, a software-TPM on the smart card, a "roaming-TPM" for use in an enterprise, and general experimentation on the correct definition of security primitives for future TPM designs.

References

1. Trusted Computing Group TPM Specification Version 1.2 Revision 103 (2007), https://www.trustedcomputinggroup.org/specs/TPM/
2. England, P., Peinado, M.: Authenticated operation of open computing devices. In: Batten, L.M., Seberry, J. (eds.) ACISP 2002. LNCS, vol. 2384, pp. 346–361. Springer, Heidelberg (2002)
3. Sparks, E.R.: A Security Assesment of Trusted Platform Modules. Dartmouth College, Technical Report. TR2007-597
4. Halderman, J.A., et al.: Lest We Remember: Cold Boot Attacks on Encryption Keys. In: Proc. 2008 USENIX Security Symposium (2008)
5. Bruschi, D., et al.: Attacking a Trusted Computing Platform. Improving the Security of the TCG Specification. Technical Report. Università degli Studi di Milano. Milan (2005)
6. England, P.: Practical Techniques for Operating System Attestation. Proceedings of Trust (2008)
7. Costan, V., et al.: The Trusted Execution Module: Commodity General-Purpose Trusted Computing. In: Eighth Smart Card Research and Advanced Application Conference
8. Offline dictionary attack on TCG TPM weak authorisation data, and solution. In: Chen, L., Ryan, M.D., Grawrock, D., Reimer, H., Sadeghi, A., Vishik, C. (eds.): Future of Trust in Computing, Vieweg & Teubner, 2008 (2008)
9. Sarmenta, L.F., et al.: Virtual Monotonic Counters and Count-Limited Objects using a TPM without a Trusted OS (Extended Version), Mit Technical Report MIT-CSAIL-TR-2006-064 (2006)
10. George, P.: User Authentication with Smart Cards in Trusted Computing. In: Arabnia, H.R., Aissi, S., Mun, Y. (eds.) Security and Management, SAM 2004, pp. 25–31. CSREA Press, Las Vegas (2004)
11. Balacheff, B., et al.: A trusted process to digitally sign a document. In: Proceedings of the 2001 workshop on New security paradigms. pp. 79–86 (2001) 1-58113-457-6
12. Giraud, J.-L., Rousseau, L.: Trust Relations in a Digital Signature System Based on a Smart Card. In: Proceedings of 23rd National Information Systems Security Conference, Baltimore
13. Costan, V.: The Trusted Execution Module Commodity General-Purpose Trusted Computing. In: The Eighth Smart Card Research and Advanced Application Conference
14. Grawrock, D.: The Intel Safer Computing Initiative: Building Blocks for Trusted Computing, 1st edn. Intel Press (2006) 0976483262
15. Kauer, B.: OSLO: Improving the Security of Trusted Computing. In: Proceedings of the 16th Usenix Security Symposium (2001)
16. McCune, J.M., et al.: Flicker: An Execution Infrastructure for TCB Minimization. In: Proceedings of the ACM European Conference on Computer Systems (EuroSys 2008) held in Glasgow (2008)

ACPI: Design Principles and Concerns

Loïc Duflot, Olivier Levillain, and Benjamin Morin

DCSSI 51 bd. de la Tour Maubourg 75700 Paris Cedex 07 France

Abstract. ACPI (Advanced Configuration Power Interface) allows operating systems to efficiently configure the hardware platform they are running on and deal with power management tasks. These tasks used to be achieved by the BIOS because it was the only platform component to know which specific chipset or device registers dealt with power management. In this paper, we illustrate how this shift in the global power management model introduces additional threats, especially for trusted platforms, by showing how rootkits can use ACPI to conceal some of their functions. We also study the relationship between trusted computing blocks and ACPI.

Keywords: ACPI, trusted platforms, rootkits.

1 Introduction

ACPI (Advanced Configuration and Power Interface) [8] was specified by Intel®, Hewlett-Packard, Microsoft®, Phoenix® and Toshiba to establish common interfaces for platform-independent configuration and power management. In the ACPI model, the OSPM (Operating System-directed configuration and Power Management) is the specific operating system component in charge of power management tasks. ACPI has been widely accepted as a de-facto standard to replace the former APM [16] (Advanced Power Management) approach, where power management was mostly performed by the BIOS. Pushing power management at the operating system level allows more flexibility and more complex power management schemes. However, operating systems are generic objects by nature, so the hardware platform must provide the operating system with some means of understanding how power management should be achieved on this specific platform. This is the purpose of the ACPI tables.

On a trusted platform, the trusted computing base is generally in charge of power management. If the trusted computing base is to run on several platforms, then it must make use of the ACPI tables provided by the BIOS. In this paper, we try to determine whether the trusted computing base can trust the ACPI tables, or if there is a way for an attacker to modify those tables as a means for privilege escalation on a platform, and what would be the impact of a bug in one of the ACPI tables.

It is well understood in the industrial world that ACPI is one of the most complex components to deal with from a security perspective on a trusted platform (along with System Management Mode for instance). During the 2006 Blackhat

L. Chen, C.J. Mitchell, and A. Martin (Eds.): Trust 2009, LNCS 5471, pp. 14–28, 2009.
© Springer-Verlag Berlin Heidelberg 2009

forum, John Heasman [6] presented how it is possible to design an ACPI-based rootkit. However, to our best knowledge, our paper is one of the first attempt to study the initial design flaws and to present a comprehensive proof-of-concept of an ACPI rootkit-like function that can be triggered by external hardware events (laptop lid opening, power adapter plugged and removed twice in a row for instance).

In section 2, we present the way ACPI works on a traditional computer and show how ACPI is handled on a Linux system. Section 3 gives a description of the flaws in the ACPI model that make it possible for an attacker to use ACPI to conceal rootkit functions. In section 4, we present an actual proof-of-concept of an ACPI rogue code that allows an attacker to install a remanent backdoor on a Linux-based laptop that will be triggered when the power adapter is plugged and unplugged twice in a row. In section 5, we describe how the problem can be handled on so-called trusted platforms. Section 6 concludes the paper.

2   ACPI Design Principles

For the sake of simplicity, we only consider in this paper traditional x86 and BIOS-based computer platforms.

2.1   Traditional PC Architecture

Figure 1 shows a traditional PC architecture. User code (trusted computing bases, operating systems, applications) run on the CPU [10]. The chipset component is in charge of hardware devices management. The northbridge [9] part of the chipset is connected to main system memory (RAM) and to the graphic adapter. The southbridge [14] part of the chipset is connected to other devices (network interface controller, sound device, USB devices) through various communication buses. Power management of a device is achieved at the hardware level by modifying the content of configuration registers hosted by the chipset (northbridge, southbridge or both depending on the device) and in the device itself. Those registers can be accessed from the CPU using several different mechanisms [13]:

- some registers are mapped by the chipset into the main system memory space. Those so-called Memory-Mapped I/O registers can thus be accessed by the CPU in the same way as RAM is, but at different addresses;
- some registers are mapped into a separate 16-bit bus. These registers are called Programmed I/O (PIO) registers. They are given an address in the PIO space and can be accessed from the CPU using "in" [11] and "out" [12] assembly langage instructions;
- the chipset can also choose to map configuration registers into the PCI configuration space [17]. One way to access those registers is to use two dedicated PIO registers, 0xcf8 and 0xcfc, by specifying the PCI address of the register (composed of a bus number, a device number, a function index and an offset)

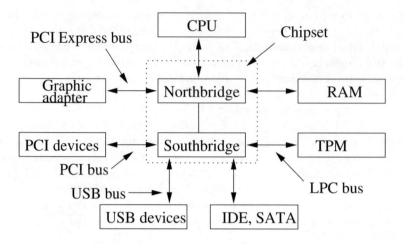

Fig. 1. Traditional PC architecture (example Pentium® 4-based architecture)

in the 0xcf8 register and reading (resp. writing to) the 0xcfc register to read (resp. write) the content of the PCI register.

2.2   ACPI Components

In the model, the chipset itself does not attempt to configure power management registers. Configuration is actually initiated by software components running on the CPU. At boot time, the BIOS is likely to configure the hardware, while operating systems or trusted computing bases are in charge of power management once the boot process is over.

In the ACPI model, the platform provides an ACPI BIOS, several ACPI registers that are accessed for power management purpose (they can be either Memory Mapped registers, Programmed I/O registers or PCI configuration registers), and ACPI tables that basically specify how ACPI registers should be accessed.

ACPI tables have different types and purposes:

- the Root System Description Table (RSDT) contains a set of pointers to the other tables. The address of the RSDT is provided by the Root System Description Pointer (RSDP), which must be stored in the Extended BIOS Data Area (EBDA), or in the BIOS read-only memory space. The OSPM will only locate the RSDP by searching for a particular magic number (the RSDP signature) that the RSDP is required to begin with;
- the Differentiated System Description Table (DSDT), the address of which can be determined thanks to the pointer provided by the RSDT, contains those methods that should be used by the component in charge of power management and specifies how the power characteristics of the devices shall be modified. The ACPI specification only defines the methods that are available for each device and their meaning. Actions defined in the methods are

machine-specific. The DSDT is written in AML (ACPI Machine Langage) [8], which can be disassembled into a more comprehensible language, called ASL (ACPI Specification Langage)[1];

   – many other tables are also provided, but for the sake of simplicity, we will not give details on them.

ACPI does not standardise power management at the software level, but operating systems are advised to include the following components to perform power management tasks:

   – an Operating System-directed configuration and Power Management component (OSPM) running at the kernel level should be in charge of the overall power management strategy;

   – an ACPI driver and AML interpreter should be used by the OSPM to execute the contents of the methods specified in the DSDT;

   – device drivers should optionally make use of the AML interpreter to perform power management independently of the OSPM.

ACPI components and their relationships with the kernel are summarized in Figure 2.

2.3 DSDT Basic Structure

The DSDT describes those devices that support power management. Devices are organized in packages in a tree-like structure. Several standardized packages are located under the root (labelled \) of the tree, such as the _PR Processor tree package, which stores all CPU related objects and the _SB System Bus tree package, which stores all bus-related resources. PCI resources (e.g., PCI0, PCI1) are located in the _SB package. In turn, devices can be defined in other devices' subtrees. For instance, IDE or USB controllers can be accessed in the tree below the PCI0 device; the path to the USB0 host controller on the DSDT tree is thus _SB.PCI0.USB0. Power management-related methods are the leaves of the tree. For example, the method that allows the USB0 controller to transit to the S5 power state is _SB.PCI0.USB0._S5. Most method names are defined in the ACPI standard, so that the OSPM knows which method to call. Example of such standard methods are given in [8].

Power management basically works as follows: in response to some hardware-triggered event, or based on its own policy, the OSPM can initiate a power management-related action by executing the corresponding AML method in the DSDT. For instance, in order to put one of the USB controller in the S5 power state, the OSPM simply has to run the _SB.PCI0.USB0._S5 method.

2.4 ACPI Machine Language and ACPI Source Language

AML-written tables can be disassembled in ACPI source language (ASL) using for instance the ACPIca tools [1]. The ASL language provides basic constructs in

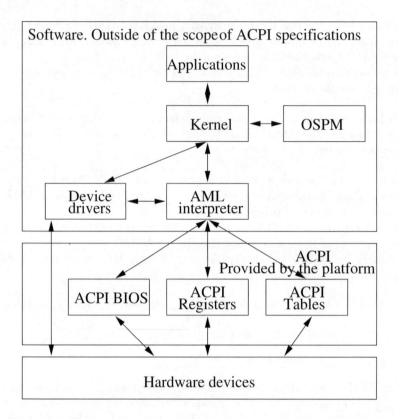

Fig. 2. ACPI architecture

order to define ACPI registers and methods. Logical and arithmetic operations on registers, branching instructions and loops are available. Special commands are also available, like the `Notify()` command, which can be used by the OSPM to send messages to other parts of the operating system. Section 2.5 shows how Notify events are handled under Linux.

The ACPI registers are defined by the ASL `OperationRegion()` command. Memory, PCI configuration and PIO spaces can be mapped as ACPI registers. Different fields of each ACPI register can be given a name using the `Field()` command (see 2.5).

2.5   Use of ACPI in Practice: Linux Example

In this section, we study how ACPI is handled by an ACPI-compliant Linux system. This will be useful as most of the examples we give in the next sections will be related to Linux systems.

ACPI software in Linux is mostly composed of two different parts:

– a kernel service which includes an AML interpreter, ACPI drivers for different devices (e.g, fan, CPU, batteries) and part of the OSPM. The modular structure of the Linux kernel allows for a selection of devices that are handled by the kernel using ACPI;

- a userland service called acpid (ACPI daemon) that is functionally part of the OSPM. acpid is configured through a set of configuration files stored in the /etc/acpi directory, each of which specifying the expected system behavior when an ACPI "Notify" event for a particular device is received. For instance, the /etc/acpi/power file can be used to configure acpid so that whenever a power button event is received, the shutdown command is executed.

The Linux kernel also allows the user to define an alternate DSDT file, different from the one specified by the BIOS. This function is quite convenient as it allows the DSDT to be modified, e.g. for debug purposes.

The easiest way to force the kernel to use a custom DSDT is through the use of an "initial RAM disk" (initrd). An initrd is usually used by the bootloader of a Linux system to load kernel modules that are required to access the root file system (SATA or IDE drivers, file system-related modules for instance) when they are not shipped with the kernel. But the initrd can also be used to provide a custom DSDT to the kernel. For the kernel to use a custom DSDT, all we have to do is create an initrd file with the following command[1] and provide the initrd to the bootloader.

```
mkinitrd --dsdt=dsdt.aml initrd.img 2.6.17
```

The DSDT used by the system is accessible via the /proc/acpi pseudo-file. It is then possible to disassemble the DSDT of the system and then reassemble the output ASL file without modifications. On some computers, this simple operation fails. On the example below, we disassemble the DSDT file (called "dsdt") of an actual desktop system through the iasl -d dsdt command. The ASL file corresponding to the DSDT is written in the dsdt.dsl file. Next, we compile the dsdt.dsl file into AML. Ideally, the output file should be identical to "dsdt" . However, the compiler shows unexpected compilation errors. This is symptomatic of ACPI tables that do not comply to the standard, despite being written in AML.

```
#iasl -d dsdt
Loading Acpi table from file dsdt
[...]
Disassembly completed, written to "dsdt.dsl"
#iasl dsdt.dsl
dsdt.dsl    286:      Method (\_WAK, 1, NotSerialized)
Warning  1079 -       ^ Reserved method must return a value (_WAK)
dsdt.dsl    319:           Store (Local0, Local0)
Error     4049 -      ^ Method local variable is not initialized (Local0)
dsdt.dsl    324:           Store (Local0, Local0)
Error     4049 -      ^ Method local variable is not initialized (Local0)
```

---

[1] The code that is presented below has been tested for a Linux 2.6.17 kernel.

```
ASL Input:   dsdt.dsl - 4350 lines, 144392 bytes, 1678 keywords
Compilation complete. 2 Errors, 1 Warnings, 0 Remarks, 382 Optimizations
```

It is also possible to copy the system DSDT and change the definition of ACPI registers. If we map kernel structures such as system calls to ACPI registers, or define new ACPI registers, compiling the modified DSDT does not cause any warning. It is then possible to update the initrd of the system in order for the modified DSDT to be used by the system after the next reboot. The following code describes how to define such new ACPI registers. The first OperationRegion() command defines an ACPI register called LIN corresponding to a byte-wide PCI configuration register. The second OperationRegion command defines a system memory 12-byte wide ACPI register called SAC composed of three 4-byte registers defined through the following Field() command called SAC1, SAC2 and SAC3.

```
/* PCI configuration register : */
/* Bus 0 Dev 0 Fun 0 Offset 0x62 is mapped to LIN */
Name(_ADR, 0x00000000)
OperationRegion(LIN, PCI_Config, 0x62, 0x01)
Field(LIN, ByteAcc, Nolock, Preserve) { INF,8 }

/* System Memory at address 0x00175c96 */
/* (Setuid() syscall) is mapped to SAC */
OperationRegion (SAC, SystemMemory, 0x00175c96, 0x000c)
Field (SAC, AnyAcc, NoLock, Preserve)
  { SAC1,32, SAC2,32, SAC3,32 }
```

3   Security Issues with ACPI

In this section we study different security issues related to ACPI. The ACPI model seems to be the most important security flaw. Indeed, the OSPM must trust the content of the ACPI tables supplied by the BIOS in order to run ACPI code. Actually, the OSPM has no particular way to determine whether ACPI tables are genuine or not. Also, the OSPM has no means to properly identify what the ACPI registers are. As ACPI does not provide any ACPI register identification scheme, the OSPM cannot ensure that the methods defined in the DSDT actually manipulate *only* ACPI registers, so the OSPM can merely trust those methods.

One could argue that OSPMs have the possibility to correctly identify ACPI registers. If the OSPM knows that a particular network adapter is plugged in for instance, it should be able to know which specific configurations of the device are related to power management and which are not. If the OSPM was able to differentiate ACPI registers from regular chipset or device registers then the OSPM could enforce a simple access control policy and would refuse to read or modify the content of any non-ACPI register even if instructed to do so by one of the methods of the DSDT. However, as stated in introduction, ACPI has been precisely introduced to define common interfaces and make sure that platform- specific information (for instance the location of ACPI registers) is pushed in ACPI tables for the operating system to configure the platform without an in-depth understanding of the semantics of the chipset or devices registers. In other words, ACPI would be useless if the OSPM knew enough of the platform details to identify the ACPI registers.

One could also argue that the OSPM not being able to identify ACPI registers is not a security issue, as computer programs have to trust higher-privilege or to some extent previously booted components. What we wanted to stress out here is the fact that ACPI could have been designed differently at the hardware or platform level to allow OSPMs to differentiate ACPI registers from other registers. What's more, the paradigm forcing OSes to trust previously booted software tends to be challenged by new technologies using hot reboot (this matter is discussed in section 5).

We now look at the problem from the chipset point of view. The chipset is able to know the location and the purpose of most ACPI registers, but it does not know when the OSPM is running on the CPU, nor can it distinguish ACPI-related access to the registers from non-ACPI-related accesses. From the chipset perspective, a userspace code attempting to modify a register is not different from the OSPM, so there is no way for the chipset to enforce that the OSPM be the only component to access ACPI-related registers and that OSPM cannot access non-ACPI-related registers.

At this point, one could argue that it is not the job of the hardware to make security-related decisions. Here again our point is that the fact that neither the OSPM nor the chipset can serve as a policy enforcement point seems a major design problem. Additionally, it seems fair to note that the chipset is already used as a policy enforcement point to restrict access to security-critical memory areas such as the SMRAM [3], so using the chipset to make the platform more secure would not really be that innovative.

As a summary, neither the chipset nor the OSPM can decide whether an action is legitimate or not: the OSPM is not able to determine if the registers it is accessing are indeed ACPI because it blindly trusts the content of the DSDT, and the chipset cannot know what software component is trying to access a particular resource because all software components running in protected mode look the same to the chipset.

The lack of policy enforcement point makes it impossible to detect misbehaviors of the ACPI sub-system:

- it is impossible to detect a bug in the DSDT that would incorrectly define an ACPI register (remember that disassembling the DSDT and reassembling it on some computers reveals AML errors);
- it is impossible to detect live modifications of the DSDT image the OSPM is using.

Other security issues exist even if they can probably be considered of lesser importance. First, device drivers are allowed to access the content of the DSDT and perform ACPI-related tasks. The fact that the OSPM and the device drivers could be independently accessing the same registers could lead to inconsistencies and to incorrect system behavior. For instance, the OSPM could consider that some device is in a particular state when the device driver itself has configured the device differently. Also, the fact that the OSPM has to actually look for the Root System Description Pointer signature to be able to locate the structure is quite debatable from a security point of view. OSPMs probably do not look for multiple RSDP structures, so an OSPM is likely to use the first RSDP matching the signature. The fact that the OSPM is indeed able to identify the actual RSDP relies on the assumption that there is no way for an attacker to insert a rogue RSDP with a correct signature in memory before the genuine RSDP. This assumption actually does not prove easy to guaranty.

4   Design of a Rootkit Function

The overall principle of an ACPI rootkit has been presented by John Heasman [6]. According to the author, designing an ACPI rootkit triggered by external hardware events (e.g., lid closing, power adapter plugging or removing) was still an open problem. In this paper, we present a proof-of-concept code that allows a rogue rootkit-like function to run whenever the power adapter is pulled and replugged twice in a row. We also study the limits of the ACPI model and conclude that ACPI rootkits detection is a complex problem.

4.1   ACPI Rootkit Motivations

An attacker controlling the content of the DSDT could:

- add devices in the DSDT, create new ACPI registers corresponding to any memory zone, or PIO register;
- modify existing methods behavior, create additional methods.

This attack assumes that the attacker has enough privileges to modify the DSDT used by the OSPM. For instance, the attacker can attempt a live modification of the DSDT the OSPM is using or, alternatively, interfere with the DSDT load process (for instance by flashing the BIOS or modifying the boot loader) in order for the OSPM to load the tainted DSDT. On most operating systems, an attacker will only be allowed to do so if she is granted maximum privileges (ring 0). Therefore, this attack shall not be useful in a privilege escalation scheme; on the other hand, modifications of the DSDT can be useful to kernel- level rootkits.

Kernel-level rootkits are malwares which try hard to ensure both their stealthiness and resilience. Indeed, an attacker needs her rootkit to hide its presence from the user and the operating system and also remain in memory, even if part of the rootkit is removed by some antivirus software. It has been shown in [4] that rootkits could hide functions inside of the SMI handler. SMI handler is a component running in the CPU System Management Mode [3] and that is virtually inaccessible from operating systems. Another possibility for the rootkit is to modify one of the methods of the DSDT to make sure that each time this method is launched by the OSPM, functions of the rootkit get executed.

4.2   Sample ACPI Rootkit Rogue Function

As a proof-of-concept of what is described above, we show how it is possible for an attacker to design an ACPI rogue code for a Toshiba Portégé M400 laptop using a Linux Mandriva 2008 [15] system. This rogue code is intended to trigger a backdoor every time the power adapter plug is pulled and replugged twice in a row; the backdoor grants superuser privileges to subsequent user logins, no matter what the user id is.

In order to do so, the attacker can create a new device TEST and define a new ACPI register called INF corresponding to an otherwise unused chipset register[2]. This chipset register is a PCI configuration register (bus 0, device 0, function 0, offset 0x62). It is byte-wide, readable and writable and is not used by any other software component (including BIOS). Such a device can be defined as below[3]:

```
Scope(\_SB.PCI0){
Device(TEST){
          Name(_ADR, 0x00000000)
          OperationRegion(LIN, PCI_Config, 0x62, 0x01)
          Field(LIN, ByteAcc, Nolock, Preserve)
          { INF,8 }
          Method(_S1D,0, NotSerialized)
          { Return(One)}
          Method(_S3D,0, NotSerialized)
          { Return(One)}
          [...]
     }}
```

On Linux-operated laptops, the _STA (Status Request) function of the BAT1 device is used by the OSPM to check the status of the main battery, so it is supposed to be executed quite frequently (experiments have shown that it is invoked around once every 10 seconds).

The _PSR (Power Source) function of the ADP1 device is called when the power adapter is unplugged or plugged in. This function is used by the system to determine what the current power sources are. The attacker can use the newly created INF ACPI to keep track of the number of times the _PSR function has been executed in a row without the BAT1._STA function being called. This can be achieved by means of the following modifications. The BAT1._STA function is modified to ensure that each time BAT1._STA is executed, the INF ACPI register is set to 1. This can be done by using the Store() ASL command. Of course,

---

[2] The attacker could alternatively have used an unused memory space, as for example the BIOS keyboard buffer, located at physical addresses 0x41a to 0x43e.

[3] The device presented does not only contain the INF register, but also some standard methods, defined for every ACPI device. Even if these methods may not be necessary for the TEST device to be defined in the DSDT, they make it resemble real devices.

it is possible to modify other functions[4] in the same way as BAT1._STA to make
sure that the INF ACPI register is set to 1 as often as possible.

```
Device(BAT1){
        [...]
        Method (_STA, 1, NotSerialized)
        {
            Store(0x1 , \_SB.PCI0.TEST.INF)
                [...]
        }
}
```

The attacker also has to modify different functions and registers of the ADP1
device. A new ACPI register is created, which corresponds to the memory location where the setuid() syscall is stored (more precisely to the part of the
setuid() syscall where the effective user id is set).

```
Device (ADP1)
        { [...]
            /* Map setuid() syscall. 0x00175c96 is the physical address */
            /* of the part of setuid() to be modified by the backdoor */
            OperationRegion (SAC, SystemMemory, 0x00175c96, 0x000c)
            Field (SAC, AnyAcc, NoLock, Preserve)
            {
                    SAC1, 32,
                    SAC2, 32,
                    SAC3, 32
            }
[...]
```

The ADP1._PSR function is also modified to increment INF.

```
[...] /* In ADP1 device */
Method (_PSR, 0, NotSerialized)
{           /* if INF = 4 then modify setuid() */
            If (LEqual (\_SB.PCI0.TEST.INF, 0x4))
            {
                    Store(0x90900000, SAC3)
                    Store(0x0, SAC2)
                    Store(0x014c80c7, SAC1)
            }
            /* increment INF */
            Increment (\_SB.PCI0.TEST.INF)
            Return (\_SB.MEM.AACS)
}
[...] /* ADP1 device continues */
```

---

[4] Determining experimentally which functions are called often requires modification
of the DSDT to make sure that each function of the DSDT writes a different value to
the INF register when called, and tracking accesses to the INF registers (modification
of the ACPI driver).

If the INF ACPI register reaches the value 4, meaning that `ADP1._PSR` has been called four times in a row (unplugged and plugged again in twice in a row) without the `BAT1._STA` function being called in the meantime, the backdoor gets executed. The backdoor modifies the `setuid()` system call (which is called by the authentication process every time a user logs on the system) in such a way that any user obtains the superuser identity instead of her own identity (i.e. is granted maximum privileges) if authentication succeeds. This is achieved by modifying 12 bytes of `setuid()` code at physical address `0x175c96` (mapped in the `SAC1`, `SAC2`, `SAC3` ACPI registers) to make sure that the effective identity of the user is set to root. The values to be written depend on the version of the kernel, here the assembly language instruction `movl $0, 0x14c(%eax)` (where `0x14c(%eax)` corresponds to the memory location of the effective user id for this version of the kernel) are to be added, followed by two `nop` operations for opcode alignment purposes.

```
/* Without backdoor activation */    /* After backdoor activation */
Mandriva Linux Release 2008.0        Mandriva Linux Release 2008.0
Kernel 2.6 on an i686 / tty1         Kernel 2.6 on an i686 / tty1
Login: user                          Login: user
Password:                            Password:

$id                                  #id
uid=500(user) [...] euid=500(user)   uid=500(user) [...] euid=0(root)
$whoami                              #whoami
user                                 root
```

4.3   Limitations and Countermeasures

In the previous sections, we have shown that creating an ACPI rootkit-like function is possible. However, there are a couple of important limitations:

- an ACPI rootkit is machine-specific. It requires modification of the DSDT, the content of which is strongly related to the machine hardware;
- an ACPI rootkit most likely needs to be operating system-specific. The ability to create a generic and operational ACPI rootkit on a platform independently of the operating system type still needs to be verified. The ACPI `_OS` object or the ACPI `_OSI` command can help identify OSes but of course it is possible for the operating system to lie about its version;
- after a reboot, the OSPM reloads the DSDT from the one provided by the platform, unless the rootkit ensures that a modified one is loaded instead. ACPI rootkit functions will thus require knowledge of relatively important parts of the operating system or of the BIOS;
- modifications to ACPI tables that survive reboots are likely to be detected if TPM-based [18] schemes or analyzers that look for an obviously wrong behavior (mapping between an ACPI register and a system call for instance) are used. Static or dynamic code analysis tools can indeed be used to detect anomalous behaviors in the methods defined in ACPI tables, look for the

definition of ACPI registers that are not legitimate and recover ACPI tables used by the system. Of course, the efficiency of such a tool would depend on its knowledge of the operating system and the underlying hardware platform. Unfortunately, dynamic analyzers will not be efficient against kernel-level malicious codes, which would deactivate them before modifying ACPI tables.

Overall, static analyzers seem by far the best countermeasures to detect modifications of ACPI tables that survive reboots. Static analyzers can also be used to detect bugs in BIOS-provided ACPI tables. Such tools should be run after each BIOS update. Alternatively, one could also propose that the BIOS vendors cryptographically sign the ACPI tables. The signature would be verified at boot time by the BIOS itself to make sure that ACPI tables have not been modified. Such a scheme would probably not be really efficient as an attacker that would manage to modify ACPI tables would also probably have enough privileges to deactivate the signature verification function unless this function is immutable. Signature schemes will also not provide any protection against bugs in BIOS-provided ACPI tables. Detecting live modifications of the DSDT will be almost impossible as long as the content of the DSDT will be executed by the OSPM with the highest privilege level as it is the case for most classical operating systems. Possible means to protect trusted platforms against malicious functions hidden inside of the DSDT are described in the next section.

5   Impact on a Trusted Platform

The principle of a trusted platform is to identify a set of hardware and software components called "trusted computing base" (TCB). The model is that trust in the trusted computing base is sufficient to gain trust in the whole platform. On the contrary, if the trusted computing base was not working according to its specification, there would be no way to trust the platform. The trusted computing base include at minimum the Trusted Platform Module (TPM) [18], the CPU and the chipset of the platform and the software component of highest privilege (in most cases a small virtual machine monitor running different guest operating systems with reduced privileges in parallel). Different initiatives aim at limiting the size of the trusted computing base [7]. For the time being, even the BIOS itself can be put outside of the trusted computing base (using TxT [5] and Presidio technologies [2] for instance).

The ACPI specification advises the OSPM to be part of the software component with the highest privilege level. On a so-called trusted platform, the trusted computing base is thus generally the component in charge of power management. In order to do so and to remain generic, the trusted computing base will have to make use of ACPI tables which means that ACPI tables such as the DSDT will be included in the trusted computing base. Of course, if TPM and CRTM are used, ACPI tables can be measured at boot time. But measurements cannot ensure that tables will not be modified in the future by a rootkit. Measurements will ensure table integrity but will not give a way to trust their content.

But how can the trusted computing base determine that there is no bug or rogue function in the ACPI table provided by the platform that will modify the behavior of the platform? ACPI static analysis tools can be used but they will not help against live modification of the ACPI tables. Dynamic tools may also be used inside of the trusted computing base but could also be deactivated by a rootkit beforehand.

The best solution so far for a trusted platform would be to move to a new paradigm where the component in charge of power management is not the trusted computing base but a non privileged operating system running on top of the trusted computing base. This way, the OSPM running methods described in ACPI tables will not have enough privileges to modify security critical structures such as the ones inside of the trusted computing base. Any such attempt will give the hand back to the trusted computing base that can for instance shut down the power management domain and report the security breach.

6   Conclusion

In this paper, we showed how it is possible in practice for an attacker to conceal functions in the ACPI DSDT table. We have provided a proof-of-concept implementation of such a function that allows an attacker to get to maximum privileges on a laptop when she pulls the power adapter twice in a row. More importantly, we have shown that the flaw was in the ACPI model that by design lacks a correct security policy enforcement point. Neither the chipset, nor the CPU will be able to detect any DSDT-based attack scheme. Possible countermeasures include static and dynamic analysis of the ACPI tables that would help detecting modifications of the DSDT by a rootkit.

The impact is even more important on trusted computing base that have to make use of ACPI tables. Correctly tackling the problem would require trusted platforms to move to a paradigm where the component in charge of power management would not be part of the trusted computing base but in a separate environment with reduced privileges. This way, any attempt to modify security critical structures by the component in charge of power management would give the hand back to the trusted computing base.

References

1. ACPI Component Architecture. Unix format test suite (2008),
   http://www.acpica.org/downloads
2. Devices, A.M.: Amd64 virtualization: Secure virtual machine architecture reference manual (2005)
3. Duflot, L., Etiemble, D., Grumelard, O.: Security Issues Related to Pentium System Management Mode. In: CanSecWest Security Conference Core 2006 (2006)
4. Embleton, S., Sparks, S.: The System Management Mode (SMM) Rootkit. In: Black Hat Briefings (2008)
5. Grawrock, D.: The intel safer computing initiative (2007)

6. Heasman, J.: Implementing and detecting an acpi bios rootkit. In: Blackhat federal 2006 (2006),
   www.blackhat.com/presentations/bh-federal-06/BH-Fed-06-Heasman.pdf
7. Heiser, G., Elphinstone, K., Kuz, I., Klein, G., Petters, S.: Towards trustworthy computing systems: taking microkernel to the next level. In: ACM operating systems review (2007)
8. Hewlett-Packard: Intel, Microsoft, Phoenix, and Toshiba. The acpi specification: revision 3.0b (2008), http://www.acpi.info/spec.htm
9. Intel Corp. Intel 82845 Memory Controller Hub (MCH) Datasheet (2002)
10. Intel Corp. Intel 64 and IA 32 Architectures Software Developer's Manual Volume 1: Basic architecture (2007)
11. Intel Corp. Intel 64 and ia 32 architectures software developer's manual volume 2a: instruction set reference, a-m (2007),
    http://www.intel.com/design/processor/manuals/253666.pdf
12. Intel Corp. Intel 64 and IA 32 Architectures Software Developer's Manual Volume 2B: Instruction Set Reference, N-Z (2007)
13. Intel Corp. Intel 64 and IA 32 Architectures Software Developer's Manual Volume 3A: System Programming Guide Part 1 (2007)
14. Intel Corp. Intel I/O Controller Hub 9 (ICH9) Family Datasheet (2008)
15. Mandriva. Mandriva linux one (2008),
    http://www.mandriva.com/en/product/mandriva-linux-one
16. Microsoft and Intel. Advanced power management v1.2 specification (1996),
    www.microsoft.com/whdc/archive/amp_12.mspx
17. PCI-SIG. Pci local bus specification, revision 2.1. (1995)
18. Trusted Computing Group. Tpm specification version 1.2: Design principles (2008),
    https://www.trustedcomputinggroup.org/specs/TPM/MainP1DPrev103.zip

Implementation Aspects of Mobile and Embedded Trusted Computing

Kurt Dietrich and Johannes Winter

Institute for Applied Information Processing and Communications
Inffeldgasse 16a, 8010 Graz, Austria
{Kurt.Dietrich,Johannes.Winter}@iaik.tugraz.at

Abstract. Nowadays, trusted platform modules (TPMs) are usually deployed together with desktop PCs and notebooks. However, these platforms are not the only ones that can host TPMs. Mobile and embedded platforms like cell phones can also host TPMs but may have different requirements and different use-case scenarios. In contrast to common TPMs, TPMs for mobile platforms do not need to be implemented as micro controllers, leading to different security assumptions. In order to find these differences, we have designed and implemented two approaches for mobile TPMs that are analyzed in detail in the context of this paper.

Keywords: Mobile Trusted Computing, MTMs, ARM TrustZone, Secure Element, JavaCard.

1 Introduction

Today, trusted platform modules (TPMs) are available for nearly every PC platform, ranging from desktop machines to notebooks. These TPMs provide the basic building blocks for different security services like storing integrity measurements of the installed and loaded software during boot (aka authenticated boot in the language of the TCG), authenticated reporting of these stored values to remote verifiers (aka remote attestation) or binding certain data like keys to certain platform configurations (aka sealing, binding). All of these services provide the basic building blocks for Trusted Computing (TC) enabled platforms.

Common desktop TPMs are produced in high numbers which allows TPM manufactureres to keep the prices low. However, these common TPMs are deprecated for mobile and embedded applications From a certain point of view, it seems simple to put a micro controller based TPM like the ones used on desktop machines on a mobile platform. However, each new chip on a phone's mother board increases the cost of this device, not to mention the additional power consumption of the extra chip. Consequently, it is reasonable to search for alternatives - alternatives, for example that are primarily based on features and mechanisms that embedded devices already carry as part of their base configuration. Moreover, to keep the costs for mobile TPMs at a low price, the TPMs might also be implemented only in software, raising questions about the security

L. Chen, C.J. Mitchell, and A. Martin (Eds.): Trust 2009, LNCS 5471, pp. 29–44, 2009.
© Springer-Verlag Berlin Heidelberg 2009

assumptions for these mobile-trusted-modules (MTM)s and the platforms they are used with.

The Trusted Computing Group (TCG) has published a specification that defines how mobile TPMs could be designed and which features they could provide [6]. Intentionally, this specification is written in a rather relaxed style which allows manufacturer to implement their mobile TPMs in different ways. This specification also forms the basis for the design of our prototypes and our ongoing investigations.

In this paper, we discuss our two designs for providing TC building blocks on embedded devices. Both building blocks rely on security mechanisms already hosted by the embedded devices. The first approach focuses on a software emulated mobile TPM that uses processor extensions to achieve protection from access by arbitrary applications.

One interesting fact that should be mentioned at this point is that in the sense of the TCG, MTMs might also be implemented as software security modules. The TCG sees the mobile TPM more like a *service* than a fixed micro chip. Moreover, in order to achieve more flexible and cheap implementations, MTMs are not constrained to be implemented as micro controller, but might also be implemented in software. Consequently, the question arises which level of security a pure software implementation can provide. Is it possible to achieve the same level as with microcontroller based TPMs?

Or which level is necessary for certain use-cases? Without having clear definitions about conformance and compliance of mobile TPMs, these questions are hard to answer. Details about our TrustZone based TPM can be found in Section 4.1.

The second approach (see Section 4.2), makes use of onboard smart cards. Many new mobile phones are equipped with an additional smart card (besides the SIM card) which can hold secret data like keys or certificates. These smart cards, or secure elements (SE) in the sense of the TCG, can be addressed by the mobile phone as well as from external devices via nearfield communication which offers new perspectives of secure device communication.

In both of our approaches, we try to be as close to the TCG's published specification as possible. As a result of our investigations of these two designs, we give a discussion about the pros and cons of both approaches and provide a comparison of them.

This article is organized into 6 sections. In section 3 we give an overview and explain the differences of the two kinds of mobile TPMs i.e. mobile-remote-owner-trusted-modules (MRTMs) and mobile-local-owner-trusted-modules (MLTM). In section 4, we discuss our two approaches in detail. A comparison of the approaches is given in Section 5 and finally, Section 6 briefly concludes the contribution.

2   Related Work

Different approaches how to implement MTMs are pursued by various research groups. The most important ones are introduced in the following paragraphs.

In [20], an idea to extend a SELinux based kernel in order to provide a generic domain isolation at the kernel level is proposed by Xinwen Zhang, Onur Aciicmez and Jean-Pierre Seifert. That way, the research group provides a strong and convenient mechanism to satisfy the security requirements of trusted mobile phones on isolation of engines and integrity assurance.

One of the leading mobile phone manufacturers - NOKIA - also does research on implementation aspects of MTMs. Jan-Erik Ekberg and Markku Kylänpää published a paper [10] that provides an introduction into the concept of MTMs from the device manufacturer's point of view. Furthermore, their work presents an implementation of an MTM that is based on the well-known TPM emulator from Mario Strasser [16].

In alternative approaches, hardware provided by mobile devices itself is used to provide MTM functionality. Such hardware is the SIM card every mobile is equipped with. The work discussed in [3] uses a JavaCard applet loaded on a SIM card or on-board smart card. The Applet emulates MTM features and makes use of the hardware support of smart cards. Furthermore, this approach benefits from the smart cards design as they provide shielded locations and protected capabilities per se. This MTM supports MRTM as well as MLTM functionality.

And finally, in [18] a design for a software emulated mobile-trusted-module, based on the ARM TrustZone processor extension is discussed. This approach is one of the starting points used for this article.

3   Mobile Trusted Modules

One important building block of every trusted platform is the trusted platform module (TPM). Among other components like the CPU or the BIOS, the TPM has to be trusted a priori in order to create a *chain of trust* [7]. On mobile and embedded platforms, TPMs are called mobile-trusted-modules (MTMs). Although MTMs have similar features to TPMs, some differences between TPMs and Trusted Computing used on desktop machines and MTMs and Mobile Trusted Computing exist. In addition to the services discussed in the introduction section, mobile trusted computing defines another service called *secure boot*. In contrast to an authenticated boot, a secure boot aborts execution of the software - or more restrictive: the boot of the device - if the integrity check on the software that is currently being loaded fails. This fact implies that a remote party can assume that a certain software configuration is running on that device. Which software is running on the device is of special interest for mobile equipment vendors and network providers, as we will see in the following paragraphs.

In contrast to the TPM specification where we have one dedicated specification of the TPM and its features, the Mobile-Trusted-Module specification [6] defines two types of MTMs: the *Mobile Remote-owner-Trusted-Module* (MRTM) and the *Mobile-Local-owner-Trusted-Module* (MLTM), addressing different owners' needs. The difference between these two types of MTMs is that the MRTM must support mobile-specific commands as well as a subset of the TPM v1.2

commands. In contrast, the MLTM is only required to support a subset of
the TPM 1.2 commands [8]. Usually, phone manufacturers and network service
providers are the owner of MRTMs.

On the one hand, manufacturers and providers want to get secure remote access to the mobile phone by using features of the MRTM. On the other hand,
the phone's user or owner, who has physical access to the device and its applications, uses the MLTM . The different parties, called stakeholders, have different
security requirements on MTMs. Depending on the stakeholder, the MTMs are
applied in areas such as platform integrity, device authentication, mobile tick-
eting, SIMLock/device personalization, secure software download, secure access
to the UICC and payment services as well as user data protection and privacy.
A mobile platform may host more than one MTM, depending on different stakeholders and their requirements.

Precise definitions of how MTMs have to be implemented are not defined by
the TCG. Therefore, we propose two solutions with different security requirements.

4   Trusted Building Blocks

In the TCG mobile trusted computing architecture [5], MTMs are the fundamental building blocks for bringing trust into the platform. Any TCG-style trust
provisioning relies on a complete chain of trust, which ultimately roots in a mobile trusted module. As part of our research in mobile trusted computing, we
have investigated a variety of different approaches to realize such mobile trusted
modules, ranging from pure software solutions in the style of [10] to dedicated
hardware solutions in the style of PC TPMs. In this paper we want to briefly
describe two of the most promising approaches we are currently working on.

4.1   ARM TrustZone

In [1] and [2] ARM introduced a set of hardware-based security extensions to
ARM processor cores and AMBA on-chip components.

The key foundation of ARM TrustZone is the introduction of a "secure world"
and a "non-secure world" operating mode into TrustZone enabled processor
cores. This secure world and non-secure world mode split is an orthogonal concept to the privileged/unprivileged mode split already found on pre-TrustZone
ARM cores. On an ARM TrustZone core, secure world and non-secure world
versions of all privileged and unprivileged processor modes and control register coexist. Security critical processor core status bits and control registers are
typically restricted to secure-world-only access. For the purpose of interfacing
between secure and non-secure world a special Secure Monitor Mode together
with a Secure Monitor Call instruction exists. Interrupts can be handled in a
secure deterministic way on TrustZone cores. Apart from the extensions to the
processor core itself, the SoC busses in TrustZone enabled systems carry extra
signals to indicate the originating world for any bus cycles. Whenever a bus

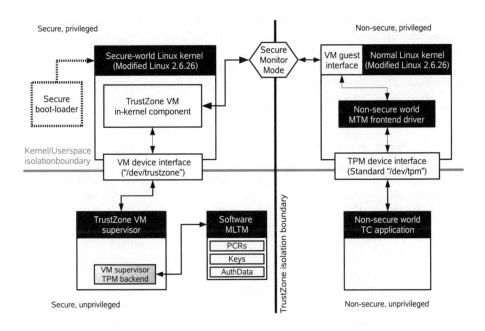

Fig. 1. Software architecture for an ARM TrustZone based trusted mobile platform

cycle is started by the core, the secure/non-secure world state is recorded and encoded into these extra signals. SoC peripherals can interpret the TrustZone extra signals to implement a low-level access control based on the secure/non-secure world distinction.

In [18], we outlined how ARM TrustZone can be used as an enabling technology to implement trusted computing building blocks on embedded platforms. The intrinsic split of the platform into a secure and non-secure partition can be efficiently leveraged to provide the isolation properties required for the protected capabilities and shielded locations of a mobile trusted module. As shown in [18], it is possible to accomplish that goal by solely relying on well known open source software projects, like the Linux kernel, as fundamental building blocks.

Figure 1 gives an overview of a simplified version of the envisioned software architecture for a mobile trusted platform. The prototype design utilizes the TrustZone secure/non-secure world boundary to create two separate domains, each running its own modified version of the Linux kernel. On the secure world side, a specialized stripped down Linux kernel is used to provide the necessary runtime environment for software based mobile trusted modules and for the components required to handle the non-secure world side. The secure world environment can be stripped down to the bare minimum of software components.

The MTMs, which execute as software processes within this tightly controlled secure world environment, can rely on the process isolation and access control features of the secure world kernel to provide the required isolation properties with respect to other secure world components.

The hardware supported boundary to the non-secure world environment is used to provide a sufficient protective shielding against any potentially malicious piece of code running on the non-secure side. There is no direct way for non-secure world code to access secure world data or code memory without explicit permissions. This is guaranteed by the TrustZone hardware extensions even for platform features like DMA, which normally cause a lot of issues on platforms without TrustZone.

Trusted Engines and the ARM TrustZone approach. A logical extension to our prototype software design, which is not shown in figure 1, is to include a re-stricted execution environment for secure bytecode or script computation within the secure world partition of the system. The TCG reference architecture for mobile trusted platforms mentions the existence of "trusted engines", without being precise on the exact nature and implementation details of these building blocks. These trusted engines are capable of performing trustworthy computa-tions on behalf of a remote stakeholder on the local mobile platform. In the TCG architecture, trust provisioning for these engines is done on the basis of mobile remote owner trusted modules (MRTMs).

The trusted engine concept can be seen as partitioning of the platform into different trust domains for the stakeholders of the platform. Since various stake-holders of a mobile platform can not be expected to ultimately trust each other, mechanisms are required to support a sufficient level of isolation and separation amongst them. Our ARM TrustZone based approach intrinsically provides two levels of separation through the TrustZone secure/non-secure world boundary. These two levels of isolation can be expected to be insufficient if a mobile trusted platform has more than two different stakeholders. Even in the case of only two stakeholders, for example a "device manufacturer" and a "device user", it is arguable whether two trust domains are sufficient.

By relying on existing software isolation technologies within the two trust domains intrinsic to ARM TrustZone, it is possible to split them into an arbitrary number of smaller trust domains.

Secure user-space process based approach. One approach to implementing trusted engines can be the combination of secure boot concepts with strong software iso-lation. In this scenario, trusted engines would be implemented as secure-world user space processes, with embedded certificates. In order to guarantee that only trusted code is executed within secure world, the secure world operating system has to enforce mandatory validation of these certificates before allowing any secure user-space processes to run. Depending on the availability of cryp-tographic and trusted computing primitives within the secure world operating system, these certificates can range from simple asymmetric signatures over the executable images to RIM certificates as proposed in the TCG mobile reference architecture.

An obvious and very simple mechanism for splitting secure user-space into smaller trust domains, is to leverage the access control mechanisms offered by standard Linux users and groups. However, depending on the complexity and nature of the task being performed by a trusted engine it can be desirable to have a more fine grained approach to access control. As an example, a trusted engine might be comprised of a set of collaborating user-space processes, which run at different privilege levels.

To support fine grained access control together with strong software isolation, frameworks like SELinux can be used. The authors of [20] propose a SELinux based system, to implement different trust domains with mandatory access control on basis of a normal Linux platform. Their approach can be mapped to the secure and non-secure world environments of our TrustZone prototype design, in order to provide fine-grained trust domains and software isolation boundaries within the two worlds.

Comparison to software MTM solutions on general purpose processors. The TrustZone based approach to a mobile trusted module implementation discussed in the preceding section is a hybrid solution somewhere in the middle between a pure software MTM implementation and dedicated MTM hardware. A pure software MTM implementation running on a general purpose processor[1] has to solely rely on the process isolation features provided by the operating system kernel or hypervisor. In such an implementation we can expect all MTMs to run under the same kernel or hypervisor as any potentially malicious user applications. In current hypervisors like Xen [19] or microkernels like L4 [11], compartment isolation is achieved by using standard virtual memory management mechanisms available on the general purpose processor they run on. Usually, only the small hypervisor or microkernel runs in a privileged processor mode, while the compartments run in unprivileged processor modes.

In the proposed ARM TrustZone based design, the situation is slightly different due to the dual nature of the processor core. Since TrustZone effectively turns a single physical processor core into two separate virtual processors, we have the possibility to strongly separate the MTMs from any potentially untrusted user applications. The prototype design explicitly reserves the secure world environment for MTMs and tightly controlled trusted processes. Within the secure world environment, the same techniques as known from general purpose processors without TrustZone are applied to provide process isolation among the MTM processes and other trusted processes. When considering the secure world environment alone, we can give precisely the same process isolation guarantees for all secure world processes as we could on a general purpose processor only executing trusted processes.

Similarly, we can use the techniques known from general purpose processors and apply them to the non-secure world environment of the TrustZone based design. If we consider the non-secure world alone, we can achieve the same guarantees as we could on a general purpose system without TrustZone, where isolation among trusted and untrusted processes running on the general purpose processor core is provided by an OS kernel, hypervisor or microkernel.

---

[1] In this context we understand "general purpose processor" as a processor without dedicated security extensions or hardware virtualisation extensions.

The actual strengths of the TrustZone based design is the ability to create an *isolated* memory area. TrustZone memory isolation features guarantee that no non-secure world process, regardless of whether it is running in privileged or unprivileged mode, can ever access secure world memory. If there is need to perform data exchange between secure and non-secure world, only non-secure memory can be used for that purpose. Furthermore control transfer between secure and non-secure world is only possible through a strictly limited interface at the full discretion of the secure-world environment.

From a global point of view, the TrustZone design implements two independent, strongly isolated worlds with a well defined strictly controlled interface between them. Global isolation between these two worlds is provided by the intrinsic protection features of the TrustZone processor extensions. Within each of these worlds, the design achieves strong local process isolation by resorting to methods known from general purpose processors without TrustZone.

The possible combinations of these mechanisms allow for great flexibility with respect to the different trust domains on the platform. When secure-world is exclusively reserved for MTMs, with strong local isolation mechanisms in place, this design achieves protected capabilities and shielded locations, which could get close to the ones found in dedicated hardware MTM modules.

At the time of this writing it is a major part of our ongoing research to investigate the limitations of the TrustZone based design. We are currently trying to research definitive statements about which properties of dedicated hardware MTM modules can not be fulfilled with the TrustZone based design, solely relying on a software MTM implementation.

4.2   Smart Cards

In this section, the use of smart cards, or secure elements, for hosting trusted computing building blocks, is discussed. Smart cards are available on every mobile phone - either as an extra smart card or as the subscriber identity module (SIM) card. The SIM card is required for identifying the user (or better, the account that is charged for the call) to the communication network. More advanced devices that support UMTS also support the use of universal-SIM (USIM) cards which are equipped with more sophisticated security algorithms. These two types of smart cards seem to be a natural place where to host MTM functionality.

However, developers are hardly allowed to install and execute arbitrary applications on these cards. Therefore, we moved to alternatives. Other devices are equipped with on-board smart cards (e.g. Nokia 6131 NFC) which we used in our approach to host the MTM [3].

At this point, it is important to notice the difference, between a secure element and a SIM card. The secure element, is fixed on the platform - it cannot be removed. In contrast to a SIM card that can be removed from the device. All data that is stored on the secure element, remains on the platform and cannot be transferred to another device by just moving the card.

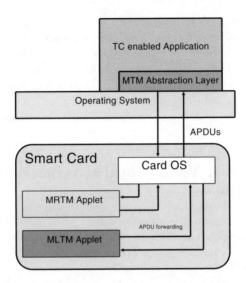

Fig. 2. Software architecture for a Smart Card based trusted mobile platform

This fact has interesting consequences. On the one hand, all data that is bound to the removable card cannot be unbound unless the correct card is reinserted again. On the other hand, data that is stored inside a secure element can be transfered to the new device. Moreover, if the data is fixed to a certain platform configuration, the new device could be forced to have the same configuration in order to get access to the stored data.

JavaCards can host different applications, called applets [13]. Typical applications use such applets to store and manage authorized access e.g. digital purses or authentication credentials. However, the card can also be used to host applets with MTM functionality.

Figure 2 shows the basic design of our prototype. The smart card (or secure element) hosts the MTM. The MTM itself is implemented as a Java Card applet that supports the processing of TCG compatible commands [8]. Common TPM functionality also includes cryptographic operations, e.g. the current MTM specification defines RSA operations to be used for asymmetric cryptography. Typically, smart cards are equipped with hardware based cryptographic support. This hardware support enables smart card applications to perform fast cryptographic operations. Fortunately, this support is also available for Java Card applets which enables them to support all required operations [6].

The communication between the host application and the smart card is done by TCG conformant commands that are split to fit into APDUs as defined in [9]. However, current available cards underlie strong restrictions from available memory (EEPROM and RAM). The approximate free available space on our reference prototype is about 76 kByte of nonvolatile memory and 8 kBytes of RAM. Furthermore, the processing of Java byte code is rather slow, which demands efficient command handling and parsing.

Many cards can host more than one applet. This fact allows the installation of multiple MTM applets and therefore allows to install a MRTM and an MLTM on the same card, providing the functionalities of both kinds of MTMs.

A major advantage when using smart cards for hosting MTM functionality is that all security properties of a certain smart card can be reused when assessing the security level of the smart card based TPM. Smart cards are well investigated in the sense of security evaluations - various security evaluations and protection profiles [17] exists.

5   Software-Based Versus Hardware-Based Mobile Trusted Modules

In this section, the different advantages and disadvantages of our approaches are discussed. Both approaches are able to provide MTM features and functionality as defined by the TCG mobile phone Specification [6] - all required commands, for MRTMs and MLTMs, can be provided.

On the one hand, software-based MTMs are a very flexible solution and can easily be adapted to certain use-case requirements. However, it is hard to determine whether a pure software or TrustZone enhanced implementation can provide *shielded locations* and *protected capabilities* that form the core requirements of TPMs as required by the TCG [7].

On the other hand, shielded locations are supported by secure elements per se. The design of current TPMs and MTMs originally stems from the designs of smart cards which makes it easy to prove that the requirement for shielded locations and protected capabilities can be achieved by secure elements. Moreover, protected capabilities can be established by implementing the required command and authorization handling services as software components on the card.

5.1   Architectural Implications

A smart card based approach, where the execution of MTM specific operations is separated between main CPU and a MTM specific processor, has other consequences as the execution of such operations together with arbitrary applications on a just one single CPU. The first approach provides an absolute separation of the MTM functionality.

The second approach relies on specific platform features that can provide hardware enforced separation and protection of processes or, in some cases, software based isolation via the operating system or assumptions of the compiler system. Examples therefore are the L4, micro kernel based architecture and the Microsoft research operating system *Singularity* [15].

Roots-of-Trust. Important base components of all trusted platforms are the *roots-of-trust*. Not all of these roots are provided by the MTM, they can be provided by the BIOS or a piece of software that does verification operations, for example. Therefore, it is reasonable to investigate possible impacts on these roots by our designs.

It is obvious to see that the smart card approach provides a root-of-trust-for-storage (RTS) and root-of-trust-for-reporting (RTR) per se. All measurement values are stored inside a protected area and all required operations for reporting this values (i.e. quote and identity operations) can be performed in the same protected area. Therefore, we can assume that the card provides RTR and RTS. However, can we put the same assumption on the TrustZone approach?

When we take a closer look at the design (see Section 4.1) we realize that the software based MTM itself relies on other roots of trust. In order to use this kind of MTM, we require a mechanism that guarantees the integrity and authenticity of the MTM implementation (i.e. Root-of-Trust-for-Enforcement (RTE)) [10]. This can be achieved by requiring the device to perform a secure boot process [6] which again includes operations that rely on a Root-of-Trust-for-Verification (RTV) and a Root-of-Trust-for-Measurement (RTM). Consequently, we require a RTV and a RTM to be present before the MTM can be securely started.

An interesting design could be the combination of both approaches. Instead of a protected place in the BIOS, the secure element could store long term secrets like the RVAI and could be used to check the integrity of the software MTM. Consequently, the RTV could then be the smart card itself. Nevertheless, a RTM is still required as the measurement process is done outside whatever MTM. This implies that the BIOS must provide means to communicate with the smart card.

Integrity Information. The integrity verification process involves RIM certificates which contain integrity information of certain software images and information of expected integrity metrics [6]. The integrity of these certificates themselves are checked by using asymmetric cryptography which can be rather time consuming and slow on mobile devices. In order to address this problem, the MPWG has introduced the concept of binding a RIM certificate to a certain MTM involving just symmetric cryptography with a key that is only known to the MTM. Using secure elements could improve this process greatly. Instead of binding the certificate to the MTM, the certificate could be stored within the MTM. Assuming that only authorized entities can update or store certificates within the element, the certificate's integrity can be seen as assured.

The benefit of this approach could be that a verifier would only have to create a hash of the RIM certificate and of the image and send it to the secure element. The secure element could then simply compare the hash certificate with the hash of the stored certificate to verify its integrity.

Moreover, the card could compare the corresponding PCR selection values stored in the certificate with the current content of the PCRs detecting aberrations between the expected and the actual platform configuration before extending the PCR, as defined in [6].

Separation. In the JavaCard MTM implementation, the processor executing the MTM code is a physically distinct entity to the processor running application code. The interface between the MTM and the application is constrained by the ISO7816 [9] smart-card interface of the secure element. Data exchange between the MTM and the application is limited to an APDU based protocol, there is no mechanism for directly sharing memory between the MTM and the application. The nature of this smartcard interface automatically forces the MTM and any other applets running inside the secure element into a passive role, with respect to the application processor.

A different situation arises when considering the TrustZone based MTM implementation. In this design, the same physical processor is shared by the MTM code and the application code. By using the TrustZone features of the physical processor core, two isolated virtual cores for secure and non-secure world are created. These two virtual cores can not be considered as a multi-core or multi-processor system with respect to parallelism. Secure and non-secure world are mutually exclusive. Whenever one of the worlds is active, the other world sleeps. Since it is undesirable to suspend all non-secure world application while an MTM running in secure world performs some longer operation, a time-sharing and pre-emption mechanism is needed. The interface between the virtual core hosting the MTM and the virtual core hosting the application is built around a system-call style secure monitor call instruction. Data exchange between the virtual cores takes place using a combination of general purpose processor registers and shared memory.

Platform Binding. The binding of the MTM to its platform is of essential interest especially for software based MTMs. While the binding in case of secure elements is given by design, the binding of software based MTMs is not. As all digital data, such as software-based MTMs, could easily be transferred or duplicated by just copying the software, efficient mechanisms are needed to protect the state of a software MTM. Apart from MTM cloning, it is necessary to provide countermeasures against MTM state rollback attacks. Furthermore, parts of the MTM state, like private or secret keys, have confidentiality requirements which need to be fulfilled.

If the target platform of the software MTM provides shielded locations, like chip-internal non-volatile secure memory, all of these issues can be solved relatively easily. depending on the available size of that memory. Such non-volatile memory could be an EEPROM or a battery buffered internal static RAM, for example.

The amount of secure memory can be very small, since only a single secret key K_{state} needs to be placed within this memory. Providing confidentiality and platform binding is easily accomplished by using the secret K_{state} key for encrypting the MTM state blob. By ensuring that no two platforms share the same K_{state} key, a binding between each platform and the MTM state blobs encrypted on that platform can be established.

The described mechanism does not enforce any requirements on the update-ability of the K_{state} key and thus also works with platforms, which already contain hardwired built-in keys. Unfortunately. this simple approach is not sufficient to prevent state rollback attacks. When the platform provides some intrinsic mechanism to support at least one monotonic counters with large capacity, state rollback issues can be mitigated, by using the value of this counter to track the current revision of the MTM permanent state block.

The need for a monotonic counter to do state revision tracking can be eliminated if the secure location used to store K_{state} is writeable. In that case, the MTM generates a new random K_{state} key each time when an updated version of the state blob needs to be stored. As a side effect, this enhanced mechanism allows the storage of monotonic counter values within the encrypted MTM state blob, residing outside secure memory.

5.2 The Role of Virtual Machines

Virtual machines play a key role to both of the designs discussed in this paper.

In the secure element based design, the primitives provided by the JavaCard framework and the Java language are used to realize protected capabilities and shielded locations for the MTM applet. Within the context of the Java environment running on the secure element, applet security and isolation is provided by the design of the JavaCard framework [14].

The JavaCard framework is designed to be usable in environments with extreme constraints on resources like memory and computational power. Todays smartcards are often based on very simple 8bit microcontrollers like 8051-derivates. Such controllers mostly lack support for features like memory protection, virtual memory or a distinction between privileged and unprivileged processor modes.

Providing process isolation for applications running natively on such a limited processor becomes next to impossible. The JavaCard VM provides a powerful yet simple solution to remedy this undesirable situation. Instead of allowing applet writers to use the potentially dangerous native instruction set of the smart card processor, it provides a safe virtual machine instruction set. The virtual machine instruction set of the JavaCard VM (cf. [14], [12]) is designed to not expose any direct means for raw pointer or memory operations. In addition the Java virtual machine specification enforces a number of restrictions on valid programs to allow bytecode verification. In the context of current JavaCards, bytecode verification is mostly done outside the card. Since special keys are required to load applets onto the card, it is still possible to guarantee that only verified applets are installed. Once the applets are installed, the card can be locked, disallowing any further applet installations.

Based on bytecode verification and the virtual machine instruction set design of the JavaCard VM, it is possible to overcome the limitations of the underlying native processor with respect to applet isolation. Under the assumption that the virtual machine implementation is correct and secure, JavaCard VMs allow powerful software-isolation without the need for equally powerful underlying hardware isolation.

When discussing the TrustZone based prototype design, we already mentioned the possibility of implementing trusted engines as user-space processes, running in the secure world environment of the TrustZone based platform. The ARM processors used in the TrustZone based design do not suffer from the same limitations with respect to memory protection and privileged instructions.

Nevertheless, trusted engines implemented as native processes can pose a threat to the entire secure world environment, especially if they have to process input from untrusted sources. Incorrectly implemented native trusted engines can give an adversary the capability of directly executing code in secure world user-space. While this does not necessarily lead to an immediate break of platform security, it can be a highly significant advantage to an adversary.

A virtual machine based approach to trusted engines offers mechanisms to tightly restrict the low-level operations which can be carried out by software running inside the trusted engine. For example, potentially unsafe low-level operations like direct raw pointer manipulation can be ruled out by appropriate bytecode design. Depending on the tradeoff between performance and security requirements, virtual machines can implement a significant amount of runtime checks and bytecode verification steps.

Examples for candidate VMs include the Java VM (J2ME, JavaCard) or the Lua VM. Especially the latter case of the Lua scripting language appears to be a quite attractive candidate due to the small size and high flexibility of the Lua programming language. It should be pointed out that Lua has already been used in designs with a similar problem setting, as demonstrated in [4].

6   Conclusion and Future Work

In this paper, we discussed two approaches for building mobile trusted modules based on existing platform features. The ARM TrustZone approach, covered in section 4.1, focuses on using special capabilities of the platform and its main processor for implementing trusted computing building blocks in software. Apart from the requirement for a sufficient processor core with ARM TrustZone support, this approach avoids dependencies on additional dedicated trusted computing hardware. In comparison to the second MTM implementation approach outlined in this paper, the TrustZone approach can not rely on the same security properties inherited from a smart card environment. We give a comparison of the TrustZone based approach to a pure software MTM solution on general purpose processors. Based on the additional memory and process isolation features offered through TrustZone, we conclude that the TrustZone approach allows a finer-grained set of possible trust boundaries and domains. Moreover, we conclude that software MTMs running in a secure world environment and exclusively using secure world memory, can provide protected capabilities and shielded locations which are potentially stronger than their counterparts in the general purpose processor without TrustZone features.

Finally, we argue that the TrustZone based approach has the potential for matching the security properties of a dedicated hardware based MTM implementation closer than a software MTM implementation on a general purpose processor can do.

The second approach discussed in the paper is based on a dedicated secure element found on the platform. As mentioned at the beginning of section 4.2, such secure elements are already deployed in a number of mobile phone platforms. Again, this JavaCard oriented approach focuses on reusing the existing secure element for hosting trusted computing building blocks, without creating the need for additional special purpose hardware. In this approach, mobile trusted module functionality is implemented in a dedicated smart card environment, sharing some similarity with the TPM modules available in many desktop PC systems. This MTM implementation approach inherits the security properties established by the JavaCard framework and its smart card nature. We conclude that protected capabilities and shielded locations of the smart card based MTM implementation approach closely match their counterparts found in existing TPM modules. We can not yet make a definitive and exhaustive statement on the difference between the security properties of the JavaCard MTM and the TrustZone-based software MTM. Properties of ARM TrustZone suggest that the software MTM implementation can achieve characteristics close to the JavaCard MTM's security properties at least for a subset of these properties. The precise limits of the security properties of both approaches discussed in this paper are part of ongoing and future research. It is an open question whether the MTM implementations discussed in this paper are compliant and/or conformant to the TCG specifications. Since there is no publically available test suite for MTMs at the time of this writing, we can not yet decide if our implementations are compliant to the TCG specifications.

Unfortunately, there is no protection profile for MTMs available either, thus it is not possible to make any assertions about the conformance of our implementations to the TCG specifications at the time of this writing.

References

1. Alves, T., Felton, D.: TrustZone: Integrated Hardware and Software Security - Enabling Trusted Computing in Embedded Systems (July 2004),
   http://www.arm.com/pdfs/TZ_Whitepaper.pdf
2. ARM Ltd. TrustZone Technology Overview. Introduction,
   http://www.arm.com/products/esd/trustzone_home.html
3. Dietrich, K.: An integrated architecture for trusted computing for java enabled embedded devices. In: STC 2007: Proceedings of the 2007 ACM workshop on Scalable trusted computing, pp. 2–6. ACM, New York (2007)
4. Ekberg, J.-E., Asokan, N., Kostiainen, K., Rantala, A.: Scheduling execution of credentials in constrained secure environments. In: STC 2008: Proceedings of the 3rd ACM workshop on Scalable trusted computing, pp. 61–70. ACM, New York (2008)
5. Trusted Computing Group Mobile Working Group. TCG Mobile Reference Architecture Version 1.0 Revision 1. Specification (June 12, 2007),
   http://www.trustedcomputinggroup.org/specs/mobilephone/
   tcg-mobile-reference-architecture-1.0.pdf
6. Trusted Computing Group Mobile Working Group. TCG Mobile Trusted Module Sepecification Version 1 rev. 1.0. Specification (June 12, 2007),
   https://www.trustedcomputinggroup.org/specs/mobilephone/
   tcg-mobile-trusted-module-1.0.pdf
7. Trusted Computing Group TPM Working Group. TPM Main Part 1 Design Principles. Specification, Specification version 1.2 Level 2 Revision 103 (July 9, 2007),
   https://www.trustedcomputinggroup.org/specs/TPM/mainP1DPrev103.zip

8. Trusted Computing Group TPM Working Group. TPM Main Part 3 Commands. Specification, Specification version 1.2 Level 2 Revision 103 (July 9, 2007), https://www.trustedcomputinggroup.org/specs/TPM/mainP3Commandsrev103.zip
9. International Organisation for Standardisation. ISO/IEC 7816-4, Part 4: Interindustry commands for interchange (2005)
10. Kylänpää, M., Ekberg, J.-E.: Mobile Trusted Module (MTM) - an introduction (November 14 (2007), http://research.nokia.com/files/NRCTR2007015.pdf
11. Open Kernel Labs. OKL4 microkernel source code, release 1.5.2., http://wiki.ok-labs.com/images/2/20/Okl4_release_1.5.2.tar.gz
12. Lindholm, T., Yellin, F.: The Java Virtual Machine Specification. Second Edition, http://java.sun.com/docs/books/jvms/second_edition/html/VMSpecTOC.doc.html
13. Sun Microsystems. Java Card Technology. Overview, http://java.sun.com/products/javacard/
14. SUN Microsystems. Java Card Platform Specification 2.2.2. Specification (March 2006), http://java.sun.com/products/javacard/specs.html
15. Microsoft Research. Singularity (2008)
16. Strasser, M.: TPM Emulator. Software package, http://tpm-emulator.berlios.de/
17. SUN. Javacard protection profile (May 2006)
18. Winter, J.: Trusted computing building blocks for embedded linux-based arm trustzone platforms. In: STC 2008: Proceedings of the 3rd ACM workshop on Scalable trusted computing, pp. 21–30. ACM, New York (2008)
19. XEN Hypervisor, http://xen.org/
20. Zhang, X., Aciicmez, O., Seifert, J.-P.: A trusted mobile phone reference architecture via secure kernel. In: STC 2007: Proceedings of the 2007 ACM workshop on Scalable trusted computing, pp. 7–14. ACM, New York (2007)

Modeling Trusted Computing Support in a Protection Profile for High Assurance Security Kernels

Hans Löhr[1], Ahmad-Reza Sadeghi[1], Christian Stüble[2], Marion Weber[3], and Marcel Winandy[1]

[1]Horst Görtz Institute for IT-Security, Ruhr-University Bochum, Germany
{hans.loehr,ahmad.sadeghi,marcel.winandy}@trust.rub.de
[2]Sirrix AG, Bochum, Germany
stueble@sirrix.com
[3]Bundesamt für Sicherheit in der Informationstechnik (BSI), Bonn, Germany
marion.weber@bsi.bund.de

Abstract. This paper presents a Common Criteria protection profile for high assurance security kernels (HASK-PP) based on the results and experiences of several (international) projects on design and implementation of trustworthy platforms. Our HASK-PP was motivated by the fact that currently no protection profile is available that appropriately covers trusted computing features such as trusted boot, sealing, and trusted channels (secure channels with inherent attestation).

In particular, we show how trusted computing features are modeled in the HASK protection profile without depending on any concrete implementation for these features. Instead, this is left to the definition of the security targets of a an IT product which claims conformance to the HASK-PP. Our HASK protection profile was evaluated and certified at evaluation assurance level five (EAL5) by the German Federal Office for Information Security (BSI).

1 Introduction

Industrial and governmental IT applications pose a high degree of assurance on the security of the deployed IT products. Consequently, appropriate evaluation means are desired to verify product claims. In this context, *Common Criteria* standards [1] are established methodologies to provide assurance that the process of specification, implementation and evaluation of an IT security product has been conducted in an appropriate, rigorous and standard manner. In particular, protection profiles (PP) define a set of requirements for a specific class of products that must be fulfilled by any product that is certified as compliant to the profile.

For secure operating systems, a small number of protection profiles exist. However, until recently, the existing protection profiles either model only specific aspects such as access control models, or they define the operating system

L. Chen, C.J. Mitchell, and A. Martin (Eds.): Trust 2009, LNCS 5471, pp. 45–62, 2009.
© Springer-Verlag Berlin Heidelberg 2009

on a very low level. In particular, these protection profiles do not consider important security aspects that can be realized by the emerging trusted computing technology such as secure booting, trusted channels, or data binding.

For example, the *Trusted Computing Group* (TCG), an industrial initiative aiming at the realization of trusted computing, has specified security extensions for commodity computing platforms. The core TCG specification is the *Trusted Platform Module* (TPM) [2], currently implemented as cost-effective, tamper-evident hardware security module embedded in computer mainboards. It allows a platform to provide evidence of its integrity, cryptographically bind data to previously taken integrity measurements, and protect cryptographic keys in shielded hardware. Based on these functionalities, a secure operating system can realize more advanced protection for applications and more reliable evidence of its trustworthiness to external entities like remote parties.

Using a TPM to realize the mentioned security properties is only one option. Alternative solutions are possible based on other hardware security modules like secure coprocessors [3, 4] or smartcards. Hence, to enable the certification of secure systems providing these security properties on an abstraction level allowing end-users to compare security products, a new protection profile incorporating trusted computing becomes necessary.

Contribution. In this paper, we present a Common Criteria protection profile for high assurance security kernels (HASK-PP) [5], based on experience established over several years during the design and development of security kernels in projects such as EMSCB [6], OpenTC [7], and SINA [8]. Moreover, we discuss certain aspects of this protection profile and explain the background of decisions made during the development. The HASK-PP incorporates a number of novelties, compared to existing protection profiles:

- Secure and authenticated boot abstraction (trusted boot)[1]
- User data binding (trusted storage)
- Secure channels with evidence on integrity of endpoints (trusted channels)
- Minimal core security requirements
- High flexibility for implementation

Although one important input to the PP development was trusted computing technology, a strong requirement of the PP development was to keep it implementation-independent. Moreover, a key driver was to minimize the core security requirements, particularly regarding user management and auditing. Only minimal requirements were defined in order to also allow products that do not have (multiple) users or do not need extensive auditing (e.g., embedded devices). The definition of additional security requirements is intentionally left to the specification of security targets of concrete products. All together, this allows a wide range of platforms such as servers, desktop systems, and embedded devices, which can be evaluated according to the HASK protection profile.

---

[1] We explain the differences between secure and authenticated boot in Section 4.1. In general we use the term *trusted boot* as an abstraction for both.

The protection profile was evaluated and certified at evaluation assurance level five (EAL5) by the German Federal Office for Information Security (BSI).

Outline. In Section 2, we introduce goals and design principles of the development of this protection profile and discuss related and previous work. We also briefly introduce the Common Criteria and relevant terminology. Section 3 presents an overview of the high assurance security kernel protection profile (HASK-PP). We show in Section 4 how trusted computing features are modeled in the protection profile, in particular trusted boot, trusted storage, and trusted channels. Finally, we conclude the paper in Section 5 with a brief summary and an outlook on future work.

2   Toward a Protection Profile for Security Kernels

2.1   Goals and Design Principles

The overall goal of the HASK protection profile was to define evaluation criteria for security kernels that provide functions for the management and separation of compartments operating on top of the security kernel. Examples of product types that may implement these functions are

- Microkernels,
- Virtual machine monitors, and
- Logical partitioning products.

The protection profile was developed based on the experiences with different security kernels covering certain aspects to be considered by HASK:

- *Turaya* [9]: A microkernel-based security kernel for desktop and mobile IT products based on COTS components. An open-source version of the Turaya security kernel has been developed in the EMSCB [6] project partly funded by the German Ministry of Economics and Technology.
- *OpenTC* [7]: A hypervisor-based security kernel for clients and servers, using trusted computing technology. OpenTC is a research project partly funded by the European Union.
- *SINA* [8]: A high-assurance "Secure Inter-Network Architecture" developed by the German Federal Office for Information Security (BSI).

High-level abstraction of trusted computing features such as remote attestation and binding were among the results of these projects. We derived our requirements for a protection profile from these insights. In addition to the security functionality of traditional security kernels (such as access control, audit, etc.), three important functions must exist in a product claiming compliance with the HASK protection profile: (1) trusted channel, (2) trusted storage, and (3) trusted boot.

The first function is the ability to "prove" a "trust status" to a remote trusted IT product and to verify the correctness of a status submitted by a remote trusted IT product. This status shows that the product is authentic, has not been modified, and is "fresh" (i. e. the status information received has not been replayed from a previous status information potentially intercepted by an attacker). Based on this information, trusted channels between trusted IT products can be established.

The second function allows to bind user data to compartments resp. the security kernel itself (trusted storage). This function can be used to prevent adversaries from bypassing security policies by modification of applications or the operating system. It was deliberately not the goal to prescribe which method is used to implement these functions. However, a product compliant to the protection profile requires hardware, software, or firmware in its environment that is able to ensure the integrity of the security kernel and its data during start-up.

Hence, the third function provides a trustworthy bootstrap mechanism (trusted boot), which supports the other two functions in providing evidence that the product has started in the intended manner. Figure 1 shows the abstract view of a security kernel and our goals.

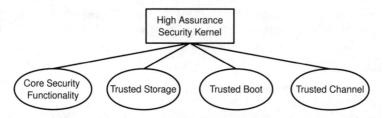

Fig. 1. Abstract functionality of a high-assurance security kernel. "Core Security Functionality" includes separation and access control.

Another important design principle of the HASK-PP was to keep it as minimal as possible to allow a wide range of different realizations, but prevent 'trivial' realizations that do not provide the intended security property from being able to claiming compliance. In fact, the tightrope walk between minimalism and exclusion of trivial realizations was one of the most challenging tasks during the development of this protection profile.

2.2   Common Criteria Basics and Terminology

The *Common Criteria (CC)* are an international standard that aims at permitting comparability between the results of independent security evaluations [1]. The CC provide requirements for security functionality of IT products and assurance measures for the security evaluation of these products. The *Common Criteria Recognition Agreement (CCRA)* regulates international recognition of certificates, and about two dozen countries – including the USA, Canada, UK, Germany, France, Japan, and many others – are currently members of the CCRA.

During security assessment, a given product, the *target of evaluation (TOE)*, is evaluated according to a set of assurance requirements with respect to a *security target (ST)* that defines the security requirements for this TOE. An *evaluation assurance level (EAL)* is a pre-defined set of assurance requirements. The CC specify seven levels (from EAL1 to EAL7), where levels with higher numbers include all requirements from the preceding levels. All hardware, software, and firmware that is necessary for the security functionality of the TOE is called *TOE security functionality (TSF)*. The security requirements that have to be fulfilled by the TSF are called *security functional requirements (SFRs)*. The CC offers a set of classes of pre-defined SFRs, from which designers of security targets can choose. SFR classes are grouped according to security functionality like, e.g., data protection, security management, identification and authentication, auditing.

A *protection profile (PP)* specifies implementation-independent security requirements for a class of TOEs (whereas an ST is implementation-dependent). An ST for a concrete TOE can claim compliance to a PP; in this case, the compliance to the PP is assessed during security evaluation. Protection profiles are particularly important to compare different IT products, since they specify a minimum set of security requirements that must be fulfilled. Of course, the ST for each product can provide additional security features.

2.3 Related Work

The concept of security kernels was explored some decades ago [10–14]. The basic idea is to implement security-critical functionality, i.e., mediating the access to resources according to a security policy, (i) separated from other functionality, and (ii) in a ideally small kernel which allows for the verification of its correctness. The validation and formal verification of security kernels was analyzed and conducted by several works as well [15–18].

Separation kernels can be seen as a subclass of security kernels. They have only limited functionality. Typically, a separation kernel divides the system into separated partitions running virtual machines. Several commercial companies develop separation kernels, such as LynuxWorks [19], Green Hills Software [20], and Wind River Systems [21]. There is also prior work in formal specification and verification of separation kernels [22, 23].

Recently, a protection profile for separation kernels (SKPP) [24] has been introduced and certified in the US. This protection profile has been designed for *high robustness* environments, i.e., it mainly addresses security evaluations at EAL6 and EAL7. The protection profile itself does not claim conformance to a specific evaluation assurance level, but specifies assurance requirements both from EAL6/EAL7, and explicitly defined requirements. Regarding security functional requirements, on the one hand, the focus of SKPP is restricted to the security functionality of separation kernels. In contrast to this, HASK-PP covers a wider range of security functionality, and in particular includes trusted computing functionality. On the other hand, SKPP includes the hardware in the TOE and specifies very detailed security requirements. In contrast, the focus of HASK-PP is more restricted in this sense, since it excludes the hardware from the TOE and leaves more flexibility for concrete implementations. For a discussion of SKPP and its development, see e.g., [25, 26].

Levin et al. [27] compare security kernel and separation kernel architectures with regard to multi-level security. Moreover, they introduce least-privilege separation kernel as a third class of architecture, which supports the security requirements of the SKPP.

In the past, conventional operating systems like various Linux distributions, Unix variants, and versions of Microsoft Windows have been evaluated according to the the *Controlled Access Protection Profile (CAPP)* [28], the *Labeled Security Protection Profile (LSPP)* [29] and the *Role-Based Access Control Protection Profile (RBAC-PP)* [30]. However, these protection profiles target lower evaluation levels[2] and only address the limited aspect of access control models.

3   Overview of HASK-PP

In this section we first describe the architecture and functionality of the TOE (Section 3.1). Then we present an overview of the main components of the protection profile, namely threats and assumptions (Section 3.2) as well as security objectives and security functional requirements (Section 3.3). Finally, we discuss our decision for the evaluation assurance level (Section 3.4).

3.1   Security Kernel Architecture and Functions

The HASK protection profile specifies the security functional and assurance requirements for a class of security kernels that allow executing multiple separated compartments on a single trusted system. Each compartment can behave like a single platform separated from each other with the TOE enforcing this separation and controlling the communication between compartments as well as with external entities in accordance with a defined policy (an overview is shown in Fig. 2). Note that the notion of compartments in the protection profile is a generic concept. A compartment is not necessarily a virtual machine, it can be any set of processes within a security domain. Any product claiming compliance with this PP must provide the necessary security functionality with a high degree of assurance to its users.

To control the communication of external entities with compartments as well as the communication between compartments, the TSF manages a set of *communication objects* that can be assigned to compartments. Communication objects are (on hypervisor-based security kernels) an abstraction for virtual network connections between virtual machines or external networks, and (on microkernel-based security kernels) an abstraction for interprocess-communication between compartmentalized (groups of) processes. Those communication objects allow the

---

[2] While the PPs themselves are certified according to EAL2 and 3, recent evaluations of operating systems according to these profiles achieved EAL4+. However, they are still far from reaching EAL5.

TSF to control which external entities and other compartments a compartment can communicate with and how this communication is protected. Protection of communication is defined by security attributes assigned to communication objects. Those attributes can define characteristics of the communication link like the set of external entities one can communicate with using this communication object, the kind of protection for the communicated data requested from the TSF when using the communication object (integrity protection, confidentiality protection, authentication of the communication peer).

In addition to the communication objects, the TOE also manages *storage containers* of persistent or volatile storage. Those may be whole disks, disk partitions, disk sectors, etc. where the technology to implement those containers (magnetic disks, flash disks, memory disks etc.) is not relevant for the protection profile.

The security kernel has the following (abstract) set of functions:

- Management of compartments (creation, deletion, starting, changing attributes)
- Management of objects, which are at least containers and communication objects (creation, deletion, changing attributes, defining and managing access control policies)
- Management of resources, which are at least processor time and memory (assignment to compartments, setting resource limits, controlling resource limits)
- Generation and verification of information that reliably shows the integrity of the security kernel, a compartment managed by the security kernel, or specific data. We call such information *evidence of integrity*.

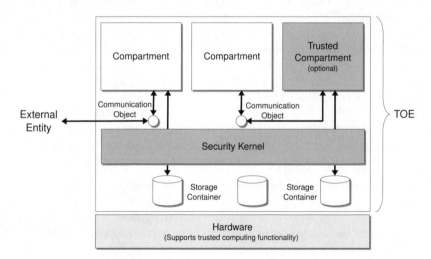

Fig. 2. TOE architecture. Dark gray colored parts implement the TSF.

A security kernel that is compliant to the protection profile needs to implement both mandatory and discretionary access control (MAC/DAC). The DAC policy must at least allow to specify "access" and "no access", and the MAC policy must at least allow separating two compartments from each other such that no information flow between them is possible.

The security kernel (based on hardware functionality required by assumptions in the PP) must be able to protect its integrity, the integrity of compartments, and the integrity of storage containers during runtime. Integrity of the security kernel is obviously required to guarantee the proper operation of the TSF. Integrity of compartments is required for trusted communication channels (see below). Integrity of storage containers is required to prevent unauthorized modification of data when this container is mounted to a compartment.

In a similar way, the system must be able to protect the confidentiality of the security kernel, the confidentiality of compartments, and the confidentiality of storage containers.

Furthermore, the security kernel must be able to provide *trusted channels* between compartments or between compartments and external entities. For a trusted channel, the security kernel has to ensure that the communication link provides integrity and confidentiality protection of the data transferred over the channel, and the identification and authentication of the communication partners must be ensured.

3.2 Threats and Assumptions

The main threats against the TOE include unauthorized access to objects or unauthorized information flow between subjects. Additionally, we considered threats that target to manipulate the TSF or TSF data, including replaying of an older state, e.g., a backup, or influencing the TSF to generate false evidence of the integrity of the TSF or its data. This also includes threats against the TOE environment, e.g., manipulation by installing malicious devices drivers accessing critical hardware functions, or external entities trying to access confidential TSF or user data by starting the TOE outside its intended operational environment.

To address the threats, we stated corresponding security objectives for the TOE and its environment. The latter is important because a security kernel in software alone cannot guarantee or verify its integrity without the assistance of security hardware functionality. In order to be **implementation-independent**, we did not include security functional requirements for the hardware. Instead, we stated **assumptions on the operational environment** in being able to

- support the TOE in producing evidence of the integrity of the TSF code and data during the boot process (`A.INTEGRITY_SUPPORT`);
- allow the TOE to store information such that it cannot be accessed by the TOE where the configuration has been manipulated in an unauthorized way (`A.BIND`[3]);

---

[3] In TCG terminology, the TPM sealing function can provide such a feature. Other implementations may be based on, e.g., secure coprocessors [3].

– provide a function the TOE trusts that is able to generate evidence of the integrity of a remote trusted IT product only if it is correct (A.REMOTE_TRUST).

The assumptions A.INTEGRITY_SUPPORT and A.REMOTE_TRUST are needed to show the status of integrity at load-time of the TOE. Combined with the integrity protection features of the TSF during runtime, one can derive the integrity status of the running TOE and compartments executed on the TOE.

Of course, for secure operation of the TOE, we assume the environment to

– provide mechanisms for separation of the TSF and other subjects or functionality (A.SEPARATION_SUPPORT);
– not contain backdoors (A.HW_OK);
– not be able to start the TOE in an insecure way without this being detectable (A.NO_TAMPER); and
– not have subjects allowed to perform administrative functions and misusing their privileges (A.NO_EVIL).

3.3   Security Objectives and Security Functional Requirements

The security objectives address protection of objects on the one hand (access control to user data, information flow control between compartments, secure data exchange, management of security attributes, resource limitation to avoid denial of service), and protection of the TSF itself on the other hand (TSF and TSF data integrity and confidentiality). Moreover, the TOE must be able to audit defined potentially security-critical events.

To address the security objectives of the TOE, we defined security functional requirements, which can be assigned to four groups: (i) core security functionality (realizing access control, security management, audit, etc.), (ii) trusted storage, (iii) trusted boot, and (iv) trusted channels. See Figure 3 for an overview (note that the SFRs in the groups overlap because some SFRs are addressing more than one objective).

The core security functionality can be divided into four subgroups[4]. (1) Access control and information flow control includes SFRs for data protection, user identification and authentication, and consistency of TSF data when shared between TSF and another trusted IT product. (2) Resource limitation: As a minimal requirement we include maximum quotas for memory and processor time in order to avoid excessive resource consumption. (3) Audit defines that the TOE must be *able* to audit the following events at minimum: start/stop of audit functions, modifications of security policy enforced by TOE, rejected attempts to perform management operations, and integrity violations of TSF or user data. We did not want to dictate a long list of audit events because some products may not have such strong audit requirement, but should be covered

---

[4] We introduce the subgroups only as orientation to reflect the objectives in this paper. The reader can find the exact mapping of SFRs to security objectives in the protection profile.

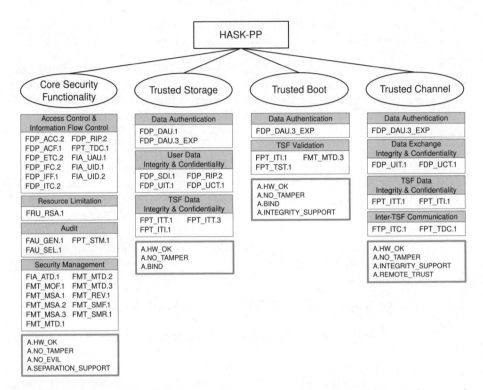

Fig. 3. Overview of the HASK-PP with logical grouping of the security functional requirements and assumptions. See Appendix A for the complete list of SFRs with their names (such as "Basic Data Authentication" for FDP_DAU.1).

by the HASK-PP, too. The actual selection of events to be audited is up to the security target of a concrete product (and can have even more audit events if necessary).

Finally, (4) security management consists of management of security attributes for subjects and objects, management of TSF data, and management of security roles. The inclusion of these SFRs in the HASK-PP was originally not the focus (because we wanted to minimize the requirements), but they were a result of dependencies between SFRs. For instance, FDP_ACF.1 (security attribute based access control) requires FMT_MSA.3 (static attribute initialization).

We discuss the modeling of the objectives trusted storage, trusted boot, and trusted channel in Section 4.

3.4   Security Assurance

The HASK-PP has been developed against the most recent version 3.1 Revision 2 of the Common Criteria to ensure its usefulness in the future. It is fully conformant to CC part 3 by selecting the EAL5 package of security assurance requirements.

EAL5 was chosen as a *minimum* level of assurance for different reasons: The architecture of the TOE in HASK-PP addresses systems with exposure to untrustworthy and unauthorized entities and with high value of the data stored and processed by the system. A sufficient level of assurance must be selected to provide system users with appropriate assurance that the system will be able to withstand such threats. The TOEs claiming conformance to the HASK-PP are expected to provide high assurance against the threats assumed in the PP. Robust and reliable separation of compartments requires a level of assurance that includes the evaluation of possible covert channels between unrelated compartments. In this context, testing and vulnerability analysis of the whole TSF is necessary. The whole architecture of a security kernel managing compartments should be implemented in a lean, modularized fashion as required by the EAL5 assurance level. This means to have well-structured internals, a functional specification which is at least semi-formal, and a development process that follows clear implementation standards and defines unambiguous use of development tools.

EAL5 was also deemed appropriate because it shall provide a platform for other secure services implemented in compartments managed by the TOE. Since such services may be certified at assurance levels above EAL4, the underlying platform must not provide weaker assurance.

EAL5 was deemed to be *sufficient* as a minimum level because levels above EAL5 are usually achievable only with extremely high efforts and costs. This allows security kernels to be evaluated and certified according to HASK-PP for commercial application scenarios that do not require the highest levels of assurance. Of course, the security target for any specific product may specify a higher evaluation level. However, the PP itself was only certified at EAL5.

4   Trusted Computing Functionality in HASK-PP

4.1   Modeling Trusted Boot

To be able to provide the "trust status" of the product configuration as required by the HASK-PP, a trustworthy bootstrap architecture is required to convince remote parties about this status. One basic concept towards the development of a trustworthy bootstrap architecture is the so-called chain of trust which has been introduced by Arbaugh et al. [31]. The core idea is that every component involved in the boot process measures the integrity of the succeeding one before it transfers control to it. If the bootstrap process is started by a trusted component (a trusted root host), it is guaranteed that modifications of components involved in the boot process can be detected by the preceding component. Since the relevant product configuration might not be limited to the security kernel itself, we include requirements for loading and starting compartments in the description of the trusted boot process.

In this context, it is possible to distinguish two types of *trusted boot* mechanisms that mainly differ in the way how the measurement results are used:

Definition 1 (Secure Boot). Secure Boot *is a security property of a bootstrap architecture ensuring that only configurations of a certain property can be loaded. If a modification is detected, the bootstrap process is interrupted.*

The term 'property' used in this definition only identifies a set of configurations, e.g., a list or a signature key certifying allowed configurations. An example implementation of secure boot, as proposed by Arbaugh et al., is to verify the integrity of a succeeding component according to a given reference value. If the verification fails, the boot process is halted or an error function is executed [32].

Definition 2 (Authenticated Boot). Authenticated Boot *is a security property of a bootstrap architecture ensuring that remote parties can verify properties of the booted configuration.*

We use the term trusted boot to refer to both secure and authenticated boot. In contrast to secure boot, authenticated boot is not actively influencing the boot process. An example implementation of authenticated boot, e.g., as proposed by the TCG, is to securely store measurement results (i.e., hash values) of the components involved in the boot chain within the Trusted Platform Module (TPM) and attest the values over an authentic channel.[5]

Although both concepts are very similar, they fulfill slightly different security requirements: Secure boot ensures that only valid configurations are loaded. Local users can therefore assume that the platform is in a trustworthy state if the bootstrap process finished successfully. Remote parties, however, can in general not make any assumptions about the loaded platform configuration. In contrast, authenticated boot allows remote parties to verify the platform's configuration. But because any configuration can be loaded, local users can in general not make any assumptions about the current platform configuration. To securely verify the current platform configuration, further mechanisms such as secure hardware tokens or software mechanism are required.

In general, such a trustworthy bootstrap architecture can be realized using different combinations of technologies and assumptions. Typical examples are smartcards, the TPM, a tamper-evident device, or the assumption that adversaries do not have physical access to the platform.

Since such a bootstrap architecture cannot be realized without assumptions regarding the IT-environment (i.e., hardware or environmental assumptions), the HASK-PP models it using the assumptions A.BIND and A.INTEGRITY_SUPPORT. To allow a compliant product to implement authenticated boot, the assumption A.INTEGRITY_SUPPORT only requires that a manipulated security kernel is not able to generate false evidence of its own integrity. The assumption A.BIND requires that there must be a possibility for the TSF to store data and code in such a way that it can be loaded only if the integrity of the TSF is intact. This allows to implement secure boot.

---

[5] Note that neither authenticated boot, nor secure boot can protect the confidentiality of information under the assumptions that hold for common PC architectures, i.e., the adversary has access to the harddisk. The reason is that both bootstrap architectures do not provide protected storage.

In the protection profile, several security requirements are related to trusted boot. Existing security functional requirements (SFRs) from the CC have been used to require validation of the security kernel and compartments during start-up. This includes that only secure values for memory and CPU time assigned to a compartment are accepted, that the TSF runs a suite of self tests when loading a compartment that requires integrity evidence, and that any modifications between shut down and start-up of the system (e.g., due to manipulations of the hard disk when the system is shut off) can be detected.

Most notably, one extended SFR, FDP_DAU.3_EXP "controlled data authentication", has been defined specifically for the HASK-PP. This requirement states that the TSF must provide the capability to generate evidence that can be used as a guarantee of the integrity of objects. Moreover, it allows the security target of a concrete product to specify conditions under which such evidence is generated, and subjects must be provided with the ability to verify such evidence. This extended SFR allows the security kernel to extend the "chain of trust" (which must be rooted either in hardware or in the operational environment, as expressed by the assumptions mentioned above) up to individual compartments started by the security kernel. Furthermore, it is also relevant for other trusted computing features, such as trusted storage and trusted channels discussed in the following sections.

HASK-PP requires only that the IT-environment offers a mechanism to check the integrity of the security kernel either before (e.g., by a tamper-resistant cover) or during (e.g., with a TPM) loading it. Which alternative is used is left for the specific implementation to decide.

4.2   Modeling Trusted Storage

A security kernel claiming compliance to the HASK-PP must provide *trusted storage*, according to the following definition:

Definition 3. Trusted storage *is storage where* confidentiality, integrity, *and* freshness *(i.e., protection against replay attacks) of stored data is provided, and where the* integrity of the TOE accessing the data *is ensured (in order to prevent other software, such as alternative or modified operating systems, from accessing the data).*

To support trusted storage, a security kernel needs special support from the operational environment, which is reflected in the PP as assumption A.BIND. This assumption requires that the security kernel can store information in such a way that it cannot be accessed by a manipulated TOE (or by software with a different configuration). In concrete systems, A.BIND is usually fulfilled by special hardware features.

Moreover, the security kernel has to ensure that confidentiality and integrity of the data are protected both when the system is running, and when it is offline. Furthermore, it must be infeasible for an attacker to modify the system, or to obtain confidential information from the system in order to get access to the protected data. Additionally, the security kernel must provide a capability to authenticate storage containers, and to verify the integrity of the entity (e.g., compartment) accessing the data. These requirements are expressed by SFRs from the Common Criteria classes FDP (user data protection) and FPT (protection of the TSF), together with the requirement FDP_DAU.3_EXP (cf. Section 4.1).

Several possibilities exist to implement trusted storage in real systems. One such possibility is based on a TPM, however, other concepts for trusted computing, e.g., based on proprietary security modules that are not compliant to the TCG specifications, might use different approaches to realize trusted storage.

Trusted storage with the TCG specifications. In the terminology of the TCG, *sealing* denotes the encryption of data with a key that can only be used by a specific TPM under strictly defined conditions: During sealing, the user can specify values for the evidence of integrity that has to be present inside protected registers of the TPM for decrypting (*unsealing*) the data. During unsealing, the TPM checks the content of these registers and refuses to decrypt if the current evidence deviates from the required values. Sealing provides integrity and confidentiality of the data, as well as integrity of the TOE. To support freshness, monotonic counters, another feature of the TPM, can be used.

4.3   Modeling Trusted Channels

The possibility to establish trusted channels has to be provided by any security kernel claiming compliance to HASK-PP.

Definition 4. *A trusted channel is a channel between two entities that provides integrity, confidentiality, and authenticity of the transmitted data, and ensures integrity and authenticity of the end points.*

Hence, a trusted channel allows the communication partners to receive integrity (attestation) information from their peers. A trusted channel may either provide mutual attestation (i.e., integrity measurements of both end points are transmitted), or only the integrity of one end point is verified. Several solutions for trusted channels based on the TCG specifications have been proposed in the literature [33–37].

To keep the protection profile general and implementation-independent, we need to formulate abstract requirements for the trusted channel, without excluding any specific realization.

The hardware and environmental assumptions which are required for a trusted channel are the availability of a mechanism for the TOE to produce evidence of its own integrity (A.INTEGRITY_SUPPORT) and the availability of a mechanism (that must be trusted by the TOE) providing a similar feature for the remote entity (A.REMOTE_TRUST).

The mandatory functionality of the security kernel to support trusted channels are required by SFRs from the CC for integrity and confidentiality of user data and TSF data during transfer, security functional requirements from the CC for inter-TSF communication, and the component for controlled data authentication that has been introduced specifically for HASK-PP (FDP_DAU.3_EXP).

The distinctive feature of *end point integrity* provided by trusted channels is expressed by requiring *assured identification* of the end points in the CC component FTP_ITC.1 ("Inter-TSF trusted channel"). Here, the term *assured identification* includes integrity verification.

5   Conclusion

In this paper, we describe the first Common Criteria protection profile for a secure operating system with support for enhanced security features, as they are provided by trusted computing technology. The protection profile is general and abstract, thus covering a wide class of IT products without fixing specific mechanisms and leaving a maximum of flexibility and freedom for concrete implementations.

We show how trusted computing features like trusted boot, trusted storage, and trusted channels can be expressed in a generic way by a protection profile, and we point out the relation to existing concepts like the TCG specifications. Moreover, we present and explain the motivation behind the protection profile and important design decisions.

Since the protection profile has been certified, it can be used as a guideline for the design of real systems by security architects. Proof-of-concept implementations and other results from projects like EMSCB, OpenTC, and SINA provide a starting point for developing a security kernel that can be evaluated and certified according to the HASK-PP.

Acknowledgment

This work has been partially funded by the European Commission as part of the OpenTC project [7]. We would like to thank Helmut Kurth and Gerald Krummeck from atsec information security for their invaluable contribution in writing the protection profile, and the anonymous reviewers for their thoughtful comments on this paper.

References

1. Common Criteria for Information Technology Security Evaluation, http://www.commoncriteriaportal.org/thecc.html
2. Trusted Computing Group: TPM Main Specification Version 1.2 rev. 103 (July 2007), https://www.trustedcomputinggroup.org
3. Smith, S.W., Weingart, S.: Building a high-performance, programmable secure coprocessor. Computer Networks 31(8), 831–860 (1999)
4. Yee, B.S.: Using Secure Coprocessors. PhD thesis, School of Computer Science, Carnegie Mellon University, CMU-CS-94-149 (May 1994)

5. Kurth, H., Krummeck, G., Stüble, C., Weber, M., Winandy, M.: HASK-PP: Protection profile for a high assurance security kernel (2008),
   http://www.sirrix.com/media/downloads/54500.pdf
6. European Multilaterally Secure Computing Base, http://www.emscb.de
7. Open Trusted Computing, http://www.opentc.net
8. Sichere Inter-Netzwerk Architektur (SINA),
   http://www.bsi.bund.de/fachthem/sina/index.htm
9. Sadeghi, A.R., Stüble, C., Pohlmann, N.: European multilateral secure computing base - open trusted computing for you and me. Datenschutz und Datensicherheit DuD 28(9), 548–554 (2004)
10. Schroeder, M.D.: Engineering a security kernel for Multics. In: SOSP 1975: Proceedings of the fifth ACM symposium on Operating systems principles, pp. 25–32. ACM, New York (1975)
11. Walter, K.G., Schaen, S.I., Ogden, W.F., Rounds, W.C., Shumway, D.G., Schaeffer, D.D., Biba, K.J., Bradshaw, F.T., Ames, S.R., Gilligan, J.M.: Structured specification of a security kernel. In: Proceedings of the international conference on Reliable software, pp. 285–293. ACM, New York (1975)
12. Chittenden, B., Higgins, P.J.: The security kernel approach to secure operating systems. In: ACM-SE 17: Proceedings of the 17th Annual Southeast Regional Conference, pp. 136–137. ACM, New York (1979)
13. Ames Jr., S.R., Gasser, M., Schell, R.R.: Security kernel design and implementation: An introduction. Computer 16(7), 14–22 (1983)
14. Karger, P.A., Zurko, M.E., Bonin, D.W., Mason, A.H., Kahn, C.E.: A retrospective on the VAX VMM security kernel. IEEE Transactions on Software Engineering 17(11), 1147–1163 (1991)
15. Kemmerer, R.A.: Formal verification of the UCLA security kernel: abstract model, mapping functions, theorem generation, and proofs. PhD thesis (1979)
16. Millen, J.K.: Security kernel validation in practice. Commun. ACM 19(5), 243–250 (1976)
17. Rushby, J.: Design and verification of secure systems. In: SOSP 1981: Proceedings of the 8th ACM Symposium on Operating Systems Principles, pp. 12–21. ACM, New York (1981)
18. Silverman, J.M.: Reflections on the verification of the security of an operating system kernel. In: SOSP 1983: Proceedings of the ninth ACM symposium on Operating systems principles, pp. 143–154. ACM, New York (1983)
19. DeLong, R.J.: LynxSecure separation kernel – a high-assurance security RTOS. Technical report, LynuxWorks, San Jose, CA (May 2007)
20. Green Hills Software Inc.: INTEGRITY PC Technology (November 2008),
   http://www.ghs.com/products/rtos/integritypc.html
21. Wind River Systems Inc.: Wind River High-Assurance Solutions for Aerospace & Defense. Whitepaper (February 2008), http://www.windriver.com/products/product-verviews/PO_MILS_Solution_Feb2008.pdf
22. Martin, W.B., White, P.D., Taylor, F.S.: Creating high confidence in a separation kernel. Automated Software Engineering. 9(3), 263–284 (2002)
23. Heitmeyer, C.L., Archer, M., Leonard, E.I., McLean, J.: Formal specification and verification of data separation in a separation kernel for an embedded system. In: CCS 2006: Proceedings of the 13th ACM conference on Computer and communications security, pp. 346–355. ACM, New York (2006)
24. Information Assurance Directorate: U.S. government protection profile for separation kernels in environments requiring high robustness (SKPP) (2007),
   http://www.niap-ccevs.org/cc-scheme/pp/pp.cfm/id/pp_skpp_hr_v1.03

25. Nguyen, T., Levin, T., Irvine, C.: High robustness requirements in a common criteria protection profile. In: IEEE International Information Assurance Workshop (2006)
26. DeLong, R.J., Nguyen, T., Irvine, C., Levin, T.: Toward a medium-robustness separation kernel protection profile. In: ACSAC 2007. IEEE Computer Society Press, Los Alamitos (2007)
27. Levin, T.E., Irvine, C.E., Weissman, C., Nguyen, T.D.: Analysis of three multilevel security architectures. In: CSAW 2007: Proceedings of the 2007 ACM workshop on Computer security architecture, pp. 37–46. ACM, New York (2007)
28. National Security Agency: Controlled access protection profile (CAPP) (1999), http://www.niap-ccevs.org/cc-scheme/pp/id/PP_OS_CA_V1.d
29. National Security Agency: Labeled security protection profile (LSPP) (1999), http://www.niap-ccevs.org/cc-scheme/pp/id/PP_OS_LS_V1.b
30. Reynolds, J., Chandramouli, R.: Role-based access control protection profile (RBAC-PP), CygnaCom Solutions, Inc. and National Institute of Standards and Testing (1998), http://www.niap-ccevs.org/cc-scheme/pp/id/PP_RBAC_V1.0
31. Arbaugh, W.A., Farber, D.J., Smith, J.M.: A secure and reliable bootstrap architecture. In: Proceedings of the IEEE Symposium on Research in Security and Privacy, Oakland, CA, pp. 65–71. IEEE Computer Society Press, Los Alamitos (1997)
32. Arbaugh, W.A., Keromytis, A.D., Farber, D.J., Smith, J.M.: Automated recovery in a secure bootstrap process. In: Proceedings of the Symposium on Network and Distributed Systems Security (NDSS 1998), San Diego, California, pp. 155–167 (2008)
33. Goldman, K., Perez, R., Sailer, R.: Linking remote attestation to secure tunnel endpoints. In: Proceedings of the 1st ACM Workshop on Scalable Trusted Computing (STC 2006), pp. 21–24. ACM, New York (2006)
34. Stumpf, F., Tafreschi, O., Röder, P., Eckert, C.: A robust integrity reporting protocol for remote attestation. In: Proceedings of the Second Workshop on Advances in Trusted Computing (WATC 2006) (Fall 2006)
35. Sadeghi, A.R., Wolf, M., Stüble, C., Asokan, N., Ekberg, J.E.: Enabling fairer digital rights management with trusted computing. In: Garay, J.A., Lenstra, A.K., Mambo, M., Peralta, R. (eds.) ISC 2007. LNCS, vol. 4779, pp. 53–70. Springer, Heidelberg (2007)
36. Gasmi, Y., Sadeghi, A.-R., Stewin, P., Unger, M., Asokan, N.: Beyond secure channels. In: Proceedings of the 2nd ACM Workshop on Scalable Trusted Computing (STC 2007), pp. 30–40. ACM, New York (2007)
37. Armknecht, F., Gasmi, Y., Sadeghi, A.R., Stewin, P., Unger, M., Ramunno, G., Vernizzi, D.: An efficient implementation of trusted channels based on OpenSSL. In: Proceedings of the 3rd ACM Workshop on Scalable Trusted Computing (STC 2008), pp. 41–50. ACM, New York (2008)

A   Security Functional Requirements

The security functional requirements of the HASK-PP originate all from Common Criteria V3.1 Release 2, part 2, with the exception of FDP_DAU.3_EXP, which is an extended requirement defined in the protection profile. Table 1 summarizes the security functional requirements of HASK-PP.

Table 1. Security functional requirements in HASK-PP

SFR	Title
FAU_GEN.1	Audit data generation
FAU_SEL.1	Security audit event selection
FDP_ACC.2	Complete access control
FDP_ACF.1	Security attribute based access control
FDP_DAU.1	Basic data authentication
FDP_DAU.3_EXP	Controlled data authentication
FDP_ETC.2	Export of user data with security attributes
FDP_IFC.2	Complete information flow control
FDP_IFF.1	Simple security attributes
FDP_ITC.2	Import of user data with security attributes
FDP_RIP.2	Full residual information protection
FDP_SDI.1	Stored data integrity monitoring
FDP_UCT.1	Basic data exchange confidentiality
FDP_UIT.1	Data exchange integrity
FIA_ATD.1	User attribute definition
FIA_UAU.1	Timing of authentication
FIA_UID.1	Timing of identification
FIA_UID.2	User identification before any action
FMT_MOF.1	Management of security functions behavior
FMT_MSA.1	Management of security attributes
FMT_MSA.2	Secure security attributes
FMT_MSA.3	Static attribute initialization
FMT_MTD.1(1)	Management of TSF data
FMT_MTD.1(2)	Management of TSF data for communication objects
FMT_MTD.2	Management of limits on TSF data
FMT_MTD.3	Secure TSF data
FMT_REV.1	Revocation
FMT_SMF.1	Specification of management functions
FMT_SMR.1	Security roles
FPT_ITI.1	Inter-TSF detection of modification
FPT_ITT.1	Basic internal TSF data transfer
FPT_ITT.3	TSF data integrity monitoring
FPT_STM.1	Reliable time stamps
FPT_TDC.1	Inter-TSF basic TSF data consistency
FPT_TST.1	TSF testing
FRU_RSA.1	Maximum quotas
FTP_ITC.1	Inter-TSF trusted channel

Remote Attestation of Attribute Updates and Information Flows in a UCON System

Mohammad Nauman[1], Masoom Alam[1], Xinwen Zhang[2], and Tamleek Ali[1]

[1] Security Engineering Research Group,
Institute of Management Sciences, Peshawar, Pakistan
{nauman,masoom,tamleek}@imsciences.edu.pk
[2] Samsung Information Systems America, San José, USA
xinwen.z@samsung.com

Abstract. UCON is a highly flexible and expressive usage control model which allows an object owner to specify detailed usage control policies to be evaluated on a remote platform. Assurance of correct enforcement is mandatory for the establishment of trust on the remote platform claiming to implement UCON. Without such an assurance, there is no way of knowing whether the policies attached to the objects will be enforced as expected. Remote attestation, an important component of Trusted Computing, is highly suitable for establishing such an assurance. Existing approaches towards remote attestation work at a very coarse-grained level and mostly only measure binary hashes of the applications on the remote platform. Solutions at this level of abstraction cannot provide assurance to a challenger regarding behavior of a remote platform concerning enforcement of the owner's policies. In this paper, we provide a new remote attestation technique which allows a challenger to verify two important behaviors of a UCON system enforcing its policies. These two behaviors are the attribute update behavior and information flow behavior. Measuring, storing and reporting these behaviors in a trusted manner is described in detail and a mechanism for the verification of these behaviors against the original UCON policies is provided. The end result is a flexible and scalable technique for establishing trust on attribute updates and information flow behaviors of a remote UCON system.

Keywords: Information flow, remote attestation, usage control, security.

1 Introduction

Usage control deals with issues concerning usage of protected objects based on the policies of the object owner. While traditional *access control* models deal with authorization issues such as who may access an object, *usage control* models address issues concerning use of objects such as duration of each use, the number of usages and ability to re-distribute etc.

UCON [1] is a highly expressive usage control model which adds *continuity* of access decisions and *mutability* of attributes at the model level. Its major

L. Chen, C.J. Mitchell, and A. Martin (Eds.): Trust 2009, LNCS 5471, pp. 63–80, 2009.
© Springer-Verlag Berlin Heidelberg 2009

strength lies in the ability to specify elaborate usage control policies to be evaluated on a remote platform. This strength of UCON to operate on a remote platform is also a source of concern. Since the owner of the object releases it to a remote platform, she has no way of ensuring that the policies attached to it will be enforced as specified. Trusted computing [2] proposes an innovative approach for establishing trust on a remote platform in such a scenario. This approach, called Remote Attestation, allows a *challenger* to verify that the behavior of a *target* platform is trustworthy. Existing approaches towards remote attestation include low-level techniques of presenting binary hashes of executables to the challenger [3,4], middle-level approaches of mapping system configurations to generic properties by a trusted third party [5] and a high level mechanism of measuring individual components of a policy model for the establishment of trust [6]. The low- and middle-level techniques allow a challenger to statically determine the identity of the applications running on the client and properties of the system in general. They do not enable measurement of dynamic behavior of a target application on the client. Moreover, it has been widely accepted that binary hashes of executables alone are insufficient for reasoning about trustworthiness of a platform [4,7]. Low-level binary hash based techniques are, therefore, not suitable for remote attestation of a UCON system.

Consider for example, a UCON policy, which specifies that, "a media file can only be played once by an individual in the public relations office for two minutes only and that each usage has to be logged". Clearly, it is impossible to deduce, from the hash of an executable alone, that this policy will be enforced correctly by the application.

For deducing such intricate details of an application's behavior, Alam et al. have proposed Model-based Behavioral Attestation [6] i.e. attestation of a policy model being followed by the target application for a specific purpose. This technique proposes the decomposition of the behavior of a policy model into its individual components and measuring these individual behaviors. If the behavior of each of the components can be attested by the challenger, the whole system can be deemed as trustworthy. Model-based Behavioral Attestation has specified three behaviors of a UCON policy model – active subject/object behavior, attribute update behavior and state transition behavior. We note that the procedure for the measurement of these behaviors is not a part of the Model-based Behavioral Attestation framework.

In this paper, we specify a technique for measurement, storage and reporting of the attribute update behavior and its verification against the challenger's policies. Attribute updates are an integral part of the UCON model and heavily influence usage decisions [8]. Successful remote attestation of attribute update behavior would provide confidence to the challenger regarding the trustworthiness of a target platform.

We also identify another UCON model behavior – information flow behavior – which captures the possible information flows between objects in a UCON system. Attesting the trustworthiness of information flow behavior would provide assurance that no illegal information flows occurred on the client end during the usage of the owner's resources. Such assurance is critical in systems of a distributed nature [9]. Similar to the attribute update behavior, we provide a detailed mechanism for the measurement, storage, reporting and verification of the information flow behavior.

Contributions: Our contributions in this paper are as follows: 1) We describe a mechanism for recording arbitrary data structures in the TPM as opposed to binary hashes of executables only. 2) We detail a procedure for measuring the behaviors of attribute updates and information flows in a UCON system. 3) We provide a means of verifying the behavior tokens returned by the target application on the challenger side against the original UCON policies.

Outline: The rest of the paper is organized as follows: In Section 2, we provide background about the UCON model and describe the formal model used for our attestation purposes. Behavioral Attestation is introduced in Section 3. Our UCON system attestation is described at length in Section 4 with attribute updates and information flows covered in Sections 4.1 and 4.2 respectively. Previous work related to this paper is mentioned in Section 5. Finally, we conclude our work and present future directions in Section 6.

2   UCON

UCON [1] is a Usage CONtrol model, which builds heavily on traditional access control models. It incorporates dynamic usage of protected objects and changes in decisions to allow further access to these objects as a result of usage. This extension is achieved through the introduction of two novel features: access decision continuity and attribute mutability.

In a UCON system, the user initiates a request for an object protected by the UCON system. The access decision depends on the policies and constraints for the particular *subject*, *object* and *right* combination, identified by (s, o, r). The request can either be granted or denied. Even if the request is initially granted, the usage session does not end. The coupling of attribute mutability and access decision continuity means that due to the usage of the protected object, the attributes of the subject and/or object may change. As a result of this change, the decision to allow access might also be reversed. The usage session remains at state *accessing* as long as the constraints allow the continued use of the object. If the user ends the usage, the usage session moves to state *end*. If, however, the constraints lead to a denial of access after some time, the state moves to *revoked* and the user is no longer allowed access to the object. Figure 1 shows the states in the UCON usage session [1].

Zhang et al. [10] have formally specified the UCON model at a very abstract level. However, this formalization is not suitable for the purpose of information flow analysis and attestation of attribute updates. Instead, we use another formalization of UCON by Zhang et al. [11] which has been formulated for safety analysis of the UCON model. Safety analysis of UCON is essential for our behavior verification step. For the verification of behaviors collected on the target platform, we create a benchmark on the challenger side, which requires the safety problem of UCON to be decidable. However, Zhang et al. [11] have shown that the safety problem in general UCON is undecidable. They have defined the safety problem of a subset of UCON which includes only authorization predicates. This subset is termed as $UCON_A$. A formal model of $UCON_A$ is defined in which a UCON system is composed of *subjects*, *objects*, *rights*, *permissions primitive actions* and *policies*. Sets of subjects, objects and rights are denoted by S, O and R respectively and $S \subseteq O$. A *permission* is a triple of (s, o, r) where $s \in S$, $o \in O$ and $r \in R$. An attribute a of an object o is denoted by $o.a$. The set of attributes is shared by all objects and is denoted by ATT. Attributes are mapped to their values using an assignment: $o.a = v$, where $v \in dom(a) \cup \{null\}$.

A UCON system state is a pair (O, σ) where O is the set of objects and $\sigma : O \times ATT \rightarrow dom(ATT) \cup \{null\}$ is a function which maps each attribute of each object to a value or `null`. The initial UCON state is denoted by (O_0, σ_0).

A primitive action changes the system state. The three primitive actions in $UCON_A$ are *createObject*, *destroyObject* and *updateAttribute*. On the application of any of these actions, the state of a system is said to change from t to t' where t is the state before the application of the action and t' is the state after the action has been performed. In any given state t, the permission function ρ_t maps a pair (subject, object) to a set of rights according to their attribute values in state t.

A UCON policy consists of a name, two parameter objects (usually a subject and an object), an authorization rule and a sequence of primitive actions.

$$policy\_name(s, o):$$
$$p_1 \wedge p_2 \wedge \ldots \wedge p_n \rightarrow permit(s, o, r)$$
$$act_1; act_2; \ldots; act_k$$

If one of the primitive actions in a policy is a *createObject* action, the policy is called a creating policy. The set of policies in a system is denoted by C. Changes to a system state occur as a result of application of a policy. For two UCON system states, (O_t, σ_t) and $(O_{t'}, \sigma_{t'})$, $t \twoheadrightarrow_c t'$ denotes that there exists a pair of objects (o_1, o_2) where $o_1 \in O_t$ such that policy $c(o_1, o_2)$ can be applied to t and changes the state to t'. Moreover, $t \twoheadrightarrow_C t'$ if $\exists c \in C.t \twoheadrightarrow_c t'$ and $t \rightsquigarrow_C t'$ if there

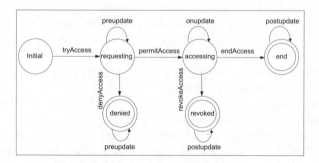

Fig. 1. The UCON Model States

exists a sequence of states $t_1, t_2, \ldots, t_n$ such that $t \twoheadrightarrow_C t_1 \twoheadrightarrow_C t_2 \ldots \twoheadrightarrow_C t_n \twoheadrightarrow_C t'$. $t \rightsquigarrow_C t'$ or simply $t \rightsquigarrow t'$ is called the *transition history* from t to t'.

Zhang et al. have proven that the safety problem in this general model of $UCON_A$ is undecidable [11]. In order to render the safety problem decidable, Zhang et al. propose some restrictions on the system. Different structures have been defined in the form of *ground policies*, *attribute update graph* and *attribute creation graph* to formalize these restrictions.

A set of *ground policies* generated from a UCON policy 'c' denotes all the evaluations of the policy c with possible attribute tuples of the object parameters which satisfy the predicates in the authorization rule of c. Assume $ATT = \{a\}$ and $dom(a) = \{1, 2, 3\}$ and the following UCON policy:

$c(s, o)$:
  $s.a > o.a \rightarrow permit(s, o, r)$
  $updateAttribute \quad o : o.a = o.a + 1$

Grounding this policy generates the following three *ground* policies:

$c(s : (a = 3), o : (a = 2))$:
  $true \rightarrow permit(s, o, r)$
  $updateAttributeTuple \quad o : (a = 2) \rightarrow (a = 3)$

$c(s : (a = 3), o : (a = 1))$:
  $true \rightarrow permit(s, o, r)$
  $updateAttributeTuple \quad o : (a = 1) \rightarrow (a = 2)$

$c(s : (a = 2), o : (a = 1))$:
  $true \rightarrow permit(s, o, r)$
  $updateAttributeTuple \quad o : (a = 1) \rightarrow (a = 2)$

Note that for attribute tuples for which the predicate is not true (e.g. $s : (a = 1), o : (a = 1))$, no ground policy is generated.

A *create ground policy* is a ground policy, which contains a *createObject* action in its body. In such a policy, the attribute tuple of the first parameter object is termed as *create-parent attribute tuple* and that of the second is termed as *create-child attribute tuple*. An *Attribute Creation Graph (ACG)* is a directed graph with nodes all possible attribute tuples and an edge from create-parent attribute tuple to a create-child attribute tuple if there exists a corresponding ground policy for these tuples.

Similarly, in a ground policy which updates an attribute tuple, the old attribute tuple is called the *update-parent attribute tuple* and the updated tuple is called the *update-child attribute tuple*. An *Attribute Update Graph (AUG)* is a directed graph with nodes all possible attribute tuples and edges from update-parent attribute tuple to update-child attribute tuple if there exists a corresponding ground policy for these tuples.

Using these structures, Zhang et al. [11] have shown that a UCON$_A$ system with finite attribute domains is decidable if the ACG is acyclic, the AUG has no cycles containing a create-parent attribute tuple and in each creating ground policy, the attribute tuples of both the parent and child are updated. Usefulness of UCON$_A$ systems with these restrictions has been shown. For a detailed discussion and proofs of these statements, we refer the reader to [11].

In the next sections, we describe how a UCON$_A$ system with these restrictions can be remotely attested using dynamic behaviors of the system recorded during enforcement of policies.

3   Behavioral Attestation

Traditional attestation techniques [3,4,5] rely solely on the binary hashes of applications running on the client. A chain of trust is established from the core root of trust (i.e. the Trusted Platform Module) to the application. However, all of these techniques measure the target application statically without considering its inner working [6]. A recent technique, Model-based Behavioral Attestation (MBA) [6], proposes a high-level framework for measuring the internal working of the target application based on the dynamic behaviors of the different components of the application. We note that the MBA framework relies on the existence of a small *monitor* module in the target application as part of the Trusted Computing Base (TCB)[1].

The monitor, being a part of the TCB, can measure the dynamic behavior of the rest of the application in a trusted manner. During an attestation request, the monitor sends these measurements to the challenger where they can be verified. If the behavior depicted by these measurements is compliant with the object owner's policy, the challenger can be assured that the security policy is indeed being enforced as expected. For the dynamic behaviors reported by the monitor to be trusted, there are two requirements.

1. The monitor module has to be verified for correctness using formal methods. While formal verification of large systems is a complex procedure and quickly becomes infeasible [13], verification of small components is easier and can yield many benefits. The monitor is a relatively small component and its formal verification adds significantly to the confidence in the correctness of the functionality and subsequently to its reported measurements.
2. Its hash has to attested using traditional attestation techniques such as IMA [3] or PRIMA [4]. In other words, this dynamic attestation technique is not exclusive of traditional attestation mechanisms but supports them by providing an added level of confidence through attestation of internal working of the application and its dynamic behavior.

The rest of the paper describes details of implementation of this monitor in a target application enforcing UCON policies. We discuss the measurements to

---

[1] TCB is the collection of software and hardware components which are responsible for enforcing security policies on a platform [12].

be made for the dynamic behavior of attribute updates and information flows in the application and the mechanism for reporting these changes to the challenger in a trusted manner. We also describe how the reported behavior can be verified against the challenger's policy to ensure that the information flows and attribute updates in the target UCON application are occurring as expected.

4   UCON System Attestation

UCON is primarily concerned with usage of an object after it is released to a remote platform. The owner of the object may not have control over the usage of the object. It is therefore imperative that she be able to establish trust on the remote platform. Without the assurance of trustworthiness of the UCON system on the remote platform, there is no way of ensuring that the UCON policy attached to the object will indeed be enforced as expected [6].

We focus on two aspects of a UCON system implementation in this contribution:

1. Attributes play an important role in a UCON system. Attribute mutability is a core feature of UCON which lends the model its flexibility and expressive power. The challenger needs to be able to verify remotely that attribute updates occurring on the client are compliant with the policies.
2. To ensure that no information leakage can occur, the challenger needs a mechanism for remotely attesting possible information flows on the target. Information flows not allowed by the policies of the challenger may lead to a leakage of information to unauthorized parties. By having the client report all possible information flow to the challenger in a trustworthy manner, possible information leakage can be successfully detected.[2]

To formulate a framework for these two requirements, we define two *behaviors*. The first requirement is captured by the *attribute update behavior (AU)* and the second is captured by the *information flow behavior (IF)*. Each of these behaviors is monitored by the Behavior Manager (BM) which is a part of the UCON engine on the client end (cf. Section 3). The BM captures dynamic behavior of attribute updates and possible information flows and is capable of communicating these behaviors to the challenger in a trustworthy manner.

Figure 2 depicts the architecture of remote attestation of a UCON system. When a target application on the client requests an object, the server, upon successful authorization of the client, attaches a UCON policy to the object and releases the *protected object* to the client. The object is registered with the UCON decision engine on the client. During the usage of the object, usage authorization decisions and any updates which need to be performed are communicated to the Behavior Manager. The Attribute Update Manager records proofs for the attribute update behavior *AU* and the Information Flow Manager records proofs for the information flow behavior *IF*. During an attestation challenge,

---

[2] In this contribution, we focus on explicit information flows. Implicit information flows, such as those through covert channels, are not addressed.

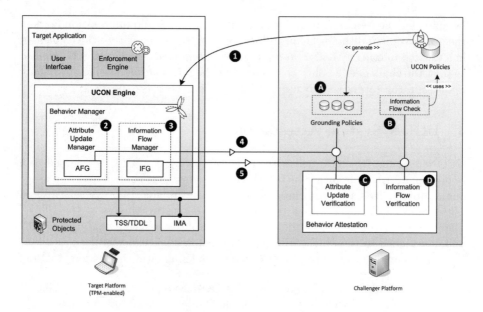

Fig. 2. Remote Attestation of a UCON System

the Behavior Manager collects these behavior proofs and reports them to the challenger.

Upon receipt of these two behaviors, the challenger performs two behavior verification procedures. The attribute update verification module utilizes the original UCON policies to generate ground policies (cf. Section 2) which are used to verify the trustworthiness of the attribute update behavior (cf. Section 4.1). The same set of UCON policies are utilized by the information flow attestation mechanism to verify the information flow behavior using an information flow check algorithm (cf. Section 4.2).

The details of storing and reporting the two behaviors in a trusted manner on the target platform and the verification mechanisms utilized on the challenger side are described below.

4.1   Attribute Update Behavior

For capturing the attribute update behavior, the BM implements one or more *Attribute Update Procedures (AUPs)* which are responsible for updating attributes on the client end. The procedures take two inputs, either of which can be an attribute of an object or a constant.

Individual calls to an attribute update procedure and subsequent attribute updates are recorded through a graph structure called the *attribute flow graph*. This structure stores the relationship between updated attributes and the attributes used as inputs for this updation. Formally:

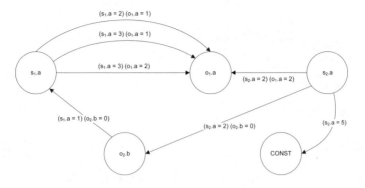

Fig. 3. Attribute Flow Graph Example

Definition 1 (Attribute Flow Graph). *The Attribute Flow Graph (AFG) is a directed multi-graph (G,V) where G is a set of nodes representing object attributes or a constant and V is a set of edges representing attribute updates. An edge directed from $o_i.a$ to $o_j.b$ denotes an update of $o_i.a$ and is labeled with $(o_i.a = dom(ATT)), (o_j.b = dom(ATT))$. The label captures the values of $o_i.a$ and $o_j.b$ before the update takes place. The special node called CONST is used to denote all constants.*

Figure 3 shows a graphical representation of the AFG. Note that there may be more than one attribute updates involving the same set of object attributes but with different values. An attribute update involving a constant is represented by an edge from the target attribute to the $CONST$ node.

To capture the AFG in a trustworthy manner, we employ the constructs of Trusted Computing. The initial value of the the AFG (i.e. null) and any subsequent changes to it are stored in an *Attribute Update Log (AUL)*. At startup, the BM initializes the AUL with an initialization token $INIT$. It monitors all calls to the *AUPs* and whenever a call is received, it creates an *entry* in the AUL. Any change to the AUL is stored in a Platform Configuration Register (PCR) of the TPM by taking a hash of the entry and extending the PCR through *pcr_extend* (cf. Figure 4). The hash of the update procedure (AUP_x) responsible for performing the specific update is also recorded in the PCR through *pcr_extend*. The new value of the PCR after an update is calculated as:

$$PCR_{AUL_\epsilon} = SHA\text{-}1(\ SHA\text{-}1(PCR_{AUL_{\epsilon-1}}\ ||\ SHA\text{-}1(AUL_\epsilon))\ ||SHA\text{-}1(AUP_x))$$

During an attestation challenge, the BM receives a nonce from the challenger and submits the nonce to the TPM through a Trusted Software Stack (TSS) [14,15,16]. It requests the TPM to perform a quote over the given PCR and nonce. The quoted value of the PCR is sent to the challenger along with the AUL for verification.[3]

---

[3] The interested reader may refer to [17] for a detailed description of the quote operation over a PCR.

```
INIT                                  // initialize the AUL
s1.a:o1.a:s1.a=2:o1.a=1::AUP1         // update by AUP1 involving s1.a and o1.a
s1.a:o2.b:s1.a=1:o2.b=0::AUP2         // update by AUP2 involving s1.a and o2.b
s1.a:o1.a:s1.a=3:o1.a=1::AUP1         // ...
s2.a:CONST:s2.a=5::AUPY               // update by AUPY involving s2.a and a constant
s1.a:o1.a:s1.a=2:o1.a=2::AUPX         // ...
s2.a:o1.a:s2.a=2:o1.a=2::AUP2         // ...
s2.a:o2.b:s2.a=2:o2.b=0::AUP1         // ...
```

Fig. 4. Sample Attribute Update Log

Capturing the dynamic behavior of updates is a relatively simple task. Once the attribute update log is received by the challenger, it has to be verified against the policy to ensure that all attribute updates occurring on the client comply with the policies of the challenger. The challenger utilizes the grounding procedure, defined in Section 2, for this compliance checking.

In order for the attribute updates occurring on the client to be considered as trustworthy, the challenger needs to be able to verify that, for each update, there exists a ground policy (generated as a result of grounding of the policies sent to the client), which requires the update performed at the client end. It also requires the hash of the update procedure responsible for performing the update to be trusted. The first step for the verification of attribute update behavior is the verification of the signature performed by the client's TPM on the PCR value. This ensures that the PCR values can be trusted to be signed by a genuine TPM and not by a software masquerading as a TPM. The second step is to verify the Attribute Update Log (AUL) against the PCR value returned. This is a similar operation to the verification procedure used by the Integrity Measurement Architecture [3]. Hashes of entries in the AUL and those of the update procedures are concatenated in sequence to give the final value of the PCR. For each entry AUL_ϵ in the AUL, the PCR value at AUL_ϵ is given by:

$$\mathrm{PCR}_{AUL_\epsilon} = \mathrm{SHA\text{-}1}(\ \mathrm{SHA\text{-}1}(\mathrm{PCR}_{AUL_{\epsilon-1}} \parallel \mathrm{SHA\text{-}1}(AUL_\epsilon))\ \parallel \mathrm{SHA\text{-}1}(AUP_x))$$

where AUP_x is the procedure performing the update recorded in AUL_ϵ. If the final value of the computation matches the value of the PCR returned by the target's TPM, the challenger can be assured that the AUL has not been tampered with and can be used for verification of the target's behavior.

The next step in the attribute update behavior verification is to verify each attribute update operation against the ground policies to ensure that no illegal attribute updates have occurred on the target platform and that the hash of the update procedure responsible for performing the updates is a known good one. For each attribute update, represented by edges in the AFG, there must exist a ground policy which updates the target (object, attribute) pair using the source (object, attribute) pair in the AFG. Attribute updates involving constants must be verified against the $CONST$ node against the values required by the ground policies. Formally:

$$\forall v \in V. \exists c_n \in C_n. \exists uo \in c_n.target(uo) = target(v)$$
$$\wedge \exists s \in sources(uo).s = source(v)$$
$$\wedge \forall o.a \in v.value(o.a) = avalue(o.a, uo)$$

where uo is an update operation in a ground policy c_n, $target(uo)$ is the output of the update operation, $sources(uo)$ are the inputs to the update operation uo, $value(o.a)$ returns the value of the attribute a of object o during the update procedure and $avalue(o.a, uo)$ returns the attribute value of $o.a$ from the attribute tuple of uo.

If the above condition is satisfied by the complete AFG, the challenger can be assured that all attribute update operations performed on the client have been in compliance with the UCON policies. We define the trustworthiness of the attribute update behavior $\mathcal{AU}$ as:

$$\mathcal{AU}.\text{behavior} = trusted \text{ iff}$$
$$\forall v \in V. \exists c_n \in C_n. \exists uo \in c_n.target(uo) = target(v)$$
$$\wedge \exists s \in sources(uo).s = source(v)$$
$$\wedge \forall o.a \in v.value(o.a) = avalue(o.a, uo)$$
$$\wedge \forall a \in \text{AUP}_x.\ a.behavior = trusted$$

In essence, attribute update behavior is trusted if and only if 1) all attribute updates taking place on the target machine are allowed by some ground policies generated from the original usage policies of the challenger and 2) all the procedures responsible for performing attribute updates on the target are also trusted.

4.2   Information Flow Behavior

For the measurement of the information flow behavior, the Behavior Manager utilizes an Information Flow Manager. This component of the UCON implementation is responsible for maintaining a structure called the Access Rights Graph (ARG). The ARG records information about which objects have been granted access rights to other objects. Formally:

Definition 2 (Access Rights Graph). *An Access Rights Graph (ARG) is a directed graph (H, W) where H is a set of nodes representing the objects and W is a set of edges representing rights. An edge from h_1 to h_2 labeled r denotes the rights r assigned to h_1 on h_2 at some point in the usage history where $h_1, h_2 \in H$, $r \in 2^R$ and R is the set of rights.*

Figure 5 shows a graphical depiction of the ARG. To store and later report this structure in a trusted manner, the BM utilizes a technique similar to that used for capturing the AFG. The initial (empty) value of the ARG is stored in a *Access Rights Log (ARL)*. The ARL is initialized as empty by setting it to the value $INIT$. Any decisions by the UCON decision module are captured by the ARL. If an access is granted to a subject s on an object o for right r, nodes s and o are added to the ARG, if they are not already present. An entry is made in the ARL for recording the addition of the nodes. An edge, directed from s

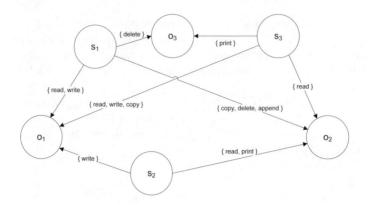

Fig. 5. Access Rights Graph Example

to o is added to the ARG and labeled $\{r\}$ if such an edge doesn't already exist. If the edge already exists, right r is added to the set of rights on the edge. An entry is made in the ARL corresponding to the addition of the right for s on o. Figure 6 shows an example ARL created as a result of different usage decisions.

Whenever an entry is appended to the ARL, its hash is calculated by the Information Flow Manager and stored in the PCR through *pcr_extend*. During an attestation challenge, the ARL and this PCR value is returned to the challenger where verification of these structures against the challenger's UCON policies takes place.

For the verification of the ARL on the challenger side, we utilize an *information flow check* algorithm which utilizes the same semantics as the UCON *safety check* algorithm presented by Zhang et al. [10]. The first step, as in the verification of the ARL, is to verify the signature by the TPM to ensure that the PCR values returned are from a genuine TPM and that the ARL is trusted. Every entry ARL_ϵ in the ARL is concatenated in sequence to give the final value of the PCR as:

$$\mathrm{PCR}_{ARL_\epsilon} = \mathrm{SHA\text{-}1}(\mathrm{PCR}_{ARL_{\epsilon-1}} \parallel \mathrm{SHA\text{-}1}(ARL_\epsilon))$$

Verification of the entries in the ARL provides assurance to the challenger that the ARL has not been tampered with. The individual entries in the ARL are

```
INIT                    // initialize the ARL
ADD|s1                  // add a new subject s1
ADD|o3                  // add a new object o3
ASSIGN|s1:o3:delete     // assign right delete to s1 on o3
ADD|o1                  // ...
ASSIGN|s1:o1:read       // ...
ADD|o2                  // ...
ASSIGN|s1:o2:append     // ...
...
```

Fig. 6. Sample Access Rights Log

Fig. 7. Information Flow Graph corresponding to ARG in Figure 5

used to re-generate the ARG on the challenger side. After this re-generation, the challenger creates an Information Flow Graph (IFG). The IFG depicts possible information flows implied by the Access Rights Graph. Formally:

Definition 3 (Information Flow Graph). *An Information Flow Graph (IFG) is a directed graph (I, U) where I is a set of nodes representing the objects and U is a set of edges representing possible information flow in the direction of the edge. An edge from i_1 to i_2 denotes that information may have flown from i_1 to i_2 where $i_1, i_2 \in I$.*

To construct the IFG from the ARG, we first define all rights as *read-like, write-like, read-write-like* or *no-impact* [18]. No-impact operations are those which cannot play a part in information flow (such as *print*) and are discarded immediately. Afterwards, all objects in the ARG are represented in the IFG. For each subject s in the ARG, an edge is created from o_1 to o_2 if a read-like (or read-write-like) operation is granted to s on o_1 and a write-like (or read-write-like) operation is granted to s on o_2. Afterwards, orphan nodes are removed from the IFG. Figure 7 shows an IFG corresponding to the ARG of Figure 5.

For the verification of possible information flows as depicted by the IFG the following procedure is adopted. For each edge on the IFG, Algorithm 1 is applied to ensure that the information flow is compliant with the policies of the challenger. The algorithm takes an initial UCON state and a set of ground policies as inputs. A finite automaton (FA) is created which maps changes to the UCON state as a result of applying non-creating ground polices (line 2). For each state in the resulting FA, a few operations are performed. First, all subjects which have been assigned a read-like (or read-write-like) right on o_1 are added to the set *reading* (lines 4,6). If one of the subjects was previously granted a write-like operation on o_2, the algorithm immediately returns *true* (line 7) as the subject would have been able to cause information to flow from o_1 to o_2.

A similar procedure is followed for write-like operations (line 9). All subjects which have been assigned a write-like operation (or read-write-like operation) on o_2 are added to the set *writing* (lines 9,11) and if one of them was previously assigned a read-like operation on o_1, the algorithm returns true immediately (line 12).[4]

Finally, creating ground policies are applied (line 15) to extend the UCON system with new objects and `InfoFlowCheck()` algorithm is called recursively (line 20) to check for possible information flows in this expanded space.

---

[4] Note that the algorithm only checks for information flow *from o_1 to o_2* and not in the other direction.

Algorithm 1. Information Flow Check Algorithm

Input: UCON$_A$ system with initial state $t_0 = (O_0, \sigma_0)$, a finite set of ground policies
and two objects, o_1 and o_2
Output: A boolean value which is true only if information can flow from o_1 to o_2

1) **InfoFlowCheck(O$_0$, t$_0$)**
2) *Construct a finite state automaton* $\mathcal{FA}$ *with objects* O_0 *and the set of non-creating*
    ground policies as in [11]
3) **foreach** $t_0 \leadsto t \in \mathcal{FA}$ **do**
4)   **collect** $\varsigma = \{x | r \in \rho_t(x, o_1) \wedge r = $ 'read' $\}$
5)   **foreach** $s \in \varsigma$ **do**
6) $reading := reading \cup \{s\}$
            // maintain a set of subjects which have been allowed to read from o_1
7)   **if** $s \in writing$ **return** true;
8)   **end for**
9)   **collect** $\varsigma = \{x | r \in \rho_t(x, o_2) \wedge r = $ 'write' $\}$
10)   **foreach** $s \in \varsigma$ **do**
11) $writing := writing \cup \{s\}$
            // maintain a set of subjects which have been allowed to write to o_2
12)   **if** $s \in reading$ **return** true;
13)   **end for**
14)   **foreach** subject s in t **do**
15)   **foreach** creating ground policy $c(s : \tau_s, o : \tau_o)$, where $\tau_s(a) = \sigma_s(o.a)$ **do**
16)   enforce $c(s : \tau_s, o : \tau_o)$;
17)   create object o and update its attribute tuple to τ_o';
18)   update s's attribute tuple to τ_s';
19)   the system state changes to t' with new object o and update attributes of
                s and o ;
20) $InfoFlowCheck(O_0 \cup \{o\}, t')$
21)   **end for**
22)   **end for**
23) **end for**

The trustworthiness of the information flow behavior $\mathcal{IF}$ is defined as:

$$\mathcal{IF}.\text{behavior} = \text{trusted iff } \forall u \in U. \;\; InfoFlowCheck(u) = \text{true}$$
$$\text{where } U \text{ is the set of edges in the IFG.}$$

Concisely, information flow behavior is trusted if and only if all possible paths
of information flow on the client comply with the challenger's usage policies.

5   Related Work

One of the earliest and most significant works analyzing information flow models is by Denning [19] in which mechanisms for information flow are formalized
using a lattice structure of labels and classes of objects. JFlow [20] is a security-
typed language providing "mostly-static" information flow control by assigning
labels to objects within the source code and ensuring that information flows

comply with the security policy of the programmer. JFlow relies on a specialized compiler and information flow controlling virtual machine for enforcement of information flow control. Haldar et al. [21] have devised a mechanism for implementing mandatory access control (MAC) mechanisms in virtual machines for controlling information flows. They propose the use of run-time policy enforcement as opposed to the mostly-static compile time checks [20] for enforcing MAC policies. Nair et al. [22] have presented an information flow control system which addresses the issue of implicit information flows. The resulting framework is capable of dynamically assigning labels to objects and propagating these labels based on information and control flow.

All of these models and mechanisms address either information flow control or audit but do not deal with remote attestation of information flows, the underlying environment or the target application. However, as can be seen, some of them deal with implicit information flows as well as explicit ones and can, therefore, help in future extensions of this work.

From the aspect of remote attestation, several works have been proposed. These include the Integrity Measurement Architecture [3], which allows a remote party to verify the trustworthiness of a target platform based on the load-time integrity of binaries on the target platform. Policy Reduced Integrity Measurement Architecture (PRIMA) [4] targets a specific application by analyzing the information flow to and from the target application but still does not address internal structures and semantics of the application. LKIM [7] is one of the few approaches, which target the dynamic behavior of a system. It verifies the integrity of a Linux kernel by measuring and reporting the target's dynamic state [23]. It has been shown to detect malicious code, which could not be detected using hashes of static code.

Gu et al. [24] have described a new approach for measuring the behavior of an application using static analysis of the source code and verification of *program execution* against this benchmark.

The attestation technique described in our contribution is significantly different from both these approaches in two respects. Firstly, we utilize the TPM hardware for *trusted* storage and reporting of measurements. Secondly, our approach utilizes the owner's *policies* for the creation of a baseline. This allows for the integrity verification of a specific application for a particular purpose, thus greatly reducing the complexity of attestation.

Semantic Remote Attestation [25] is closest to the approach described in this paper. It proposes the use of a Trusted Virtual Machine, which is established as trusted and is then expected to enforce the policies at the VM level. However, trust on the correct enforcement of the policies is implied and no mechanism for measuring the correctness of the enforcement is provided. Our technique builds on this approach and describes a detailed architecture for using run-time measurements of the behavior in a trusted manner for dynamic behavioral attestation of a target application. To the best of our knowledge, no work has been done for the attestation of attribute updates and information flows in a UCON system at this level of detail.

6   Conclusion and Future Work

Remote attestation is an integral part of Trusted Computing. It allows a challenger to establish the trustworthiness of a remote platform depending on its behavior. Recent advances in remote attestation have led us to believe that measuring the hashes of executables on the remote platform is insufficient for the establishment of trust. It is necessary to verify the dynamic behavior and internal functioning of a target application. In this paper, we have proposed a mechanism for attesting the dynamic behavior of UCON – a highly expressive usage control model. Two important aspects of UCON, attribute updates and information flow, have been described. We have presented details regarding measurement, storage and verification of these behaviors in a trustworthy manner. The model of UCON under consideration is $UCON_A$ with certain restrictions, which has previously been shown to be useful in practical scenarios. Establishment of trust on a remote party implementing this model will provide confidence to the challenger that her policies will indeed be enforced on the remote end as dictated.

This paper has introduced the novel concept and semantics of using a small 'behavior manager' component on the remote platform for collecting trust tokens used during attestation. This concept has been applied to collect and verify attribute update behavior and information flow behavior. The same technique can, with slight modifications, be applied for collecting various other types of trust tokens, such as information flows to and from other applications, system calls and input/output to storage devices, for an even more detailed inspection of the dynamic behavior of the target application. These and other behaviors are being considered for attestation of UCON and even generalized applications not following the UCON model. These form the basis of ongoing work in this research.

Acknowledgements

This research work has been supported by Grant No. ICTRDF/TR&D/2008/45 from the National ICT R&D Fund, Pakistan to Security Engineering Research Group, Institute of Management Sciences, Peshawar.

References

1. Park, J., Sandhu, R.: Towards Usage Control Models: Beyond Traditional Access Control. In: SACMAT 2002: Proceedings of the seventh ACM Symposium on Access Control Models and Technologies, pp. 57–64. ACM Press, New York (2002)
2. Trusted Computing Group, http://www.trustedcomputinggroup.org/
3. Sailer, R., Zhang, X., Jaeger, T., van Doorn, L.: Design and Implementation of a TCG-based Integrity Measurement Architecture. In: SSYM 2004: Proceedings of the 13th conference on USENIX Security Symposium, Berkeley, CA, USA, USENIX Association (2004)

4. Jaeger, T., Sailer, R., Shankar, U.: PRIMA: Policy-Reduced Integrity Measurement Architecture. In: SACMAT 2006: Proceedings of the eleventh ACM Symposium on Access Control Models and Technologies, pp. 19–28. ACM Press, New York (2006)
5. Sadeghi, A.R., Stüble, C.: Property-based Attestation for Computing Platforms: Caring about Properties, not Mechanisms. In: NSPW 2004: Proceedings of the 2004 Workshop on New Security Paradigms, pp. 67–77. ACM Press, New York (2004)
6. Alam, M., Zhang, X., Nauman, M., Ali, T., Seifert, J.P.: Model-based Behavioral Attestation. In: SACMAT 2008: Proceedings of the thirteenth ACM symposium on Access control models and technologies. ACM Press, New York (2008)
7. Loscocco, P.A., Wilson, P.W., Pendergrass, J.A., McDonell, C.D.: Linux Kernel Integrity Measurement Using Contextual Inspection. In: STC 2007: Proceedings of the 2007 ACM Workshop on Scalable Trusted Computing, pp. 21–29. ACM, New York (2007)
8. Zhang, X., Nakae, M., Covington, M.J., Sandhu, R.S.: Toward a Usage-Based Security Framework for Collaborative Computing Systems. ACM Trans. Inf. Syst. Secur. 11(1) (2008)
9. Srivatsa, M., Balfe, S.: Trust Management For Secure Information Flows. In: CCS 2008: Proceedings of the 15th ACM Conference on Computer and Communications Security, pp. 175–187. ACM, New York (2008)
10. Zhang, X., Parisi-Presicce, F., Sandhu, R., Park, J.: Formal Model and Policy Specification of Usage Control. ACM Trans. Inf. Syst. Secur. 8(4), 351–387 (2005)
11. Zhang, X., Sandhu, R., Parisi-Presicce, F.: Safety Analysis of Usage Control Authorization Models. In: ASIACCS 2006: Proceedings of the 2006 ACM Symposium on Information, computer and communications security, pp. 243–254. ACM, New York (2006)
12. Kanerva, P.: Anonymous Authorization in Networked Systems: An Implementation of Physical Access Control System. Masters Thesis. Helsinki University of Technology (March 2001)
13. Bella, G., Paulson, L.C., Massacci, F.: The Verification of an Industrial Payment Protocol: the SET Purchase Phase. In: CCS 2002: Proceedings of the 9th ACM Conference on Computer and Communications Security, pp. 12–20. ACM, New York (2002)
14. TCG Software Stack (TSS) Specifications, https://www.trustedcomputinggroup.org/specs/TSS/
15. Trusted Computing for the Java(tm) Platform, http://trustedjava.sourceforge.net/
16. Java Community Process. JSR321: Trusted Computing API for Java, http://jcp.org/en/jsr/detail?id=321
17. Alam, M., Zhang, X., Nauman, M., Ali, T.: Behavioral Attestation for Web Services (BA4WS). In: SWS 2008: Proceedings of the ACM Workshop on Secure Web Services (SWS) located at 15th ACM Conference on Computer and Communications Security (CCS-15). ACM Press, New York (2008)
18. Guttman, J.: Verifying Information Flow Goals in Security-Enhanced Linux. Journal of Computer Security 13(1), 115–134 (2005)
19. Denning, D.E., Denning, P.J.: Certification of programs for secure information flow. Commun. ACM 20(7), 504–513 (1977)
20. Myers, A.C.: JFlow: Practical Mostly-static Information Flow Control. In: POPL 1999: Proceedings of the 26th ACM SIGPLAN-SIGACT symposium on Principles of programming languages, pp. 228–241. ACM, New York (1999)

21. Haldar, V., Chandra, D., Franz, M.: Practical, Dynamic Information-flow for Virtual Machines, www.vivekhaldar.com/pubs/plid2005.pdf
22. Nair, S., Simpson, P., Crispo, B., Tanenbaum, A.: A Virtual Machine Based Information Flow Control System for Policy Enforcement. Electronic Notes in Theoretical Computer Science 197(1), 3–16 (2008)
23. Thober, M., Pendergrass, J.A., McDonell, C.D.: Improving Coherency of Runtime Integrity Measurement. In: STC 2008: Proceedings of the 2008 ACM Workshop on Scalable Trusted Computing. ACM, New York (2008)
24. Gu, L., Ding, X., Deng, R., Xie, B., Mei, H.: Remote Attestation on Program Execution. In: STC 2008: Proceedings of the 2008 ACM Workshop on Scalable Trusted Computing. ACM, New York (2008)
25. Haldar, V., Chandra, D., Franz, M.: Semantic Remote Attestation – A Virtual Machine directed approach to Trusted Computing In. Proc. of the Third Virtual Macine Research and Technology Symposium USENIX (2004)

Measuring Semantic Integrity for Remote Attestation

Fabrizio Baiardi[1], Diego Cilea[2], Daniele Sgandurra[2], and Francesco Ceccarelli[3]

[1] Polo G. Marconi, La Spezia
Università di Pisa, Italy
baiardi@di.unipi.it
[2] Dipartimento di Informatica
Università di Pisa, Italy
{cilea,daniele}@di.unipi.it
[3] ENEL SpA, Italy
francesco.ceccarelli@enel.it

Abstract. We propose a framework for the attestation of the integrity of a remote system that considers not only the configuration of the system to be attested but also its current behaviour. The resulting architecture, called Virtual machine Integrity Measurement System (VIMS), is based upon virtualization technology and it runs two virtual machines on a system to be attested, i.e. the Client (C-VM) and the Assurance VM (A-VM). A generic remote server (REM-S) accepts incoming connections and cooperates with the A-VM to authenticate and attest the integrity of the C-VM and of the software it runs. The A-VM is a shadow machine that exploits virtual machine introspection to apply a set of consistency checks on the configuration of the C-VM and on the software it currently runs. The checks depend upon the security policies that the REM-S establishes in the initial connection handshake. The REM-S defines both the complexity of checks to be applied and the frequency of their execution and it communicates the security policy to the A-VM through a control channel. Policies that can be applied range from the one that simply checks the integrity of the binaries loaded by the C-VM to those that continuously monitor the dynamic behaviour of applications to discover attacks that alter their expected behaviour. The control channel also transmits the results of the checks from the A-VM to the REM-S. As an example, remote attestation can be adopted when a client software on the C-VM tries to establish a secure channel to a REM-S on an Intranet.

After describing the overall VIMS architecture, we present and discuss the implementation and the performance of a first prototype.

1 Introduction

Intranet access has become a fundamental prerequisite for corporate users. On the other hand, network administrators cannot guarantee the confidentiality and

L. Chen, C.J. Mitchell, and A. Martin (Eds.): Trust 2009, LNCS 5471, pp. 81–100, 2009.
© Springer-Verlag Berlin Heidelberg 2009

the integrity of Intranet data that may be accessed by remote clients because little assurance about the integrity of these clients can be established. In fact, an attacker may have compromised a client application to download or modify corporate data through the remote access gained by the client. A solution to this problem requires a general notion of integrity that, first of all, should consider that a client system can be trusted only if it executes applications in a predefined set. Moreover, these applications should be continuously monitored to discover if they have been attacked. In other words, since both these applications and the underlying software can be attacked, the notion of integrity should also take into account run-time attacks against both applications and the OS rather than merely verifying that the proper binaries have been loaded.

Virtual machine Integrity Measurement System (VIMS) is an architecture that implements the proposed approach to integrity measurement and that can be adopted to protect networks by auditing endpoint configurations. VIMS evaluates the integrity of a remote host and it imposes a security policy before the platform can connect to an existing network to access some of the services it offers. In more detail, VIMS can guarantee the integrity of a client system that is trying to connect to the network, where the adopted notion of integrity includes not only the correct configuration of the system and of the software it runs, but also that the client does not execute some malware that changes the overall behaviour of its applications. To this purpose, VIMS exploits virtualization technology to enable the client system to run two virtual machines (VMs) on top of a virtual machine monitor (VMM). The Client VM (C-VM) runs the client software, such as a VPN client application to connect to a remote server (REM-S), while the Assurance VM (A-VM) is a shadow VM that applies a set of security checks on the memory of the C-VM. These checks measure, on behalf of the REM-S, the integrity of the software that the C-VM runs. The A-VM can either apply consistency checks periodically or on demand when requested by the REM-S. Furthermore, the complexity of the checks that it applies is a function of the degree of the assurance that the REM-S requires. As soon as the A-VM detects anomalous behaviour or some malware, for example a rootkit in the memory of the C-VM, it contacts the REM-S that can tear down the connection with the C-VM.

The rest of the paper is organised as follows. Section 2 introduces the main concepts underlying VIMS, such as trusted computing, virtualization, semantic attestation and discusses related works. Section 3 presents the overall architecture of VIMS. The current prototype implementation is discussed in Sect. 4. Section 5 presents a first set of performance results. Finally, Sect. 6 draws some conclusions and outlines future developments.

2   Background

After discussing some related works, this section introduces the main concepts underlying VIMS.

2.1   Related Works

Trusted Virtual Domains (TVDs) [1] [2] is an architecture where computing services can be offloaded into execution environments that demonstrably meet a set of security requirements. A TVD is an abstract union including by an *initiator* and one or more *responders*. During the process of joining, all the parties specify and confirm the set of mutual requirements and each party is assured of the identity and integrity of the computer system of the remote party. The enforcement of the attestation is delegated to virtual environments. *Terra* [3] is a VM-based architecture for trusted computing that enables applications with distinct security requirements to run simultaneously on commodity hardware. The software stack in each VM can be tailored to meet the security requirements of its applications. [4] discusses the design and implementation of Integrity Measurement Architecture (IMA), which is a secure integrity measurement system for Linux. This architecture enables a system to prove that the integrity of a program on a remote system is sufficient. IMA uses the Trusted Platform Module (TPM) to detect subversion of the measurements system by comparing a hash value stored in the TPM against the one in the measurement system audit log. UCLinux [5] is a Linux Security Module that enables TPM-based usage controls enforcement. It provides the attestation support, sealing support and protection from administrative abuse required by a trustworthy usage control system, and it does so with existing hardware and limited changes to an existing OS. [6] introduces a formal integrity model to manage the integrity of arbitrary aspects of a virtualized system. The authors describe the PEV architecture, which is based upon a model that generalises the integrity management functions of the TPM to cover not only software binaries, but also VMs, virtual devices, and a wide range of security policies. PEV enables the verification of security compliance and the enforcement of security policies. [7] discusses an access control architecture that enables corporations to verify the integrity of a remote client and establish trust into its ability to enforce a security policy before allowing the client to access corporate Intranet services. It also shows how to enforce the policy on both remote clients and VPN servers. To this end, it discusses the adoption of an integrity heart-beat that enables the VPN server to react to changes in the security properties of the remote client by updating the security policy. Pioneer [8] is a software-based platform addressing the problem of verifiable code execution on legacy computing hosts without relying on secure co-processors or CPU virtualization extensions. Pioneer is based on a challenge-response protocol between an external trusted entity (the dispatcher) and an untrusted computing platform. *Property based attestation* [9] [10] is a strategy that describes an aspect of the behaviour of the platform to be attested with respect to security-related requirements. As an example, a property may state that a platform has built-in measures to conform to the privacy laws, or that it strictly separates processes from each other, or that it has built-in functionalities to provide Multi-Level Security. A protocol and architecture for property attestation is proposed in [11]. With property attestation, a verifier is securely assured of security properties of the execution environment of the verified platform without receiving detailed configuration data. This enhances privacy and scalability because the verifier needs to be aware of only a few security properties rather than of a huge number of acceptable configurations. *Semantic integrity* [12] is a measurement approach targeting the dynamic state of the software during execution and, therefore, providing fresh measurement results. Similar to the adoption of language-based virtual machines for remote attestation of dynamic program properties [13], this approach can provide increased flexibility for the challenger, because the integrity monitor can examine the current state of a system to detect semantic integrity violations. This technique alone will not produce complete results as it does not attempt to characterise the entire system. However, it does offer a way to measure the integrity of portions of the target not suitable for measurement by hashing. Prima [14], which is an extension of the Linux IMA system, measures information flow integrity that can be verified by remote parties.

2.2   Trusted Computing

One outstanding framework of integrity measurement is that endorsed by the Trusted Computing Group (TCG), an industry consortium that defines specifications for hardware and software components [15]. The standard TCG measurement is the computation of SHA-1 cryptographic hash of critical components as they are loaded into the system. The TCG guidance for measurement includes the Trusted Platform Module (TPM) as a hardware device to securely store and report measurement values in the form of a SHA-1 hash. This architecture provides a good model for determining the integrity during software initialisation. Moreover, the TPM is becoming standard on several personal computing platforms. However, this framework does not address issues such as loss of platform integrity due to run-time attacks against the system. If the system environment can be attacked through either its interfaces or the hardware and software environment, this issue requires not only to measure the integrity of an executable stored in a file, but also to periodically measure the integrity of the software running in memory [16]. This approach poses new problems because, first of all, the well-known execution environment initialised at boot time, and that provided a safe environment for the measurement, cannot be reproduced without rebooting the system. Second, if the applications virtual memories are updated after they have been loaded, their hash value change as well. Finally, some run-time data updates cannot be correctly represented through hash values.

TPM and vTPM. In systems equipped with a TPM chip [17] [18], the TPM acts as a root-of-trust in the process that builds and setup the software environments and it ensures that a system has loaded its software properly. Moreover, it protects secrets such as asymmetric keys or it can be used to encrypt symmetric keys. The TPM has a set of registers that it protects from the system software and it implements two operations on each register content: *extend* and *quote*. The former operation takes a value V as input and computes the SHA-1 hash of the current register content appended to V. Instead, a quote operation generates a message with the register contents and signs it with a key protected by the TPM.

The vTPM [19] [20] extends the functionalities of the TPM in a virtualized environment, where several VMs can run distinct OSes on the same platform. The vTPM is a virtual extension of the TPM that enables the VMM to emulate the features of the TPM, by exporting to each VM a virtual implementation of the TPM having the same interface of the TPM.

2.3   Virtualization and Semantic Attestation

A Virtual Machine Monitor (VMM) is a thin software layer that runs on top of a physical machine and that creates, manages and monitors Virtual Machines (VMs), i.e. execution environments. Each VM emulates, at software, the behaviour of the underlying physical machine. In this way, a VMM can run different OSes in parallel.

To apply consistency checks on the OS kernel of a system and on the processes it runs in a robust and transparent manner, several proposed solutions exploit virtualization technologies [21]. Virtualization enhances the robustness of controls and guarantees a transparent monitoring by running two VMs on the same physical machine, e.g. a monitored VM and a privileged VM. The former runs the system and the processes to be monitored, while the latter is a distinct VM that can access the memory of the other VM to apply a set of security checks on any region in this memory, i.e. the privileged VM has full access to the memory space of any other VM to apply virtual machine introspection [22]. These checks verify the integrity of the software that the monitored VM runs and they implement a form of *semantic attestation* because, first of all, they consider the current status of the running processes. Furthermore, they can exploit any information about the expected behaviour of a component to discover anomalous behaviour of the component itself.

3   Overall Architecture

Virtual machine Integrity Measurement System (VIMS) is a system that measures the integrity of a node as required by remote semantic attestation. VIMS integrates a set of tools for static and dynamic analysis to protect the OS kernel and the running processes of a node against attacks trying to modify their expected behaviour. The various tools of VIMS analyse the current state of the critical data structures loaded by the kernel, the kernel itself, including the modules, and the running processes.

Design Goals. VIMS is aimed at implementing a fairly general and reliable system to measure the integrity of a remote client, so that the server can be assured of the state of the remote host. The main goals of VIMS are:

1. granular checks on the integrity of the client: with respect to solutions that only exploit TPM-based functions, VIMS can apply more granular checks through a set of static and dynamic tools;
2. support for dynamic policies: as long as the client is connected to a network, its run-time state should be continuously monitored, to detect whether it has been infected by a malware after being successfully attacked. Moreover, the policy can be changed according to changes in the client configuration;
3. mutual attestation: as an example, in a peer-to-peer environment, all the parties should be mutually assured of the integrity of any other peer;
4. scalability: the overhead of an attestation should be negligible.

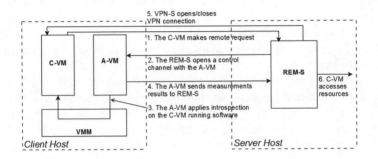

Fig. 1. Overall Architecture

VIMS Components Description. VIMS defines a set of components and a protocol that rules the information exchange among these components and define the format of the various messages. These components are (see Fig. 1): (i) the C-VM, i.e. the client virtual machine; (ii) the A-VM, i.e. the assurance virtual machine, paired with the C-VM; (iii) the REM-S, which is a generic application server. VIMS also defines a protocol. In the more general case, a client software running on the C-VM contacts the REM-S to open a connection to access some services offered either by the REM-S of by a network that the REM-S interfaces. Before allowing the client to connect and access the service, the REM-S establishes an out-of-band control channel with the A-VM of the node that runs C-VM. The IP address of the A-VM is statically known and paired with that of the C-VM. As long as the C-VM and the REM-S interact, the REM-S and the A-VM periodically exchange information through the control channel about (i) the security policy to be applied and (ii) the results of the executed checks that are used to evaluate the C-VM integrity. The protocol exploits the out-of-band control channel also to inform the REM-S that the C-VM has been compromised either before or during the communications between the C-VM and the REM-S.

VIMS may exploit the TPM and vTPM to apply the consistency checks on the C-VM starting from a valid root-of-trust, which is located in the hardware. With respect to systems that are based on TPM mechanisms only, VIMS can implement a semantic attestation that applies consistency checks based upon the semantic behaviour of the processes. In this case, a static tool is firstly applied to analyse the source code of the program run by a process to be attested. Then, the A-VM uses the output of this tool to monitor the status of the C-VM memory and the run-time system call sequence that a process produces. In this way, VIMS can apply rigorous and granular semantic checks at run-time, which are strictly more powerful that those based upon the hash of the running code only.

The A-VM exploits *virtual machine introspection* (VMI) [22] to retrieve critical data structures in the memory of the C-VM and evaluate a set of assertions on these structures. Each assertion is an invariant for the original application that constrains the values in the data structure and that is violated any time the application has been attacked. By evaluating these assertions VIMS can: (i) guarantee the integrity of critical kernel data structures; (ii) assure that a process invokes only a predefined set of system calls.

In this way, VIMS implements a semantic integrity attestation because by applying rigorous and granular semantic checks that are more powerful than those based upon hashes of running code only. In fact, by monitoring the C-VM's current behaviour, the A-VM monitors not only the binaries that have been loaded by the OS, but also their dynamic integrity.

The A-VM can apply alternative security policies, which can be parametrised according to: (i) the frequency of the execution of security checks; (ii) their granularity, i.e. which data structures and software code need to be checked for integrity. VIMS exploits the features of the TPM to build a hash chain on the client system. This hash chain is used to measure a predefined sequence of code loads, such as the authenticated boot of the VMM and of the kernel of the A-VM from the BIOS and boot-loader. The TPM provides measurements that indicate that the VMM is safely started, so that it can initialise the local A-VM to assure it is started in a safe state. The A-VM enables the REM-S to retrieve these hash values, which are called *measurements*. This list is protected by the A-VM and cannot be accessed by the C-VM. In this way, the REM-S can establish trust at first into the A-VM measurements and then into the run-time properties of the C-VM.

After the A-VM has been safely initialised, it periodically applies virtual machine introspection to check the integrity of the software run by the C-VM. The A-VM uses the message returned by the TPM quote operation to send an authenticated hash chain to the REM-S to validate the integrity of the code contained in the hash chain that belongs to the client.

Threat Model. As far as concerns the definition of the threat model, the most important feature is the availability of a TPM. If the TPM is not available on the system that runs the C-VM and the A-VM, a transparent root-of-trust cannot be guaranteed. In this case, the reliability of integrity measurements can be guaranteed if and only if:

- the VMM is trusted; this requires that no remote software interface is open to an adversary and its state cannot be altered by a physical access to the system;
- the public and private keys of the A-VM cannot be tampered with or, in case of the private key, disclosed;
- the REM-S is trusted: this is fairly reasonable, since we assume the server runs in a controlled environment.

On the other hand, if the client subsystem is equipped with a TPM, then the main assumptions to trust VIMS measurements are:

- TPM and CPU are trusted;
- the BIOS that initiates chain of measurements of the VMM and of the A-VM is trusted;
- Memory cannot be hacked at run-time (e.g. via DMA).

Obviously, in both cases, the C-VM is untrusted, so it may be infected by malware, and so on. The A-VM and the REM-S initially establish trust based on certificates signed by a trusted Certification Authority.

Formal Model. We have defined a formal model to deduce which chains of trust can be created and which components can be trusted according to the trust relations among components, i.e. C-VMs, A-VMs and TPM in the system. The model defines a partially ordered set of tests, i.e. checks to be applied to a component, and of policies, where a policy is a pair including a set of tests and a frequency to apply such tests. Then, each component c can define:

a) a set of trusted components $trusted(c)$;
b) a policy to be applied to trust a component that does not belong to $trusted(c)$;
c) the policy it can apply to each other component. An empty policy denotes that c cannot test a component;
d) $invoke(c, p)$, which is a set of components that can use c to apply a policy p to other components, i.e. they can invoke the policy that c can apply to other components;
e) a policy to be applied to a component that does not belong to $invoke(c)$ but want to use c.

For each instance of the model, we can compute, for each component c, the set of components c trusts. This set is computed as the fixed point of a set of equations that relates the set of components that c trusts and those that c can invoke to apply a policy. In practice, the computation of the fixed point corresponds to that of the transitive closure of the two sets for all the components. Several versions of the model can be defined and the main difference is related to the component that has to invoke a test. In one version, a component a invoke a policy applied by b to be trusted by c. In another version, c invokes the policy applied by b to check whether a may be trusted.

A physical architecture and a mapping of the various components onto this architecture defines an instance of the model because, as an example, a VM may trust other VMs that run on a physical node only if this node includes a TPM component or a VM can test another one, e.g. it can apply a non empty policy, only if both the VMs run on the same node. The formal model makes it possible to prove in advance, given an architecture, a mapping and a version of the model, whether a chain of trust between two components exists. Furthermore, the proof is automatic because the computation of the fixed point of the set of equations can be fully automated.

A more general model may also consider the communication among components so that a component a trusts another component b only if there are $c_1, \ldots, c_n$ components that a trusts and that can guarantee the confidentiality and/or the integrity of communications between a and b.

3.1   C-VM Measurements

We describe now in more detail how VIMS measures the integrity of the C-VM and the corresponding interactions among the various VIMS components.

To verify the integrity of the C-VM, VIMS implements the following steps:

1. verification of the initial C-VM integrity by applying a set of measurements to its configuration. These measurements consist of a set of hash computations of the code of running processes and of the C-VM kernel, i.e. critical data structures, code and kernel modules. If the client system is equipped with vTPM, VIMS can extend the root-of-trust to the physical platform;
2. the A-VM communicates the results of the measurements to the REM-S;
3. as soon as the REM-S has received the A-VM measurements, it can choose the security policy to be applied. To determine an optimal compromise between the attestation level and the corresponding overhead, the range of possible policies varies from the one that periodically computes the hashes on the running software to the one that monitors the sequences of OS invocations by critical C-VM processes. Furthermore, the assurance level is dynamic, i.e. after receiving a set of measurements the REM-S can change the assurance level to better satisfy its security requirements.

The C-VM runs unmodified client software, and it does not need to be aware of being checked by a distinct VM so that the semantic attestation may be *fully transparent to the C-VM*. To measure the integrity of the C-VM, starting with the TPM, the following steps are required. Firstly, the TrustedBoot [23] is loaded and the TPM applies a set of measurements on the boot-loader, so that from now on all the steps can be measured from boot to kernel loading and its modules. Attestation requires that the measurements of the C-VM are certified through the keys protected in the TPM and that the remote party can establish trust on the client integrity based upon these measurements. By computing the hash of the running software, signed by the private key of the TPM, the remote party can be assured of the trustworthiness of the data received. In this way, VIMS creates a chain-of-trust from the BIOS up to the VMs that certifies the integrity of the VMM and of the A-VM. Then, further controls can be periodically applied through virtual machine introspection as requested by the REM-S. The corresponding results are exchanged through the attestation protocol between the A-VM client and the attestation module on the REM-S.

3.2 A-VM

The A-VM should be something relatively self-contained and non-changing. Moreover, it should run a minimal kernel without any Internet service and the functionalities it implements should not be directly accessed by any user. Moreover, a stable trusted A-VM may help in attesting to a variety of C-VM applications. The REM-S must trust that the A-VM is not misbehaving.

The A-VM directly accesses and examines the memory of the C-VM through virtual machine introspection to detect attacks or erroneous updates of client applications or of the underlying OS. After the A-VM has been safely initialised by the VMM, it applies a set of introspection checks to the pages storing the kernel code, the system call dispatch table, the interrupt descriptor table, and other critical kernel data structures that should never be modified. Hence, the A-VM periodically computes their hashes to check they have not been changed. Moreover, the A-VM retrieves the list of the kernel modules and verifies both their integrity and that they are authorised kernel modules. These checks are also applied to critical user-level applications on the C-VM, such as the VPN client, anti-virus software and the likes. If the current hash of a running application or of a kernel module differs from the stored values, the REM-S tears down the connection. Furthermore, the A-VM can also evaluate a set of invariants on data structures or on the sequence of invocations of an application to discover anomalous values due to an attack. Anytime the behaviour of a process differs from the one computed by a static analysis of the application source code, the current C-VM behaviour is flagged as anomalous. VIMS static tools over-approximate the process behaviour so that no false positives can occur. The A-VM manages a database that stores a set of distinct security policies that it applies on request by the REM-S. Each policy defines the granularity level of the controls, that in turn determines the measurements to be applied, and their frequency.

3.3 Attestation Protocol

The very basic steps of the attestation protocol among the C-VM, the REM-S and the A-VM are (see Fig. 1):

1. the C-VM requires the REM-S to establish a connection to access some resources;
2. the REM-S opens a control channel with the A-VM after the usual credentials checks;
3. the REM-S starts the attestation protocol with the A-VM and it transmits a list with the initial parameters;
4. the A-VM applies introspection to retrieve measurements on the objects inside the list; afterwards, the A-VM verifies the correspondence among the hash of the code of the running processes and kernel structures;

5. the A-VM returns to REM-S, on the control channel, the results of the hash that have been computed;
6. in case of successful results, the REM-S set on the A-VM the security policy that the A-VM should apply and connects grants the access to C-VM.

Further features of the protocol are: (i) the control channel between the A-VM and the REM-S exists as long as the C-VM and the REM-S are connected; (ii) the A-VM can apply specific consistency checks on the C-VM on request by the REM-S; (iii) the database of measurement configurations on the A-VM can be extended at run-time through proper REM-S requests; (iv) the REM-S can request a specific action after a timeout has been elapsed.

4   Current Implementation

Xen [24] 3.1.0 is the adopted technology to create the virtual machines based on Debian Etch 4.0 with Linux kernel 2.6.18. We adopted the tool described in [25] to define the semantic checks to be applied to the critical processes running on the C-VM, and an introspection library [26] to compute the assertion on the C-VM memory.

The following A-VM modules have been developed either to implement the attestation protocol or to apply the measurements:

- assurance module: a client plugin, running on the A-VM, to manage the remote attestation protocol;
- a vTPM module interface (if TPM is present);
- a database for measurements and security policies;
- an interface for the low-level introspection function.

The following REM-S modules have been implemented:

- an attestation module;
- a database for measurements and policies;
- an OpenVPN plugin [27];
- a plugin for ghttpd web-server;
- a vTPM module interface.

The modules to execute the attestation protocol have been implemented in Java. The attestation library on the server-side is composed of 4 Java classes of about 1500 lines of code, whereas the assurance module on the client-side is about 1000 lines of Java code, including a small wrapper to interface with the introspection functions.

The following sections discuss two test-cases we have implemented. In the first one, the C-VM used a VPN client to access a remote Intranet through a VPN server executing on the REM-S. The Intranet hosted critical SCADA devices that could be remotely accessed and monitored. We have modified the VPN server to handle the remote attestation protocol and applied the static tool to a VPN client to define its profile that is used by the A-VM to monitor its run-time

Table 1. Example of Attestation Response

```
<attestation>
  <response>
    <overallresult>suspicious</overallresult>
    <nonceid>89892345</nonceid>
    <AssuranceIp>192.168.1.1</AssuranceIp>
    <reqpolicy>timeout</reqpolicy>
    <timemillis>20000</timemillis>
    <assurancelevel>4</assurancelevel>
    <measuresaggregate>
      <measureschain>
        <measure>
          <idmeasure>TPM-Boot</idmeasure>
            <hash>7844e409c39fad83bb65f7dac4c8a53e</hash>
            <status>trusted</status>
            <object>TPM.Measure</object>
            <name>boot</name>
        </measure>
        <measure>
          <idmeasure>0</idmeasure>
            <hash>7844e409c39fad83bb65f7dac4c8a53e</hash>
            <status>trusted</status>
            <object>kernel.struct</object>
            <name>idt_table</name>
        </measure>
        ................
        <measure>
          <idmeasure>78</idmeasure>
            <hash>0000e409c39fad83bb65f7dac4c8a53e</hash>
            <status>trusted</status>
            <statusprofile>wrong</statusprofile>
            <object>process</object>
            <name>modprobe</name>
        </measure>
      </measureschain>
    </measuresaggregate>
  </response>
</attestation>
```

behaviour. In the second case, a browser accessed a simple web-server which has been extended to exploit the attestation module.

Java SSL libraries and TPM/J [28] has been used to access the TPM values. Moreover, Java SSL libraries have been used to create the secure connections and to define the services of interest, i.e. the client interaction either to create a VPN connection or to send a HTTP request to REM-S. Finally, OpenVPN and the web-server have been extended with plugins to enable remote attestation.

4.1 Attestation Module

The attestation module on the REM-S is at the core of the attestation protocol, and it is used to initialise the protocol and to exchange messages between the REM-S and the A-VM. The protocol is triggered each time a C-VM requires the REM-S to open a connection, such as a VPN to the remote network or a HTTP request to a web-server in the considered examples. Before allowing the client to connect, the REM-S exploits the attestation module, which is a daemon service waiting for input to start the handshaking phase. In the VPN connection, this module is an OpenVPN plugin that starts up the daemon as soon as it receives a request through the function `ConnectionRequest(IPClient)`. The attestation module, once activated, maps the IP address of the requesting C-VM into the IP address of the corresponding A-VM, and it opens a connection to it.

The handshaking among the REM-S and the A-VM includes the mutual authentication and the exchange of the initial protocol parameters. If the handshake is successfully completed, the A-VM applies the initial set of measurements to the C-VM and sends to the REM-S a message including the results of the checks and the hashes computed by the TrustedBoot. The message is signed with the private key of the A-VM to prevent manipulation of the results. To attest the A-VM integrity and discover the current C-VM configuration, the attestation module on the REM-S compares the results against those in the database and defines an initial security level. This level is communicated to the A-VM that stores it in its database and it applies the monitoring according to the adopted security policy.

The attestation module can apply one of two policies, based on a XML-encoded policy (see Tab. 1 for an example of an attestation response from the A-VM): (i) on-demand or (ii) timeout-based. In an on-demand policy, the REM-S can request specific measurements to the A-VM, such as semantic checks on a running process, as long as the C-VM and the REM-S are connected. Instead, in a timeout-based policy, the A-VM periodically applies a set of checks and sends to the REM-S the corresponding results.

A-VM / REM-S Interactions. Currently, the protocol between the A-VM and the REM-S includes the following steps (see Fig. 2):

1. `ConnectionRequest(username, password)`:
   − open a connection from the C-VM to the REM-S;
   − check user's credentials;
2. `ConnectionRequest(Username, IP)`; the Attestation module is activated;
3. if in the previous step the client is authenticated, then the attestation module uses `Retrieve(A-VM Information, C-VM IP)` to query the database;
4. the attestation module queries its database to retrieve the IP address of A-VM though the `Response(A-VM IP)` function;
5. `OpenConnection(A-VM IP)`: the attestation module establishes a control channel with the A-VM;
6. [sign_A-VMKey] `AttestationHandshake(Ip_REM-S, nonce)`: the attestation module sends the handshake message with some parameters, signed with the public key of the A-VM;
7. [sign_REM-SKey] `AttestationResponse(ResultsChain({ProcIDs = results}, {KernelStructures=results}, {TPM_measures}), nonce)`: the A-VM computes hash values of the running applications and the A-VM compares these results against those in its database. It sends the result to REM-S chained with the measurements of the underlying system done by the TPM;

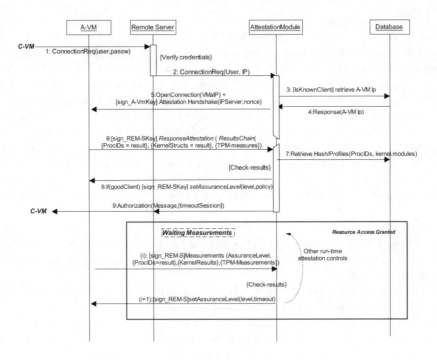

Fig. 2. Attestation Protocol Overview

8. **Check-Results**: the attestation module compares each result sent by the A-VM against the expected one;
9. the attestation module sends the current assurance policy and level to the A-VM;
10. **[sign_A-VMKey]setAssurancePolicy(level, policy)**: the REM-S sends to the A-VM an XML configuration file storing the security policy that the A-VM should apply, e.g.: (**AssuranceLevel = 1, timeout**). The parameters of this function are:
    - **level**: the required assurance level, i.e. an ID paired with a set of controls stored in the A-VM database;
    - **policy**: The field **policy** can have the value *timeout* or *on-demand*, depending on whether the checks need to be applied for each elapsed timeout or on-demand by the REM-S.
11. **Authorization(Message, [timeoutSession])**: the REM-S opens or closes the connection with C-VM and it may set a timeout session (the field **message** is the response, e.g. HTTP:403). In case of "on-demand" policy, the A-VM may cache the next requests to apply the same checks in future. Moreover, if the policy is "timeout", the A-VM caches the timeout with the paired assurance level. When the timeout is elapsed, it applies the set of measurements associated to that level and it sends the results to the REM-S.

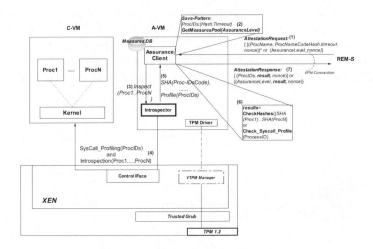

Fig. 3. C-VM: Transparent Solution

A-VM / C-VM Interactions. By exploiting the same introspection library, we have defined two distinct C-VM architectures whose names describe the kind of introspection applied on the monitored machine. In the "transparent" architecture (see Fig. 3), the monitoring is fully transparent to the C-VM and the interactions between the components are those described in the previous section. In this case, the C-VM cannot run any software that VIMS can use to establish the integrity of the C-VM. Instead, the "not-transparent" architecture (see Fig. 4), increases the amount of information that VIMS can access to measure the integrity of the C-VM at the cost of transparency. This solution embeds further functions in the introspection library to verify the integrity of the C-VM and it increases the interactions between the A-VM and the C-VM. An example is the one where the C-VM runs a collector that retrieves information from local IDSes, firewall, anti-virus and sends alerts to a director on the A-VM. In this case, some steps of the protocol between A-VM and REM-S have been modified:

- OpenConnection(A-VM IP): the REM-S requires the A-VM to open a control channel;
- the assurance module accepts requests of:
  - remote attestation from the REM-S (if the security policy is "on-demand");
  - alerts from the director.
- the requests can be:
  - [sign_A-VMKey]AttestationRequest(assuranceLevel, policy, nonce): remote attestation requests from the REM-S. This case is the same that in the transparent solution;
  - Alert(alarmCode): it happens when director sends an alert;
  - ActivateMeasures(getMeasures(alarmCode)): the assurance module, according to the code sent by the director, requires the A-VM to apply further consistency checks;

- an elapsed timeout that triggers security checks on those components listed in the policy database: the A-VM applies the measurements corresponding to the adopted assurance level and it returns to the REM-S the hashes or semantic results for each measured object.
- finally, REM-S closes the connection with the A-VM and the C-VM.

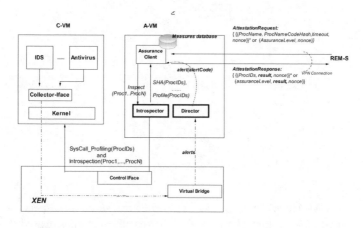

Fig. 4. C-VM: Not Transparent Solution

5   Performance Results

This section shows a preliminary performance evaluation of the current VIMS prototype. According to this preliminary evaluation, the overhead of the protocol for remote attesting the C-VM is acceptable and almost negligible anytime the A-VM only compares the computed hashes against those in its database.

Figure 5(a) shows the overhead of the IOzone [29] benchmark when the attestation requires some introspection checks with respect to the case where these checks are not applied. Timeout is the length of interval in-between two consecutive measurements, i.e. two computations of the hashes of interest. The corresponding performance degradation is fairly low.

Figure 5(b) shows the overhead computed by IOzone on the REM-S when 3 clients establish a VPN connection to the REM-S. As in the previous case, the latency of the network masks the attestation protocol overhead.

Figure 6(a) and 6(b) show the performance results of a set of tests on the simple web-server handling a set of request to a login page using HTTP. In these tests, the httperf benchmark tool [30] has been used to measure the web-server performance under stress when opening a number of HTTP connections ranging from 20 to 200, where each connection transmits 10 requests. The figures show that the response time increases significantly when attestation is applied and the REM-S load decades after about 1600 connection per sec.

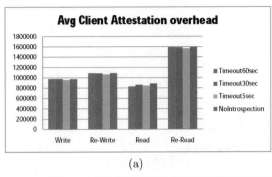

(a)

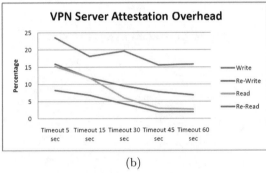

(b)

Fig. 5. Average Client Attestation Overhead(a) and VPN Server Attestation Overhead(b)

We also evaluated the overhead due to the semantic integrity checks enforced by the A-VM on the kernel code and on the software running inside the C-VM. To this purpose, the C-VM ran the VPN client while the A-VM checked the memory pages that store kernel and application code by computing their hashes and comparing them against the values in the database. Furthermore, the A-VM also monitors the system call sequence issued by the VPN client. The period of time in-between two consecutive hash computations was set to 2 seconds. The relative overhead was less than 15% in the worst case.

6 Future Works and Conclusions

A secure handling of critical information requires the continuous monitoring of the integrity of the systems that try to access such information. This, in turn, requires that these systems are highly reliable and resilient against attacks by unauthorised remote users or by malware software. In some cases, a control system can be delegated to apply integrity checks on another one, to verify that it satisfies some predefined security requirements.

In this paper we have described Virtual machine Integrity Measurement System (VIMS), an architecture to enable a network to evaluate and gain some

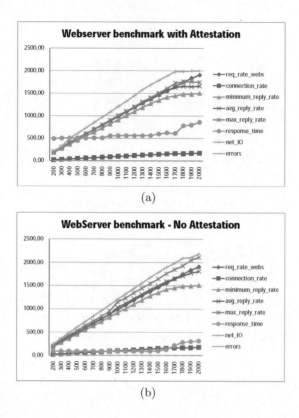

Fig. 6. Httperf Results with Attestation (a) and Without (b)

assurance about the integrity of a remote party that is willing to join the network. As an example, this happens when remote nodes wish to access a corporate VPN or when a browser is requiring resources to a web-server using HTTP. To this purpose, VIMS exploits virtualization and introspection to verify the integrity of the software components that the remote client is running and to attest it to the server that interfaces the network. Virtualization allows the client system to run a shadow VM that applies the integrity checks in a transparent way to the VM that is trying to join the private network. The adoption of VIMS may enable network administrators to protect private resources by remote systems that are trying to join the Intranet and that may be affected by spy-ware, rootkits that may infect critical resources.

An area of future research considers the exploitation of an USB dongle as a secure root-of-trust of the VMM and the A-VM to increase the portability of this architecture to those contexts where the adoption of a TPM chip gives rise to privacy concerns. Finally, VIMS can be extended with the description and implementation of a more granular user-based security policy to define the operations that remote users can invoke.

References

1. Cabuk, S., Dalton, C.I., Ramasamy, H., Schunter, M.: Towards automated provisioning of secure virtualized networks. In: CCS 2007: Proceedings of the 14th ACM conference on Computer and communications security, pp. 235–245. ACM, New York (2007)
2. Griffin, J., Jaeger, T., Perez, R., Sailer, R., van Doorn, L., Caceres, R.: Trusted Virtual Domains: Toward secure distributed services. In: Proc. of 1st IEEE Workshop on Hot Topics in System Dependability (HotDep) (2005)
3. Garfinkel, T., Pfaff, B., Chow, J., Rosenblum, M., Boneh, D.: Terra: A virtual machine-based platform for trusted computing. In: Proceedings of the 19th Symposium on Operating System Principles(SOSP 2003) (October 2003)
4. Sailer, R., Zhang, X., Jaeger, T.: Design and implementation of a TCG-based integrity measurement architecture. In: Proceedings of the 13th conference on USENIX Security Symposium, pp. 223–238 (2004)
5. Kyle, D., Brustoloni, J.C.: Uclinux: a linux security module for trusted-computing-based usage controls enforcement. In: STC 2007: Proceedings of the 2007 ACM workshop on Scalable trusted computing, pp. 63–70. ACM, New York (2007)
6. Jansen, B., Ramasamy, H., Schunter, M.: Policy enforcement and compliance proofs for Xen virtual machines. In: Proceedings of the fourth ACM SIGPLAN/SIGOPS international conference on Virtual execution environments, pp. 101–110 (2008)
7. Sailer, R., Jaeger, T., Zhang, X., van Doorn, L.: Attestation-based policy enforcement for remote access. In: CCS 2004: Proceedings of the 11th ACM conference on Computer and communications security, pp. 308–317. ACM, New York (2004)
8. Seshadri, A., Luk, M., Shi, E., Perrig, A., van Doorn, L., Khosla, P.: Pioneer: verifying code integrity and enforcing untampered code execution on legacy systems. In: SOSP 2005: Proceedings of the twentieth ACM symposium on Operating systems principles, pp. 1–16. ACM, New York (2005)
9. Sadeghi, A.R., Stüble, C.: Property-based attestation for computing platforms: caring about properties, not mechanisms. In: NSPW 2004: Proceedings of the 2004 workshop on New security paradigms, pp. 67–77. ACM, New York (2004)
10. Chen, L., Landfermann, R., Löhr, H., Rohe, M., Sadeghi, A., Stüble, C.: A protocol for property-based attestation. In: Proceedings of the first ACM workshop on Scalable trusted computing, pp. 7–16. ACM, New York (2006)
11. Poritz, J., Schunter, M., Van Herreweghen, E., Waidner, M.: Property attestation: scalable and privacy-friendly security assessment of peer computers. Research Report RZ3548, IBM Corporation (May 2004)
12. Petroni Jr., N., Fraser, T., Walters, A., Arbaugh, W.: An Architecture for Specification-Based Detection of Semantic Integrity Violations in Kernel Dynamic Data. In: Proc. of the 15th USENIX Security Symposium (2006)
13. Haldar, V., Chandra, D., Franz, M.: Semantic remote attestation: a virtual machine directed approach to trusted computing. In: VM 2004: Proceedings of the 3rd conference on Virtual Machine Research And Technology Symposium, Berkeley, CA, USA, p. 3. USENIX Association (2004)
14. Jaeger, T., Sailer, R., Shankar, U.: PRIMA: policy-reduced integrity measurement architecture. In: Proceedings of the eleventh ACM symposium on Access control models and technologies, pp. 19–28. ACM, New York (2006)
15. Pearson, S.: Trusted Computing Platforms, the Next Security Solution. Beaverton. Trusted Computing Group Administration, USA (2002)

16. Loscocco, P.A., Wilson, P.W., Pendergrass, J.A., McDonell, C.D.: Linux kernel integrity measurement using contextual inspection. In: STC 2007: Proceedings of the 2007 ACM workshop on Scalable trusted computing, pp. 21–29. ACM, New York (2007)
17. Bajikar, S.: Trusted Platform Module (TPM) based Security on Notebook PCs-White Paper. Mobile Platforms Group, Intel Corporation (June 20, 2002)
18. Intel: Trusted Execution Technology,
    http://www.intel.com/technology/security
19. Berger, S., Cáceres, R., Goldman, K.A., Perez, R., Sailer, R., van Doorn, L.: vtpm: virtualizing the trusted platform module. In: USENIX-SS'06: Proceedings of the 15th conference on USENIX Security Symposium, Berkeley, CA, USA, p. 21. USENIX Association (2006)
20. England, P., Loeser, J.: Para-Virtualized TPM Sharing. In: Lipp, P., Sadeghi, A.-R., Koch, K.-M. (eds.) Trust 2008. LNCS, vol. 4968, pp. 119–132. Springer, Heidelberg (2008)
21. Dunlap, G., King, S., Cinar, S., Basrai, M., Chen, P.: ReVirt: enabling intrusion analysis through virtual-machine logging and replay. ACM SIGOPS Operating Systems Review 36, 211–224 (2002)
22. Garfinkel, T., Rosenblum, M.: A virtual machine introspection based architecture for intrusion detection. In: Proc. Network and Distributed Systems Security Symposium (February 2003)
23. SourceForge.net: Trusted Boot, http://sourceforge.net/projects/tboot
24. Dragovic, B., Fraser, K., Hand, S., Harris, T., Ho, A., Pratt, I., Warfield, A., Barham, P., Neugebauer, R.: Xen and the art of virtualization. In: Proceedings of the ACM Symposium on Operating Systems Principles (October 2003)
25. Sgandurra, D., Baiardi, F., Maggiari, D., Tamberi, F.: Transparent Process Monitoring in a Virtual Environment. In: Proceedings of the Third International Workshop on Views On Designing Complex Architectures (VODCA 2008), Bertinoro. ENTCS, Elsevier ScienceDirect (to appear) (2008)
26. Tamberi, F., Maggiari, D., Sgandurra, D., Baiardi, F.: Semantics-Driven Introspection in a Virtual Environment. In: Proceedings of the Fourth International Conference on Information Assurance and Security (IAS 2008), pp. 299–302 (2008)
27. OpenVPN: An Open Source SSL VPN Solution, http://openvpn.net/
28. TPM/J: Java-based API for the Trusted Platform Module (TPM),
    http://projects.csail.mit.edu/tc/tpmj/
29. IOzone: Filesystem Benchmark, http://www.iozone.org/
30. Mosberger, D., Jin, T.: httperf: a tool for measuring web server performance. ACM SIGMETRICS Performance Evaluation Review 26(3), 31–37 (1998)

A PrivacyCA for Anonymity and Trust

Martin Pirker, Ronald Toegl, Daniel Hein, and Peter Danner

Institute for Applied Information Processing and Communications (IAIK),
Graz University of Technology, Inffeldgasse 16a, A–8010 Graz, Austria
{mpirker,rtoegl,dhein,pdanner}@iaik.tugraz.at

Abstract. Trusted Computing (TC) as envisioned by the Trusted Computing Group promises a solution to the problem of establishing a trust relationship between otherwise unrelated platforms. In order to achieve this goal the platform has to be equipped with a Trusted Platform Module (TPM), which is true for millions of contemporary personal computers. The TPM provides solutions for measuring the state of a platform and reporting it in an authentic way to another entity. The same cryptographic means that ensure the authenticity also allow unique identification of the platform and therefore pose a privacy problem. To circumvent this problem the TCG proposed a trusted third party, the Privacy Certification Authority (PrivacyCA).

Unfortunately, currently no PrivacyCA is generally available. In this paper we introduce our freely available implementation of a PrivacyCA. In addition, our PrivacyCA is itself a trusted service. It is capable of reporting its state to clients. Furthermore, we use a novel way to minimize the Trusted Computing Base of Java-based applications in conjunction with hardware-supported virtualization. We automatically generate the service interface from a structural specification. Thus, to the best of our knowledge, we were not only first to make this crucial service publicly available, but now also provide a trustworthy service whose privacy policy can be attested to its users by employing TC mechanisms.

Keywords: Trusted Computing, Privacy, PKI, Virtualization, Java, Trusted Computing Base.

1 Introduction

Today's computing landscape is plagued by a variety of software-based attacks and threats such as viruses, phishing attacks, and trojan horses. It is increasingly difficult to find suitable countermeasures in this hostile environment. The recent rise of the concept of *Trusted Computing* introduces a way to improve the security of current computer systems. The Trusted Computing Group (TCG) specified the Trusted Platform Module (TPM), which allows to provide cryptographically qualified and tamper-resilient statements on the software configuration of a machine.

However, the use of protected cryptographic mechanisms alone is not sufficient to convince remote machines or human users that a complex software service can

L. Chen, C.J. Mitchell, and A. Martin (Eds.): Trust 2009, LNCS 5471, pp. 101–119, 2009.
© Springer-Verlag Berlin Heidelberg 2009

actually be *trusted*. To enable a decision based on the statements made by a TPM and the associated trust levels, keys need to be vouched for. This necessitates a Public Key Infrastructure (PKI). The full potential of this approach becomes apparent on the Internet, as it allows a remote, independent party to decide on the trustworthiness of a host or a particular service.

A particular incarnation of the PKI concept is the *PrivacyCA*, which serves to protect the privacy of the user in a trust-enabled networked environment. It confirms that keys are protected by a specification-compliant TPM implementation and thus may be trusted under certain conditions – but without revealing the specific identity of the TPM and the user.

It is an important aspect, that a PrivacyCA requires knowledge of private information of a computer's configuration. Therefore it must be trusted. However, until now, no architecture or implementation has considered this requirement. We describe the architecture of a PrivacyCA service, which is designed to be trusted. It not only provides privacy but is also able to attest its integrity and behavioral policy. To overcome the complexity of deciding on the trustworthiness we minimize the TCB of this Java-based service. Our approach allows for versatile application scenarios and also integrates well with other services on virtualized platforms. The reference implementations we present provide the first actually operational instance of a PKI for Trusted Computing.

Outline. The remainder of the paper is organized as follows: Section 2 gives a short introduction to Trusted Computing mechanisms and motivates the need for a trusted third party PrivacyCA service in this environment. It also discusses a set of guidelines to follow so the trustworthiness of such a service can be achieved in practice. In Section 3 we outline the most important components and processes of a Trusted Computing supporting public key infrastructure. Putting theory to practice, Section 4 presents the practical implementation experience of a PrivacyCA service and the optimizations employed. Section 5 discusses potential use cases. The paper considers related work in Section 6 and concludes in Section 7.

2   Background

2.1   Trusted Computing Platforms

The Trusted Computing Group (TCG) [27] has defined a set of specifications to evolve current computer architectures into *Trusted Platforms*. The TCG does not claim that a Trusted Platform guarantees perfect security under all conditions and for all possible applications, but rather considers a system trustworthy if it *behaves in the expected manner for the intended purpose*.

To provide a hardware anchor for trust, the Trusted Computing Group has specified the Trusted Platform Module [31]. Similar to a Smart Card, the TPM features cryptographic primitives, but is physically bound to a specific platform. A tamper-resilient casing contains hardware implementations of cryptographic operations for public-key cryptography, key generation, hashing, and random-number generation. With these components the TPM is able to enforce security policies on cryptographic keys, such as the Endorsement Key (EK) which provides it with a unique identity.

The TCG not only specifies TPM hardware but also defines an accompanying software infrastructure called the *TCG Software Stack* (TSS) [30]. The stack consists of different modules. Applications can access Trusted Computing functionality by using the Trusted Service Provider (TSP) interface. The Trusted Core Services (TCS) are implemented as a single system service. Among the main functionalities implemented in the TCS are key management, key cache management, TPM command generation and synchronisation. The TCS communicates with the TPM via the TSS Device Driver Library (TDDL).

A system configuration and therefore the system's behavior is defined by the software it executes. We consider the sum of all the software required by a specific service to form its *Trusted Computing Base* (TCB). For a typical service this includes a hypervisor, an operating system, and possibly a language-based virtual machine that executes the service. On a trusted platform, this is reflected in the *chain-of-trust* which is unique for each specific service. Here, each software component is measured before it is given control to, starting with the Core Root-Of-Trust for Measurement (CRTM), typically the BIOS. This process also covers boot loader, kernel, libraries, binary and interpreted application code and, following the transitive trust model, leads to a continuous chain of evidence.

To prevent tampering with the platform measurements the TPM stores them in a set of *Platform Configuration Registers* (PCRs). Thus, a report on the PCR state reflects the exact state of a system. Presented with such a report an external stakeholder can form an informed opinion about a system's trustworthiness. This central concept of a TC-enabled platform is known as *Remote Attestation*. The authenticity and integrity of this report must be preserved even if the TCB is compromised or the network channel is insecure. To this end, the TPM acts as Core Root-Of-Trust for Reporting (CRTR). Upon request, it performs the TPM_Quote operation which signs the PCR state with a TPM hosted signing-capable key.

This specific keys are referred to as *Attestation Identity Keys* (AIKs). The TCG specification guarantees that these keys never leave the protection of a standard-compliant TPM. To ensure that the signature on an attestation report is actually made by a TPM-protected AIK, the used key must be vouched for within the framework of a PKI. Another use for AIKs is to certify the policies of other key types.

2.2   PrivacyCA

The TCG remote attestation architecture requires that an attestant sends a very detailed description of its system state to an attester. This raises the question of privacy protection. For one thing this information might be used to facilitate attacks. Another problem is that reusing the same key for all reporting operations allows to trace the TPM and thus the platform. In some scenarios that might be

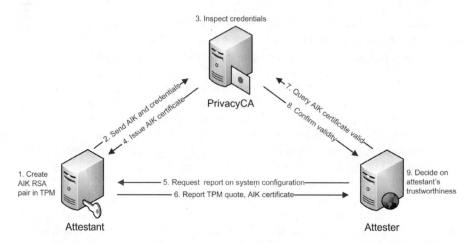

Fig. 1. Overview of AIK creation, certification and usage with a PrivacyCA. Steps 5-9 can take place at a later time and may be repeated.

a desirable feature, but typical end users should value their privacy. Therefore it is of interest, that access of independent external services cannot be correlated (i.e. to create a behavioral or marketing profile of an user).

Hence, the TCG specifications [28] define the PrivacyCA service to protect the privacy of the users. Its task is to issue AIK certificates, which guarantee that a given AIK is owned and secured by a TPM that enforces the TCG-specified policies for AIKs. It is crucial that the issued AIK certificates do not contain any kind of link to the identity of the specific TPM. By employing more than one AIK per TPM it becomes possible to mask the identity of the users.

A general overview of the life cycle of an AIK and its practical application in a remote attestation scenario is provided in Figure 1. At first, a RSA key is generated within the protection of the TPM. In order to obtain an AIK certificate for it, the trusted platform and the PrivacyCA execute a cryptographically secured protocol. A request package describing the AIK and a set of platform specific certificates is transmitted. The PrivacyCA checks the information. If the request conforms to the CA policy, an AIK certificate is returned. It is encrypted so that only the TPM indicated in the request can extract it. Now the AIK key can be used, whenever an attester requests the attestation of the trusted platform. Then the system state description, which is signed with the private part of the AIK and the AIK certificate are provided. The Attester can now verify the correctness of the signature after confirming the validity of the certificate with the help of the PrivacyCA's revocation service.

The mode of operation of a specific PrivacyCA is regulated by its policy, which defines two important properties: Who is allowed to acquire an AIK and how much information about the AIK request and the issued certificates is retained?

In a restricted deployment scenario for example, the PrivacyCA issues and validates AIK certificates only for well-known clients. This requires an initial registration step. In this case it might make sense to store all information acquired during an AIK cycle. In open scenarios, where the PrivacyCA issues certificates to a large set of customers that are not necessarily known beforehand a more liberal policy might be required. The policy options for a PrivacyCA range from "record nothing" over "know enough for the specific operation, forget details after its completion" to "store and log everything". The choice of PrivacyCA and privacy policy and consequently the intended level of privacy should be left to the end-user.

In conclusion, a PrivacyCA takes the role of a trusted third party. It must be trusted by both parties in the remote attestation process. More specifically, the attestant must be ensured that his privacy is protected in accordance to a specific policy, whereas the attester must be assured that a remote attestation report is indeed issued by a TPM.

2.3   Guidelines for Building a Trustworthy Service

In the Trusted Computing scenario envisioned by the TCG, services like a PrivacyCA take the role of a trusted third party. Ideally such a service should be provable secure. Of course, its trustworthiness not solely depends on its design, but also on its practical implementation as well. This includes the trustworthiness of the TCB it is executed on. Regrettably, the downright complexity of the overall system renders a fully formally verified approach infeasible with today's technology.

Still, by following a pragmatic combination of currently available technologies and practices, a high level of trust can be achieved. We now summarize a comprehensive set of simple, heuristically determined and generally accepted guidelines.

Guideline 1. *Apply Virtualization.*

Virtualization support allows the execution of several virtual machines in parallel on the same computer. A hypervisor or Virtual Machine Monitor (VMM) manages the compartments[1] and enforces their separation. The application of virtualization in a TC context is not a new notion [10]. It allows to isolate trusted services in compartment of their own, which helps restricting a possible subversion to a small part of the overall system.

Guideline 2. *Restrict the Trusted Computing Base to a minimum.*

Today's platforms are versatile. In regard to the trustworthiness of the platform this is a drawback. Every service with an external interface provides a point of attack. It is therefore sensible to deactivate every service and component that is not strictly necessary for the execution of the trusted service. We propose an even stricter approach: Remove every superfluous component. The rational is that even if a component does not provide a point of attack it may make security analysis and inspection of the overall system more complex.

---

[1] Note that such hardware-emulating compartments are often called "Virtual Machines". In this paper we use the term exclusively for the language-based Java Virtual Machine.

Guideline 3. *Use formal methods to proof the security of the service interface.*

A formal verification of the security of the complete TCB would be desirable. However, the level of complexity of contemporary software architectures is formidable. Yet, the main point of attack of a service is its network protocol interface, which limits the scope. Thus, we suggest to use formal and automated mechanisms for interface specification, analysis [16] and implementation.

Guideline 4. *Use a safe programming language.*

The programming language a service is written in has a paramount influence on the security properties of the service. A language that allows direct memory access through the use of pointers, or does not automatically perform range checking is inherently more unsafe than a language that does [9]. While it is possible to create safe programs in a wide variety of languages, there is a noticeable difference in the complexity and error-proneness to do so.

Guideline 5. *The source code of the service should be available to the public for inspection.*

Kerckhoff stated [14] that the security of a cryptographic system should solely rely on the secrecy of the key. The rest of the system should be open for inspection. We propose to apply a similar principle to trusted computing. Publicly available source code does not only increase the trust in a service, but in addition adds all the other advantages of public review and criticism to the development. For the same reason a trusted service should be deployed on a platform that is composed of other mature open source components.

Guideline 6. *Use Trusted Computing.*

Ensuring trustworthiness is a two-way process [23]. A client should be able to trust a service and vice versa. Trusted Computing helps to achieve this goal by measuring the platform and employing remote attestation. As mentioned above a trustworthy service should use these tools and the TPM-based capabilities available on modern platforms.

3   Trusted Computing PKI Primitives

In the following sections we outline the TCG specified components and procedures that facilitate the creation of a PKI service. We will discuss specific keys, certificates and protocols and their intended role. In this discussion, we only consider the elements relevant to the PrivacyCA concept.

Security credentials in general may be represented in different formats. The credential standard document of the TCG [33] describes credentials in the concrete instantiation of either X.509 certificates [13] or attribute certificates [8]. Additionally, some TPM functions produce binary blocks of data the internal structures of which do not conform to any standard.

3.1 Endorsement Key and EK Certificate

Every TPM hosts a unique Endorsement Key (EK). The asymmetric key pair is stored in non-volatile memory inside the TPM. It is impossible to retrieve the private part of the key. A corresponding TPM Endorsement certificate contains the public part of the key pair. This certificate represents an assertion that a certain TPM conforms with the TCG specifications and that the private Endorsement Key is indeed protected by the TPM. The Endorsement certificate is signed by the entity which created and inserted the EK.

As the Endorsement Key uniquely identifies a TPM and hence a specific platform, the privacy of the platform user or users might be at risk if the EK is employed for remote attestation operations. As a consequence, the TCG rigorously restricted the set of operations that can be performed with the EK. For instance it is used during the taking of ownership of the TPM by the user. Notably it cannot be used to sign PCR values or arbitrary data. This policy is enforced by the TPM.

3.2 Platform Certificate

A system manufacturer vouches for the components of a platform (except the TPM) with a Platform Endorsement (PE) credential. It represents an assertion that the specific platform incorporates a properly certified TPM and the necessary support components. A PE states that the platform architecture conforms to TCG specifications. A reference to the specific TPM on the platform is included.

3.3 Conformance Certificate

A platform Conformance Credential (CC) attests that the overall design of a platform satisfies the TCG specifications. It asserts the proper design of the Trusted Computing subsystem and its correct integration into the platform. The CC is described in [29], but was not updated in the newer [33] TCG specifications. The newer specification focuses on the EK, PE and AIK (see next section) credentials alone. Thus, for the scope of this paper, we consider its status obsolete and do not consider it further.

3.4 Attestation Identity Key and AIK Certificate

As an alternative to the unique and privacy sensitive EK, the TCG introduced Attestation Identity Keys (AIKs) and the associated AIK certificates. AIK certificates do not contain any information that links the certificates to the specific platform hosting the AIKs. The AIK certificates assure that the identity keys are indeed TPM hosted.

AIK protocol. In order to create an AIK certificate, the trusted client platform with a TPM and the PrivacyCA service execute a cryptographic protocol. The TCG specified the TPM interaction and the PrivacyCA actions, but did not stipulate a transmission protocol for the exchange of the request and response packets. The flow of an AIK creation is illustrated in Figure 2. The steps performed are as follows[2]

1. A client application, running on a machine equipped with a TPM, invokes the `Tspi_TPM_CollateIdentityRequest` TSS function to initiate a new AIK creation.
2. The TSS invokes the `TPM_MakeIdentity` TPM function to create a new attestation-identity RSA-key-pair (AIK). The TPM returns a structure containing the public AIK, signed with the private AIK key.
3. The TSS assembles the request to the PrivacyCA into a structure containing - amongst other information - the signed blob returned by the TPM and the EK and PE certificates of the platform. This request is encrypted with the public key of the PrivacyCA PCA_{Pub}, which must be known to the client beforehand.
4. The request is forwarded to the PrivacyCA. The PrivacyCA decrypts the request and validates its content. In doing so, it also validates the certificates contained by the request.
5. On successful validation the PrivacyCA issues an AIK certificate, encrypted with a symmetric key. The symmetric key along with a hash of the public AIK is in turn encrypted with the public key of the EK of the TPM EK_{Pub} (obtained from the EK certificate in the request). This assures that the result package can only be decrypted by the intended recipient TPM. The result is transported back to the client system.
6. The client application calls the TSS `Tspi_TPM_ActivateIdentity` function with the response from the PrivacyCA. The TSS subsequently requests the platforms TPM to decrypt the response package with the private part of the EK. If the referenced AIK is available on the TPM, the symmetric key is returned.
7. On successful completion of this protocol, the returned key is used to decrypt the response from the PCA containing the AIK certificate.

An activated AIK is a pair of an TPM identity key and the associated certificate issued by a third party PrivacyCA service. The AIK certificate attests that the key pair is bound to a TPM. It contains information fragments from both lower level certificates, EK and PE, to identify the TPM and platform model, but does not contain enough unique information to allow pinpointing to the specific physical hardware.

Additionally, an AIK certificate contains a client chosen arbitrary *label* string which allows for later recognition in a set of AIK certificates. Well defined label strings support the user of the platform in associating a key to a specific task, while they do not allow other parties to guess the identity of the platform and hence the user. This label is a specific TCG certificate extension and must not be confused with standard certificate naming fields.

---

[2] Note that some details are omitted for clarity of presentation. For a complete description please refer to the TCG specifications [28], [30] and [31].

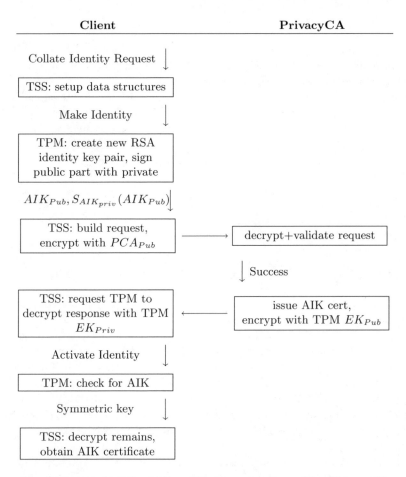

Fig. 2. Overview of the AIK certification procedure with a PrivacyCA

4   Implementations

We implement the core components of a trusted PrivacyCA service following the considerations outlined in the previous sections. Our PrivacyCA allows the creation and validation of EK and AIK certificates and also provides a simple, yet sufficient API for certificate retrieval and revocation.

We eschew the creation of a special purpose platform from scratch, instead we start out using a well maintained off-the-shelf operating system and mature library components. We based our implementation on Java running on Linux. This is a pragmatic approach which offers a good balance of prototyping speed, maturity, features, invested effort and security. We expect this concept to be versatile and trustworthy enough for all but the most security critical *intended purposes*. In the next sections we describe the implementation choices we made for each of the components in greater detail.

4.1   TCcert

As outlined in Section 3, the TCG's specification of the EK, PE and AIK certificates requires the definition of new types of certificate extensions for X.509 type certificates [33] and attribute certificates [8].

General purpose PKI tools currently do not support these extensions and we are not aware of any publicly available library that does. We present a Java library called TCcert which enables us to create these certificates. This allows us to provide the basic building blocks for a Trusted Computing PKI. The following credentials are currently supported by TCcert for certificate creation and validation

- TPM Endorsement Key (EK) credential,
- Platform Endorsement (PE) credential and
- Attestation Identity Key (AIK) credential.

4.2   A PrivacyCA Based on XML

Interaction of distinct entities connected by a network requires a common protocol understood by all participants. Several protocols exist that are already employed in PKIs and for credential management. For trusted computing a protocol should be able to support common PKI services as well as TC specific attributes, queries and data structures. The TCG considered this infrastructure problem in [32]. The two candidates mentioned are the CMC protocol [17] for X.509 certificates and the XKMS protocol [18] for XML-based credentials. The XKMS option initially appeared attractive because its ability to wrap legacy CA services designed for X.509 certificates and express certificate management in XML.

Our first PrivacyCA implementation which uses an XKMS based protocol was released at [19] in the middle of 2007. It proofs that it is possible to use an unmodified XKMS schema to encode the messages required by a TC enabled PKI. However, not all TC associated operations map to XKMS operations in a straightforward way. The AIK cycle uses pure binary data blobs and this property conflicts with the intention of using plain text XML structures. Furthermore, the proof of possession expected by certain PKI commands is not always feasible with TC keys. The TPM policy does not allow e.g. identity keys to sign arbitrary externally supplied data, as this would allow to fabricate fake trust statements. Finally, the application of this solution to a deployment scenario demonstrated that XML introduces an implementation overhead and external dependencies that significantly increase the binary size of the TCB. Therefore, we discontinued this approach.

4.3   An Efficient PrivacyCA Protocol

A PrivacyCA which offers a high level of trustworthiness requires a communication protocol that offers a complete set of PKI operations, but at the same

```
create_aik_request =
  "CREATE_AIK_REQUEST" "\n"
  "Blob: " base64 >clsbuf %save_blob "\n"
  ".\n"
  @do_create_aik_request;

create_aik_response =
  "CREATE_AIK_RESPONSE" "\n"
  "Blob1: " base64 >clsbuf %save_blob1 "\n"
  "Blob2: " base64 >clsbuf %save_blob2 "\n"
  ".\n"
  @do_create_aik_response;
```

Fig. 3. Example of formal specification for the autogenerated parser

time allows for a small-sized implementation. Keeping the guidelines discussed in Section 2.3 in mind we set out to design and build a PrivacyCA prototype by employing state-of-the-art techniques and technologies.

Communication Protocol. For a compact and robust communication protocol we devised a simple ASCII-text based solution. The basic structure of most commands is simply a command identifier followed by the data. Data items are line based, each line terminated by a new line character. The data type identifier and the actual data are separated by a colon followed by a space. Binary data payload is transmitted as Base64 encoded strings.

This is a very basic approach and thus not very prone to implementation errors. The server side parser is constructed using the Ragel state machine compiler[3], resulting in mostly automatically generated parsing code. Ragel generates executable finite state machines from a regular-expression like, formal description of the expected valid input data stream. Furthermore, it allows to generate code for multiple target languages, not only for Java, and thus we hope this encourages development of clients in alternative languages.

The following short example (cf. Figure 3) illustrates the specification of the request and response of the aik_create command which is used to generate the implementation.

Command Set. We implement a sufficient set of commands that enables our implementation to serve as a foundation for a trusted computing PKI. This also includes commands for creating and validating EK certificates, which are currently missing for the majority of shipping TPMs. Other commands allow basic tasks such as creation and revocation of AIK certificates.

Our prototype of a PrivacyCA supports the following operations to enable the identity keys concept of the TCG.

ekcert_create. This command creates a TPM endorsement certificate for a given public key. To our knowledge currently only one vendor, Infineon,

---

[3] A. Thurston, Ragel State Machine Compiler, http://www.complang.org/ragel/

supplies an EK for its TPMs. In order to support TPMs from other vendors it is necessary to supply those TPMs with EK certificates, otherwise it is unreasonable to provide them with AIK certificates.

ekcert_validate. This function validates a TPM endorsement certificate. Our PrivacyCA recognizes certificates issued by Infineon and certificates issued by our own ekcert_create command.

aik_create. implements the AIK certificate creation cycle as specified by the TCG (see section 3.4). By default, all AIK certificates issued are saved in a local storage.

aik_validate. provides a function to validate the AIK certificates issued by our PrivacyCA. The certificate to be checked is submitted by the client and the PrivacyCA returns whether the given certificate is valid.

aik_locate. offers a search function for retrieval of a specific AIK certificate. The AIK label serves as the search key.

aik_revoke. Provides the revocation of individual certificates. The copy in the local storage is removed. Thus, the certificate is no longer available for aik_locate.

tcb_quote. asks the PrivacyCA to quote itself. The PrivacyCA uses the TPM to perform a quote of the system state and returns it to the attester.

Furthermore, a trusted-third-party service like our PrivacyCA should use an end-to-end secure connection for communication with its clients. The current implementation uses unprotected communication channels, however the service can be easily upgraded with Transport Layer Security (TLS). To establish an encrypted TLS-session, we propose to use a session key derived from the same known public PrivacyCA key, which is already necessary for the aik_create command.

4.4   A Reduced Compartment Image

To facilitate the functional assessment and the security analysis of the service and its TCB, the code base should be as small as possible. Therefore, it should only include components that are crucial for its operation. This extends to even removing unnecessary parts of said components. It would be tempting to intuitively argue that fewer Lines-of-Code generally equals less defects. However, we caution that the vulnerability density is not always linear to size. Still, we believe that the overall reduction of code base complexity aids the goal of detecting and understanding security issues and furthers the goal of a trustworthy service and is thus worth exploration.

Software Layers. The TCB of our PrivacyCA service, which is written in Java, can be grouped into the following layers: PrivacyCA service, JVM/JRE, OS runtime support, OS kernel and the TPM. The top layer is our Java PrivacyCA implementation. In order for the Java bytecode to execute, a Java Runtime Environment (JRE) with a Java Virtual Machine (JVM) is required. The JVM makes use of the native environment to use system specific functions like graphics, printing and sound. The native environment is a set of high-level application

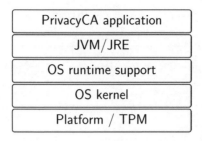

Fig. 4. The Trusted Computing Base of the PrivacyCA service consists of several layers

libraries, the C/C++ standard libraries and operating system functions. The operating system kernel implements the low-level services.

This full software stack is able to run directly on hardware as well as in a virtualized compartment, unaware of the surrounding virtualization layer. We optimized the TCB for the execution of our PrivacyCA service, by starting out with an off-the-shelf configuration and then reducing the included functionality in the respective layers to the absolute minimum. In addition, we employed free-licensed open source components only.

Java Environment. To provide the best possible Java compatibility and allow reuse of existing code we chose IcedTea[4], which is based on Sun's official OpenJDK[5]. The actual subset of the Java environment which is necessary for the PrivacyCA is small. Through the use of Java's class loading profiling feature, we identified the crucial classes. The monitoring of the system dynamic linker/loader `ld.so` produced a list of the necessary native libraries. To allow error handling, the required set of `Exception` and `Error` were also added. This approach reduces the Java runtime for a specific application to a more manageable size in the range of 10 to 20MB. Note that this approach requires manual intervention and reasonable completeness is only achievable for small applications.

We add cryptographic functionality using IAIK JCE[6] and TC support using IAIK jTSS, a pure Java TSS [26].

A Small Kernel. The minimal TCB guideline requires an OS which is small in size, yet powerful enough to support the stripped down JVM. Of the open source operating systems, GNU/Linux is widely used and actively maintained by a large global community. It is a suitable environment to host IcedTea. In addition, the kernel build system allows a fine-grained selection of only those capabilities required by our application. Our configuration consists of essential kernel functionality and a small set of drivers to enable execution directly on hardware or in a virtualized compartment environment (e.g. Xen).

---

[4] http://icedtea.classpath.org/

[5] http://openjdk.java.net/

[6] http://jce.iaik.tugraz.at/sic/products/core_crypto_toolkits/jca_jce

Table 1. Overview of the size of the PrivacyCA software components

Layer	Component	Size [kB]
OS Kernel	Linux Kernel	900
OS Runtime	BusyBox	750
	Baselayout-lite	61
C Libraries	libstdc++	3545
	uClibc	1103
	GCC Runtime	42
Java Core	Stripped Icedtea JRE	8792
Java Application	PrivacyCA Server Core	200
	lib IAIK JCE	818
	lib IAIK jTSS	312
	lib TCcert	49

A Minimal Runtime. The standard `glibc` system library uses about 20 to 25 MB disk space on a typical installation. Additional system and shell tools required for the boot process accumulate to over 3 MB. A component reduced boot process is implementable by employing the compact Busybox[7] toolkit. It supplies a minimal userland program environment. A minimal set of configuration files needed for starting and running a GNU/Linux system is provided by the sys-apps/baselayout-lite package made available from the Embedded Gentoo project[8]. Furthermore, we chose the uClibc[9] as an alternative C library with a drastically reduced footprint.

A Minimal PrivacyCA Compartment Prototype. The PrivacyCA service built from the above components is bundled into a single compartment image. Note that the privacy policy configuration is an intrinsic part of the image file. Thus it implicitly can be measured into the TPM at compartment startup. A current snapshot and associated source code is available for download from [19].

The size of the components in a current snapshot of our prototype are presented in Table 1. The complete compartment has a total size of approximately 17 Megabytes.

5   Use Cases

The general availability of a small-sized, versatile PrivacyCA compartment enables multiple deployment scenarios for further research and gathering of practical experience. We describe multiple such scenarios, where our system architecture provides added value over conventional service implementations.

Scalability of PrivacyCAs. In a future Trusted Computing-enabled Internet a PrivacyCA potentially has to serve millions of users. A certain pressure to employ

---

[7] http://www.busybox.net/
[8] http://www.gentoo.org/proj/en/base/embedded/
[9] http://www.uclibc.org/

a multitude of certificates exists as the use of more AIKs per user increases a users anonymity to service providers. This necessitates a powerful, scalable certification authority infrastructure that is capable of issuing and validating a great number of certificates.

Scalability of a PrivacyCA service can be achieved through hosting many small PrivacyCA compartments. This is done by hosting a sufficient number of compartments in parallel using virtualization technology on a set of server machines. The preservation of a services' trustworthiness is of crucial importance. The vision of such a Trusted Virtual Datacenter (TVDc) setting is an active area of research, see e.g. [25] and [5]. We are optimistic that current TVDc related research results can be adapted to construct a massively scaled trusted PrivacyCA datacenter.

Compact PrivacyCA Service for Restricted or Mobile Environments. As our PrivacyCA consists of open source components only, it is open to inspection and analysis by the community. It is also compact and self-contained: once evaluated it is easy to show that any given instance has not been changed through TC attestation mechanisms. Furthermore, self-contained services are easy to deploy, especially for in-house PrivacyCA services of organizations which presumably will precede Internet-wide use. The services' compactness also allows usage on performance restricted systems, such as trusted mobile phones [22].

Trusted Core for Large Java Applications. To increase the security of applications in the Nizza virtualization architecture, [24] suggest to extract security critical modules out of legacy applications. Each of these modules is transferred into a separate, trusted compartment called AppCore which features a small TCB. We believe that our reduced Java environment is ideally suited to implement similar modifications for Java applications.

6   Related Work

To our knowledge the first experimental public PrivacyCA service[10] was put into operation by us at IAIK in 2007. It served as a basis for the advanced version presented in this paper. In a seemingly private effort[11] another PrivacyCA was started in 2008, but with limited functional scope. Zic and Nepal [35] presented a scenario employing a prototype PrivacyCA service but to the best of our knowledge this service has not been released.

As an alternative to the trusted third party concept of a PrivacyCA, [6] proposes Direct Anonymous Attestation (DAA). TPM implementations are available, however the required software and service infrastructure has not yet been provided for. It remains a theoretical concept so far.

TC-enabled hardware platforms [7] support hardware enforced virtualization. Generally, a hypervisor like the Xen [3] virtual machine monitor or the Fiasco/L4

---

[10] http://opentc.iaik.tugraz.at/
[11] http://www.privacyca.com

[12] μ-kernel, allows the creation, execution and hibernation of isolated compartments. Modern trusted platforms [10,20,15] could in the near future employ these hardware features, given proper virtualization of the TPM [4,25,5,21].

A significant body of research on Java virtual machines and using Java as an operating system or a component thereof exists. Yet, Java is still evolving and thus older results may not reflect newer research developments or requirements. The results of [11], [34] or projects (SanOS[12]) are currently not maintained. Also, mobile Java platforms such as Sun's KVM[13] may be smaller, however their feature set is restricted and not compatible with general Java applications or libraries. More recent efforts like JNode[14] or [1] do not consider small binary size as a goal, thus resulting in a TCB that is too large for our purposes. The *Java Kernel*[15] project divides JRE libraries into separate bundles, which are later fetched at runtime as required. Reliance on a full-featured Windows environment introduces additional overhead. Anderson et al. [2] created a small sized Xen library OS running exclusively on top of the Xen hypervisor. Due to the lack of basic features it is not able to run a modern Java Runtime Environment such as OpenJDK.

7   Conclusion

This paper describes the creation of a trustworthy PrivacyCA service. We present and follow a set of guidelines that allow to achieve practical trustworthiness with a novel combination of state-of-the-art methods. These methods include formal yet compilable protocol specifications, the minimization of the TCB and the utilization of hardware-supported virtualization. Foremost, our PrivacyCA service lays the foundation for easy attestation of its state and consequently the privacy policy it guarantees to its clients.

The PrivacyCA is implemented as a self-contained image that can be executed stand-alone or by the Xen hypervisor. While the image is of minimal size, it contains a bare-bone operating system and a Java Runtime Environment. Our process can also be applied to support other services with a highly trustworthy environment. The PrivacyCA service protocol is partially auto-generated from a formal state-machine description. We outline several use-cases and incorporate the results of operating an experimental public prototype setup.

Future work will consider use cases in the context of distributed computing and advanced certification mechanisms for virtual TPMs. An integration of the newest TCG credential type, a *unified credential*[33], may stimulate new work flows. We also desire to work on closing the gap between automatic generation of an implementation and the formal security analysis of network protocols and to apply this to future extended PrivacyCA interfaces.

---

[12] http://www.jbox.dk/sanos/

[13] http://java.sun.com/products/cldc/wp/KVMwp.pdf

[14] http://www.jnode.org/

[15] http://java.sun.com/javase/6/6u10faq.jsp

Acknowledgements. The authors thank the anonymous reviewers for their insightful comments and Andreas Niederl for assisting the implementations.

The efforts at IAIK to integrate TC technology into the Java programming language are part of the OpenTC project funded by the EU as part of FP-6, contract no. 027635. The project aims at providing an open source TC framework with a special focus on the Linux operating system platform. Started as an open source project the results can be inspected by everybody, thus adding towards the trustworthiness of Trusted Computing solutions.

References

1. Ammons, G., Appavoo, J., Butrico, M., Silva, D.D., Grove, D., Kawachiya, K., Krieger, O., Rosenburg, B., Hensbergen, E.V., Wisniewski, R.W.: Libra: a library operating system for a jvm in a virtualized execution environment. In: VEE 2007: Proceedings of the 3rd international conference on Virtual execution environments, pp. 44–54. ACM, New York (2007)
2. Anderson, M.J., Moffie, M., Dalton, C.I.: Towards trustworthy virtualisation environments: Xen library os security service infrastructure. Technical Report HPL-2007-69, HP Research (2007)
3. Barham, P., Dragovic, B., Fraser, K., Hand, S., Harris, T., Ho, A., Neugebauer, R., Pratt, I., Warfield, A.: Xen and the art of virtualization. In: SOSP 2003: Proceedings of the nineteenth ACM symposium on Operating systems principles, pp. 164–177. ACM, New York (2003)
4. Berger, S., Cáceres, R., Goldman, K.A., Perez, R., Sailer, R., van Doorn, L.: vTPM: virtualizing the trusted platform module. In: USENIX-SS 2006: Proceedings of the 15th conference on USENIX Security Symposium, pp. 305–320 (2006)
5. Berger, S., Cáceres, R., Pendarakis, D., Sailer, R., Valdez, E., Perez, R., Schildhauer, W., Srinivasan, D.: TVDc: managing security in the trusted virtual datacenter. SIGOPS Oper. Syst. Rev. 42(1), 40–47 (2008)
6. Brickell, E., Camenisch, J., Chen, L.: Direct anonymous attestation. In: CCS 2004: Proceedings of the 11th ACM conference on Computer and communications security, pp. 132–145. ACM, New York (2004)
7. David Grawrock. The Intel Safer Computing Initiative. Intel Press (2006) ISBN 0-9764832-6-2
8. Farrell, S., Housley, R.: An Internet Attribute Certificate Profile for Authorization (April 2002), http://www.ietf.org/rfc/rfc3281.txt
9. Felleisen, M., Cartwright, R.: Safety as a metric. In: Proc. 12th Conference on Software Engineering Education and Training, pp. 129–131 (1999)
10. Garfinkel, T., Pfaff, B., Chow, J., Rosenblum, M., Boneh, D.: Terra: a virtual machine-based platform for trusted computing. In: SOSP 2003: Proceedings of the nineteenth ACM symposium on Operating systems principles, pp. 193–206. ACM, New York (2003)
11. Golm, M., Felser, M., Wawersich, C., Kleinöder, J.: A Java operating system as the foundation of a secure network operating system. Technical report tr-i4-02-05, Univ. of. Erlangen, Dept. of Comp. Science, Lehrstuhl 4 (2002)
12. Hohmuth, M.: The Fiasco kernel: Requirements definition. Technical Report ISSN 1430-211X, Dresden University of Technology (1998)

13. Housley, R., Polk, W., Ford, W., Solo, D.: Internet X.509 Public Key Infrastructure Certificate and Certificate and CRL Profile (April 2002), http://www.ietf.org/rfc/rfc3280.txt
14. Kerckhoffs, A.: La cryptographie militaire. Journal des sciences militaires IX (1883)
15. Kuhlmann, D., Landfermann, R., Ramasamy, H.V., Schunter, M., Ramunno, G., Vernizzi, D.: An open trusted computing architecture — secure virtual machines enabling user-defined policy enforcement. Research Report RZ 3655, IBM Research (2006)
16. Meadows, C.: Formal methods for cryptographic protocol analysis: emerging issues and trends. IEEE Journal on Selected Areas in Communications 21(1), 44–54 (2003)
17. Myers, M., Liu, X., Schaad, J., Weinstein, J.: Certificate Management Messages over CMS (April 2000), http://www.ietf.org/rfc/rfc2797.txt
18. Mysore, S.H., Hallam-Baker, P.: XML key management specification (XKMS 2.0). W3C recommendation, W3C (June 2005), http://www.w3.org/TR/2005/REC-xkms2-20050628/
19. Pirker, M., Toegl, R., Winkler, T., Vejda, T.: Trusted computing for the Java™ platform (2009), http://trustedjava.sourceforge.net/
20. Sadeghi, A.-R., Stüble, C., Pohlmann, N.: European multilateral secure computing base - open trusted computing for you and me. Datenschutz und Datensicherheit (DUD) (09/2004), pp. 548–554 (2004), http://www.trust.rub.de/media/publications/SaStPo2004Web.pdf
21. Sadeghi, A.-R., Stüble, C., Winandy, M.: Property-based TPM virtualization. In: 11th Information Security Conference (2008)
22. Schmidt, A., Kuntze, N., Kasper, M.: On the deployment of mobile trusted modules. In: Wireless Communications and Networking Conference, 2008. WCNC 2008, pp. 3169–3174. IEEE, Los Alamitos (2008)
23. Sheehy, J., Coker, G., Guttman, J., Loscocco, P., Herzog, A., Millen, J., Monk, L., Ramsdell, J., Sniffen, B.: Attestation: Evidence and trust. Technical Report 07 0186, MITRE Corporation (2007)
24. Singaravelu, L., Pu, C., Härtig, H., Helmuth, C.: Reducing TCB complexity for security-sensitive applications: three case studies. In: EuroSys 2006: Proceedings of the ACM SIGOPS/EuroSys European Conference on Computer Systems 2006, pp. 161–174. ACM, New York (2006)
25. Stumpf, F., Benz, M., Hermanowski, M., Eckert, C.: An approach to a trustworthy system architecture using virtualization (2007)
26. Toegl, R., Pirker, M.: An ongoing game of Tetris: Integrating trusted computing in Java, block-by-block. In: Proceedings of Future of Trust in Computing. Vieweg + Teubner (2008)
27. Trusted Computing Group, https://www.trustedcomputinggroup.org/
28. Trusted Computing Group. TCG infrastructure specifications, https://www.trustedcomputinggroup.org/specs/IWG/
29. Trusted Computing Group. TCG main specification version 1.1b, https://www.trustedcomputinggroup.org/specs/TPM/
30. Trusted Computing Group. TCG software stack specification, version 1.2 errata a, https://www.trustedcomputinggroup.org/specs/TSS/
31. Trusted Computing Group. TCG TPM specification version 1.2 revision 103, https://www.trustedcomputinggroup.org/specs/TPM/

32. Trusted Computing Group. TCG Reference Architecture for Interoperability (Version 1.0) (June 2005), https://www.trustedcomputinggroup.org/specs/IWG
33. Trusted Computing Group. TCG Credential Profiles Specifications (Version 1.1, rev 1.014) (May 2007), https://www.trustedcomputinggroup.org/specs/IWG
34. van Doorn, L.: A secure Java virtual machine. In: Proceedings of the 9th USENIX Security Symposium. USENIX Association (2000)
35. Zic, J., Nepal, S.: Implementing a portable trusted environment. In: Proceedings of Future of Trust in Computing. Vieweg + Teubner (2008)

Revocation of TPM Keys

Stefan Katzenbeisser[1], Klaus Kursawe[2], and Frederic Stumpf[3]

[1] Security Engineering Group,
Technische Universität Darmstadt, Darmstadt, Germany
katzenbeisser@seceng.informatik.tu-darmstadt.de
[2] Information and System Security Group,
Philips Research Europe, Eindhoven, The Netherlands
klaus.kursawe@philips.com
[3] Research Group IT-Security,
Technische Universität Darmstadt, Darmstadt, Germany
stumpf@sec.informatik.tu-darmstadt.de

Abstract. A Trusted Platform Module (TPM) offers a number of basic security services which can be used to build complex trusted applications. One of the main functionalities of a TPM is the provision of a protected storage, including access management for cryptographic keys. To allow for scalability in spite of the resource constraints of the TPM, keys are not stored inside the TPM, but in encrypted form on external, untrusted storage. This has the consequence that the actual key storage is not under control of the TPM, and it is therefore not possible to revoke individual keys. In this paper we introduce two basic methods to implement key revocation without major changes to the TPM command set, and without inhibiting backwards compatibility with the current specification. Our methods introduce no overhead for normal operation, and a reasonable small effort for managing revocable keys.

1   Introduction

One of the basic functionalities of a Trusted Platform Module (TPM) as proposed by the Trusted Computing Group [9] is the secure storage of cryptographic encryption and signature keys. By protecting these keys with hardware measures, they cannot easily be removed in offline attacks or altered through the operating system. To reduce the amount of non-volatile memory required inside the TPM, it acts as an access control device for externally stored keys rather than storing all keys itself. Only the storage root key (SRK) remains permanently in the TPM and is used to encrypt all other externally stored keys. This strategy offers the same security level as if all keys were stored internally.[1] This design choice allows to reduce the production costs of a TPM, but introduces the problem that the TPM is not able to reliably destroy externally stored keys once they

---

[1] The TPM does store other keys for internal use, especially the endorsement key; however these keys do not play a role in the context of the present paper.

L. Chen, C.J. Mitchell, and A. Martin (Eds.): Trust 2009, LNCS 5471, pp. 120–132, 2009.
© Springer-Verlag Berlin Heidelberg 2009

get compromised. Thus, if an attacker once acquires access rights to a TPM-maintained key and an encrypted version of that key, he can always access that key through the TPM hardware.

One secure way to prevent a compromised key from being used in the future is to delete the storage root key. However, this makes all non-migrateable keys maintained by the TPM unusable, which may be unacceptable in applications where a single TPM needs to manage a large number of keys. To alleviate the problem, a mechanism to revoke TPM keys is required; however, such a mechanism is not provided by the TPM specification of the Trusted Computing Group.

In this paper, we analyse two ways of implementing a TPM key revocation scheme and propose appropriate extensions to the TPM specification. It seems unavoidable to make changes to the TPM command set, as some additional verification of the validity of a key is required inside the TPM. Our methods attempt to minimise the amount of modification required, and can be implemented in a way that does not affect the compatibility of existing applications. In particular, we propose two revocation schemes: one is based on blacklisting of revoked keys, while the other one employs a whitelist approach. Both approaches require additional communication with and computation in the TPM: either loading a key has a communication complexity linear in the number of revoked keys, or revoking a key has a communication complexity linear in the number of revocable keys. In the last part of the paper, we propose to use a combination of blacklists and whitelists to ensure practicability of the key revocation scheme.

While our approach is applicable to all keys maintained by the TPM, the main application of key revocation lies in authentication keys for external services. In this application it is infeasible to guarantee that a party whose access is to be revoked can be banned from accessing the TPM—for example because he still uses the platform and is just banned from using a single service, or because an aggressive attacker may gain illicit access to a machine (the reason why keys where stored in the TPM in the first place). Thus, a mechanism is required to block the use of single keys, while other authentication keys should remain functional. In addition, a variant of the proposed protocol allows to change the authorisation information required to access a TPM key in a way that reliably invalidates old authorisation information for an attacker that holds a copy of the old TPM information; this allows for a substantially more secure key management for any application using TPM keys with a long lifetime.

2   Related Work

Efficient key revocation has been studied in various settings, especially in the context of public key infrastructures [4], or in wireless sensor networks [10]. Those applications show little connection to the TPM case though, as they usually deal with a large number of networked participants. There is relatively little work on TPM key revocation; while the Trusted Computing Group spent quite some effort on the revocability of TPMs [1] and some work has been done on key management issues such as key migration [2], we are not aware of any schemes that allow to revoke individual TPM keys.

Some authors considered TPM-based applications that share some similarities with the key revocation problem. In [3], limited trusted memory is used to store a database in untrusted storage. As in our application, it is important that an attacker cannot replay an old version of the database: in some sense, the TPM key storage can be seen as a database of keys. Sarmenta et. al. [5] propose efficient ways to implement count objects based on a TPM by using hash trees. An externally stored counter poses similar challenges as an externally stored key: it must not be possible to set the counter to an old value, while a key must contain a protected flag that marks him as valid or invalid. While it is possible to translate the hash-tree approach to key management, we believe that the problem of key revocation can be solved in a simpler way that fits better into the TPM architecture.

3   Basic Key Revocation Protocol Suite

Key revocation can be implemented either with a blacklist or a whitelist approach. While blacklists allow for an efficient (constant time) revocation of keys and introduce a performance penalty once a key is loaded into the TPM, whitelists provide fast (constant time) access to keys, but require a costly revocation operation.

A *blacklist* is an externally stored list of keys that have been revoked; integrity of the list is assured through a hash chain. The list is bound to the TPM by a cryptographic key and a register, which securely stores the last element of the hash chain within the TPM. Whenever a key is revoked, a new entry to the blacklist is created, and the TPM updates its internally stored hash. Whenever a key is loaded into the TPM, the blacklist is fed sequentially through the TPM, its integrity is checked and its entries are compared to the key to be loaded. If the key is on the blacklist, the TPM aborts the loading process. Thus, the use of a key gets expensive once a large number of keys are revoked.

In contrast, in a *whitelist* approach, a special whitelist blob, containing a (keyed) hash of a counter and the key, is produced for every key that is not revoked. Due to the use of a keyed hash, the blob is only accessible to the TPM. Inside the TPM, we need one secure counter. A key is only valid if the counter value stored in the associated whitelist key blob matches the internal TPM counter. To revoke a key, the TPM increments its internal secure counter and updates (re-creates) all non-revoked whitelist blobs by incrementing the contained counter value. This approach allows for very efficient (constant time) verification of the revocation status of a key. However, the revocation process itself is relatively complex, as the TPM needs to re-authenticate every single whitelist key blob corresponding to a non-revoked key.

In both approaches, we change the implementation of the TPM_LoadKey command. Furthermore, we require an additional command, which is used to pass the entire black- or whitelist through the TPM in a sequential manner, either during use or during revocation of the key. In the following sections, we provide implementations for both the blacklist and whitelist approach. For simplicity, the algorithm descriptions show only the input/output parameters which are accessed in the algorithms; additional parameters are given in the TPM specification [8].

For efficiency and compatibility reasons, we do not make every key revocable by default. Rather, on generation of a key, a user can choose whether a key should be revocable or not. This way, old applications can use the TPM without any modification, and the data structures needed for revocation information do not need to be bloated with keys that are not required to be revocable.

4   Blacklist Implementation

In the blacklist approach, we store an authenticated list of revoked keys in external memory. The list of keys is kept in the form of a hash chain, which allows easy authentication, sequential access and addition of new revoked keys. Furthermore, we securely store the last element of the hash chain (called *TPM.lastHash* in the sequel) inside the TPM for verification purposes; thus, only a small amount of secure persistent storage is required. Note however, that the blacklist must be stored on an external device in a way that is not accessible to an attacker, since malicious modifications (e.g., integrity changes or deletions) invalidate the whole list and allow denial of service attacks, as all revocable keys cannot be loaded in the future once the integrity of the blacklist is broken.

In order to keep the option of using non-revocable keys for less critical tasks without any performance penalties, we add a special field *revocable* to each key blob generated by the TPM. Once a key is loaded, the TPM checks the flag and only executes the standard key loading process if the key is marked as non-revocable. The *revocable* flag can be realized by introducing the new mask value 0x00000016 to the TPM_KEY_FLAGS structure [6]. As not all possible mask values are used in the current version of the specification, this can be done with minimal effort. Since the TPM_KEY_FLAGS structure is not protected by encryption, the flag also needs to be integrated to the TPM_STORE_ASYMKEY structure [6] to ensure its consistency and integrity.

In addition, another flag needs to be added to the TPM_STORE_ASYMKEY structure. This flag (called *checked* in the sequel) indicates whether a revocable key has been validated against the blacklist. This flag has the same characteristics as a semaphore and is used to deliver state information between the command which loads the key (TPM_LoadKey) and a new TPM command that validates the loaded key against the blacklist (TPM_ShowRevListElement, see below for the implementation).

Structure of the blacklist, Setup of the system. The blacklist contains the public keys of all revoked keys, authenticated by the TPM and stored in the form of a hash chain. For authentication we use the storage root key (*SRK*). Alternatively, a different key which is a direct child of the *SRK* may be utilized; this requires both the *SRK* and an additional key to be loaded into the TPM. However, since the TPM only possesses a very limited number of key slots, this concept may deplete the TPM's available key-slots and restrain the ability to load additional keys. Every element *rev_element* of the hash chain has the following structure:

$$\langle key, \text{Hash}(\text{REVOC\_LABEL} \| key \| SRK \| prevHash) \rangle ,$$

where *key* denotes the public key that is revoked, *SRK* denotes the private storage root key, REVOC_LABEL is a label that indicates that the hash value is intended solely for the construction of a revocation list, and *prevHash* denotes the hash of the previous entry in the revocation list (the latter is set to a constant value 0^k for the first list element). The usage of *SRK* in the hash makes the hash keyed: only the TPM, which is owner of the *SRK*, is able to generate hashes and verify hash values. The elements of the hash chain can easily be stored in a new TPM structure TPM_REV_ELEMENT of the following type:

```
typedef struct tdTPM_REV_ELEMENT {
    TPM_STRUCT_VER ver;
    TPM_STORE_PUBKEY pubKey;
    TPM_REV_ELEMENT_HASH Hash;
    } TPM_REV_ELEMENT;
```

The blacklist is managed by a software stack; however, only the TPM is able to operate on the blacklist.

To initialize the revocation mechanism, the hash *TPM.lastHash* (which is securely stored within the TPM) is set to 0^k, indicating the absence of a revocation list. This needs to happen whenever a new *SRK* is defined, i.e., as a part of the TPM_TakeOwnership command. Furthermore, the commands for generating keys (such as TPM_CreateWrapKey) have to be modified in order to initialize the required fields *revocable* and *checked*, where the latter one is set to FALSE by default.

Revocation of a key. A key can be revoked by a call to the new TPM command TPM_RevokeKey: the command takes the handle *keyHandle* of the key to be revoked and a handle *srkHandle* to the *SRK*. Thus, we assume that a key is available when it is revoked (this excludes the possibility of revoking keys which are not present). The command simply generates the new entry of the hash chain using the hash of the last revocation list element that is stored securely within the TPM. Furthermore, it updates this hash and returns the new revocation list entry (see Algorithm 1). Note that the command does, for performance reasons, not verify the integrity of the existing hash chain. Moreover, it does not check whether the hash chain already contains an entry for the key in question. We assume that all our commands are executed inside an established authorisation session (e.g., TPM_OSAP or TPM_OIAP) [7]. The purpose of this session is to verify authorisation and to establish an authorisation handle between the TPM and the software stack for the different keys. Since some of the commands introduced by us require authorisation of multiple keys with different authorisation knowledge, it is necessary to establish multiple authorisation sessions to the TPM. This is

---

Algorithm 1. Algorithm TPM_RevokeKey

Input : *srkHandle, keyHandle*
Output: *returnCode, revElement*

$newHash$:= Hash(REVOC_LABEL $\parallel$ *keyHandle.pubKey* $\parallel$ *SRK* $\parallel$ *TPM.lastHash*)
TPM.lastHash := *newHash*
return RET_REVOKE_KEY_ACK, *newHash*

---

similar to the TPM_ActivateIdentity command that requires two concurrent
OSAP sessions (Cf. [8], pp. 153). Note that the data-structures used here do not
directly allow to maintain a TPM-key, but replace its authorisation information
(i.e., blacklist the old version and bind the key to a new one); however, this can
easily be added if such a functionallity is desired.

Usage of a TPM key. Every TPM key that is used in an application must
be loaded by the function TPM_LoadKey. If the loaded key is revocable it cannot be directly used (*key.revocable* is set to TRUE): The TPM rather has to
check whether the key is present on the revocation list. Thus, the TPM requires the application (or the TSS) to execute a number of calls to the function
TPM_ShowRevListElement, which sequentially feeds all entries of the revocation
list through the TPM. This function checks the integrity of the hash chain and
verifies that the key to be loaded is not present on the blacklist. The function
aborts with failure (RET_FAIL) if the hash chain is invalid, requests further calls
until the end of the hash chain is reached (RET_REVOC) or returns RET_OK. In
the latter case it sets a flag indicating that the key is ready to use. Finally, to
terminate the process of loading a key, another call to TPM_LoadKey is required,
which returns the key handle for subsequent use. Note that the revocation test
is only performed when a key is loaded into the TPM, not every time it is used.
It is thus possible that a key got revoked, but still resides inside the TPM in
usable form. To alleviate the problem, it may be necessary to flush all revoked
TPM keys from the TPM cache; however, this incurs a performance penalty.

Algorithm 2 shows the necessary changes to the TPM_LoadKey command. If
the key *inKey* refers to a revocable key, it is first checked whether the revocation
list has already been tested against the given key (*inKeyPlain.Keyflags.checked*
is set to TRUE); in this case, the command performs all operations that are
normally performed when loading a key; otherwise the encrypted *inKey* structure
is returned along with the return code RET_REVOC indicating that the key needs
further processing by the function TPM_ShowRevListElement.

The implementation of the command TPM_ShowRevListElement is given in
Algorithm 3. It takes a handle to the *SRK*, the encrypted *inKey* structure returned by TPM_LoadKey, one element of the revocation list, a handle to the parent
key, and information on the authorisation session (one *Nonce* of the authorisation session for the *parentHandle*). It is necessary to integrate information of
the authorisation session to ensure that the check against the blacklist is fresh.
Thus, to successfully load a revocable key, the TPM_LoadKey command must use
parts of the same authorisation data as TPM_ShowRevListElement.

Algorithm 2. Additional performed actions of the TPM_LoadKey command

---

Input   : *parentHandle, inKey, Nonce*
Output: *returnCode, inKeyHandle, inKey*

---

inKeyPlain := Decrypt(*inKey, parentHandle*)
if *inKeyPlain.Keyflags.revocable* = TRUE **then**
    if *inKeyPlain.Keyflags.checked* = (TRUE || *Nonce*) **then**
        Continue as denoted in TPM specification
        return TPM_SUCCESS, *inKeyHandle*
    else
        inKeyPlain.Keyflags.checked := (FALSE || *Nonce*)
        inKey = Encrypt(*inKeyPlain, parentHandle*)
        return RET_REVOC, *inKey*
else
    Continue as denoted in TPM specification
    return TPM_SUCCESS, *inKeyHandle*

The algorithm validates the hash chain, assures that all subsequent calls are performed with the same public key and makes sure that the key is not present on the revocation list. For this purpose, the TPM needs to internally store two hash values: the hash (*prevHash*) of the previously validated blacklist entry and a hash of the public key (*previnKey*). Both can be realized as additional fields of the TPM_STANY_DATA structure. Once the end of the hash chain is reached (this can be realized by comparing *TPM.lastHash* with the hash of the current revocation entry), the TPM subsequently checks whether the given public key corresponds to the private key stored in the *inKey* structure. If this is the case, the label *inKeyPlain.Keyflags.checked* is changed and the *inKey* structure is returned.

Authorisation. It is not straightforward to decide which party—the TPM owner, the key owner, or even an external party—should have the right to revoke an individual key. The blacklist approach can easily be extended to allow each of the above choices; a simple modification of the TPM_RevokeKey command allows to implement the desired authorisation for key revocation, and even to decide at key creation who is allowed to revoke that particular key. An unauthorised party then simply is not able to create the corresponding blacklist entry.

Consolidation. The effort to load a revocable key increases linearly with the size of the blacklist, as all entries have to be passed through the TPM before a revocable key can be used. It is therefore desirable to have a consolidation protocol which removes the contents of the blacklist: the consolidation protocol generates a new *SRK* in parallel to the old one, copies all non-revoked keys into a new key tree under the new *SRK*, and then deletes the old *SRK*. As all old key blobs are useless without the old *SRK*, and only non-revoked keys will be transferred, the blacklist can be deleted and the TPM is again in a state with an empty blacklist.

Algorithm 3. Algorithm of the `TPM_ShowRevListElement` command

Input : *srkHandle, revElement, parentHandle,*
            inKey, Nonce

Output: *returnCode, inKey*

if undefined($prevHash$) then
$\quad$ $prevHash=0^k$

$curHash := $ Hash(REVOC_LABEL $||$ $revElement.pubKey$ $||$ SRK $||$ $prevHash$)
if $(curHash! = revElement.Hash)$ $||$ $(revElement.pubKey = inKey.pubKey)$ then
$\quad$ return RET_FAIL

if not(undefined($previnKey$)) then
$\quad$ if $previnKey$ $!=$ Hash($inKey.pubKey$) then
$\quad\quad$ return RET_FAIL

$previnKey := $ Hash($inKey.pubKey$)
$prevHash := curHash$
if $curHash = TPM.lastHash$ then
$\quad$ $inKeyPlain := $ Decrypt($inKey, parentHandle$)
$\quad$ if $inKeyPlain.Keyflags.checked = $ (FALSE $|| Nonce$) then
$\quad\quad$ if $inKeyPlain$ contains public key corresponding to $previnKey$ then
$\quad\quad\quad$ $inKeyPlain.Keyflags.checked := $ (TRUE $|| Nonce$)
$\quad\quad\quad$ $inKey := $ Encrypt($inKeyPlain, parentHandle$)
$\quad\quad\quad$ return RET_OK, $inKey$
$\quad$ else
$\quad\quad$ return RET_FAIL

else
$\quad$ return RET_REVOC

However, this approach encounters a number of practical problems. A TPM allows to store keys in a tree structure (e.g., the SRK may encrypt a user key which then itself encrypts a signature key). Thus, it may happen that a non-revocable key is used to protect a revocable key. In this case it is important to also change the non-revocable key to prevent it from being used to decrypt the old, revoked key once the blacklist is cleaned. Another problem is that the keys may have different access rights, and the appropriate key owners may not be available to authorise usage of the keys; the consolidation protocol thus would need to circumvent all access control mechanisms, which leads to additional complexity in the implementation. Finally, the key tree needs to be presented to the TPM in the right order, as parents need to be transferred before their children. While it is possible to implement a consolidation protocol that takes all above-mentioned problems into account, the added complexity may not be worth the effort. In situations where keys need to be revoked very often, a different strategy based on whitelists (as described in the next section) is much more favorable.

Hash trees. When the number of revoked keys is expected to be large, another strategy to limit the efforts of loading a key can be employed. Instead of a hash chain, the blacklist can be arranged in a tree structure. In this case, we first compute a short (e.g., 64 bit) hash of the key to be loaded, which determines the position of the key within the hash tree in the natural way: the hash is interpreted as a binary string, where each bit indicates for each level of the tree whether to continue in the left or right subtree. Every leaf node stores a hash of the form Hash(REVOC_LABEL $\|$ key $\|$ SRK), while every non-leaf node stores a hash of both children. Note that for efficiency reasons we do not store the entire tree, but omit subtrees that contain only empty leaf nodes (by replacing the entire subtree with a special node). Furthermore, the hash contained in the root of the tree is stored within the TPM.

To revoke a key, we compute the short hash of the public key which determines its position within the hash tree; subsequently, we update the path from this leaf to the root and re-create all required hashes. The new root hash of the tree is copied to the TPM. When loading a key, we have to determine whether the key is present within the hash tree. Note that, due to the fact that we know the position where a key is stored in a tree, we only need to examine one path in the tree, namely the path from the root node to the position indicated by the short hash of the key. If the integrity of this path is ensured and the key is not present in the leaf node, the key can be loaded. In this implementation both the use and the revocation of a key requires logarithmic effort.

5   Whitelist Implementation

The blacklist approach described above has the disadvantage that with an increasing number of revoked keys, the effort of loading a revocable key into the TPM increases as well. If a large number of keys needs to be revoked—for example, because a policy requires frequent key updates, or there is reason to believe that the platform has been temporarily compromised—this can quickly render usage of keys very cumbersome. A consolidation protocol can resolve this issue, but is difficult to implement. Therefore, it is worthwhile to consider the opposite approach, and implement revocation through a whitelist of allowed keys.

In this case, the TPM creates a separate *whitelist blob* for every revocable key. The whitelist blob contains a hash of the corresponding key and a counter indicating the current version of the whitelist, i.e., the number of revocation operations performed. The TPM maintains a secure counter *TPM.revCounter* which stores the current version number. A key is only declared valid if the counter value stored inside its associated whitelist blob is equal to the counter value *TPM.revCounter*. Whenever a key is revoked, the counter in all whitelist blobs corresponding to non-revoked keys must be incremented to keep them up-to-date.

As opposed to the key blob itself, the whitelist blobs are not part of the key hierarchy; rather, they are encrypted and authenticated with a dedicated key, called the whitelist root key (*WRK*), which is situated directly under the storage root key. This allows to update the whitelist without running into the same access control problems encountered in the blacklist consolidation case,

---

Algorithm 4. Additional actions performed by `TPM_CreateWrapKey`

Input   : *parentHandle, wrkHandle, keyInfo*
Output: *returnCode, wrappedKey, whitelistblob*

Set *wrappedKey.Keyflags.revocable* according to *keyInfo*
Generate key as denoted in specification
if *keyInfo.Keyflags.revocable* = TRUE **then**
 | *whitelistblob* :=
 | Hash(REVOC_LABEL || *keyInfo.pubKey* || *WRK* || *TPM.revCounter*)
return TPM_SUCCESS, *wrappedKey, whitelistblob*

---

as an update to the whitelist (a key revocation or creation of a whitelist blob for a new key) only requires access rights to the *WRK*. Using a separate *WRK* also allows for external whitelist updates: the *WRK* may be migrated onto a trusted (external) device, which is then capable of computing a new whitelist without any involvement of the TPM; the only operation required to happen inside the TPM is the counter update. This also resolves another problem encountered in the blacklist consolidation protocol: if a key is missed during the update, it is still possible to generate the new whitelist entry after the transformation.

Key creation. Key creation commands remain largely unchanged, except that a whitelist blob needs to be returned in conjunction with the key blob (note that this operation requires the *WRK* to be loaded into the TPM). The necessary modifications to the `TPM_CreateWrapKeyCommand` are shown in Algorithm 4.

Use of key. When a key is loaded, its whitelist blob must be presented to the TPM as well. The TPM hashes the public key together with the *WRK* and the current counter *TPM.revCounter* and compares the hash to the whitelist blob. Only if this hash is correct, the algorithm proceeds as in the specification (Algorithm 5 shows the implementation). Thus, preparing the key for use requires only constant time, independent of the size of the whitelist.

Algorithm 5. Additional actions performed by `TPM_LoadKey`

Input   : *parentHandle, wrkHandle, inKey, whitelistblob*
Output: *returnCode, keyHandle*

inKeyPlain := Decrypt(*inKey, parentHandle*)
if *inKeyPlain.Keyflags.revocable* = TRUE **then**
 | *hashval* := Hash(REVOC_LABEL || *inKey.pubKey* || *WRK* || *TPM.revCounter*)
 | **if** *hashval* ! = *whitelistblob* **then**
 | └ **return** RET_FAIL
Continue as in the specification
return TPM_SUCCESS, *keyHandle*

Algorithm 6. Algorithm of the `TPM_WhitelistTransformKey` command

Input : *wrkHandle, parentHandle, revokedHandle, whitelistblob*
Output: *returnCode, whitelistblob*

hashval :=
  Hash(`REVOC_LABEL` || *revokedHandle.pubKey* || *WRK* || *TPM.revCounter*)
if *hashval* = *whitelistblob* **then**
  | *whitelistblob* :=
  | Hash(`REVOC_LABEL` || *revokedHandle.pubKey* || *WRK* || *TPM.revCounter+1*)
  | **return** `TPM_SUCCESS`, *whitelistblob*
else
  └ **return** `RET_FAIL`

Revocation. To revoke a key, all whitelist blobs of non-revoked keys need to be updated (i.e., their counter values need to be incremented). This can be performed with the command `TPM_WhitelistTransformKey` (Algorithm 6), which, after appropriate authorisation, takes a key blob, increments the counter value stored in it, and returns a new blob. Once all whitelist elements are transferred, `TPM_WhitelistCommit` (Algorithm 7) must be executed, which increments the whitelist counter within the TPM. From this point on, the TPM only accepts whitelist blobs with the new counter value.

As the whitelist blob does not need to be protected by the same access control mechanisms used for the main key blob, updating the corresponding blobs does not require special authorisation. This is necessary to allow revocation of a key by a party that does not have access rights to other keys. However, calling `TPM_WhitelistCommit` is critical for the functioning of the TPM (a wrong call invalidates all keys and may result in denial-of-service attacks). It is thus required to have owner authorisation to perform a call to `TPM_WhitelistCommit`. In addition, we recommend to make *WRK* exportable, so it can be stored on an external device. This allows keys to be transferred even after a call to `TPM_WhitelistCommit`, and even to revoke keys on a temporary basis.

Algorithm 7.. Algorithm of the `TPM_WhitelistCommit` command

Input : *wrkHandle*
Output: *returnCode*

TPM.revCounter++
return `TPM_SUCCESS`

6   Combined Black- and Whitelists

As noted above, the black- and the whitelist approaches both optimise the efficiency of one of two important functions. The blacklist implementation allows key revocation with constant effort, but loading a revocable key into the TPM needs communication that is linear in the number of already revoked keys. It is possible to remove the blacklist through a consolidation protocol; however due to authentication issues this protocol is unjustifiably complex. The whitelist approach allows to very efficiently load keys into the TPM; it only requires to store a very small additional whitelist blob. The price to pay is an expensive revocation (the effort is linear in the number of revocable keys in the system). Furthermore, all key blobs must be available during revocation, unless an external trusted party is allowed to re-authenticate keys. The whitelist and blacklist approaches also differ in flexibility of authorising a key revocation. In the blacklist approach, the process of revoking a key needs the TPM to create a new blacklist entry. However, it is possible to use any desired scheme to authorise that action, and even different schemes for different keys. In the whitelist model, in contrast, an item has to be created for all keys *but* the one to be revoked, which calls for restricting the right to perform key revocation to the TPM owner.

A pragmatic approach to combine the advantages of both schemes is to use both of them in parallel. Essentially, we suggest to use the blacklist approach for normal key revocation as described above, but additionally maintain a whitelist to efficiently consolidate the blacklists. Thus, if a key is revoked, it is first put on the blacklist and the TPM will refuse to load each key on the blacklist. In addition, during the creation of a revocable key, a whitelist blob is created, and the TPM will also refuse to load any key that has no valid whitelist blob. If at any time the blacklist becomes too long (and thus, loading a key becomes inefficient), the TPM owner can consolidate the blacklist by creating a new whitelist for all keys that are not on the blacklist.

This approach requires a slightly different `TPM_WhitelistTransformKey` command, as an additional test—whether the key is present on the blacklist—must be performed. If the key is on the blacklist, no new whitelist blob is created, and the transform command instead returns an error. The second modification is that the `TPM_WhitelistCommit` command also resets the TPM internal hash value for the blacklist to 0^k. By using this approach, we gain the best of both worlds: revoking a key can be done with constant effort, while the blacklists can stay short enough to allow for efficient key usage. Furthermore, the expensive whitelist update operation only needs to be performed infrequently. Also, the scheme enables to use flexible authorisation methods to determine who is allowed to revoke a key. The only commands that necessarily need owner rights do not revoke keys themselves, but only rearrange already revoked keys to increase performance.

7   Conclusions

We have investigated two complementary approaches to implement TPM-based key revocation. While both seem to be reasonably practical on their own, the combination can achieve key revocation with a very low overhead and with minimal changes to the TPM specification. We have shown that both concepts can be realized without breaking backwards compatibility. In addition, our proposed scheme is very flexible in terms of authorising the revocation: depending on the use-case, keys can be revoked by the key owner, the TPM owner, or even by external parties.

References

1. Brickell, E.F., Camenisch, J., Chen, L.: Direct anonymous attestation. In: ACM Conference on Computer and Communications Security, pp. 132–145 (2004)
2. Kühn, U., Kursawe, K., Lucks, S., Sadeghi, A.-R., Stüble, C.: Secure data management in trusted computing. In: Rao, J.R., Sunar, B. (eds.) CHES 2005. LNCS, vol. 3659, pp. 324–338. Springer, Heidelberg (2005)
3. Maheshwari, U., Vingralek, R., Shapiro, W.: How to build a trusted database system on untrusted storage. In: OSDI 2000 Proceedings of the 4th conference on Symposium on Operating System Design & Implementation, Berkeley, CA, USA, p. 10. USENIX Association (2000)
4. Naor, M., Nissim, K.: Certificate revocation and certificate update. In: Proceedings of the 7th USENIX Security Symposium, pp. 217–228 (1998)
5. Sarmenta, L.F.G., van Dijk, M., O'Donnell, C.W., Rhodes, J., Devadas, S.: Virtual monotonic counters and count-limited objects using a tpm without a trusted os. In: STC 2006: Proceedings of the first ACM workshop on Scalable trusted computing, pp. 27–42. ACM, New York (2006)
6. Trusted Computing Group. TCG TPM Specification Version 1.2 Revision 103, TPM Main Part 2 TPM Structures. Technical report, TCG (July 2007)
7. Trusted Computing Group. TCG TPM Specification Version 1.2 Revision 103, TPM Main Part 1 Design Principles. Technical report, TCG (July 2007)
8. Trusted Computing Group. TCG TPM Specification Version 1.2 Revision 103, TPM Main Part 3 Command. Technical report, TCG (July 2007)
9. Trusted Computing Group. Trusted Platform Module (TPM) specifications. Technical report (2008), https://www.trustedcomputinggroup.org/specs/TPM
10. Xiao, Y., Rayi, V.K., Sun, B., Du, X., Hu, F., Galloway, M.: A survey of key management schemes in wireless sensor networks. Comput. Commun. 30(11-12), 2314–2341 (2007)

Securing the Dissemination of Emergency Response Data with an Integrated Hardware-Software Architecture

Timothy E. Levin[1], Jeffrey S. Dwoskin[2], Ganesha Bhaskara[3],
Thuy D. Nguyen[1], Paul C. Clark[1], Ruby B. Lee[2],
Cynthia E. Irvine[1], and Terry V. Benzel[3]

[1] Naval Postgraduate School, Monterey, CA 93943, USA
{levin,tdnguyen,pcclark,irvine}@nps.edu
[2] Princeton University, Princeton, NJ 08544, USA
{jdwoskin,rblee}@princeton.edu
[3] USC Information Sciences Institute, Marina Del Rey, CA 90292
{bhaskara,tbenzel}@isi.edu

Abstract. During many crises, access to sensitive emergency-support information is required to save lives and property. For example, for effective evacuations first responders need the names and addresses of non-ambulatory residents. Yet, currently, access to such information may not be possible because government policy makers and third-party data providers lack confidence that today's IT systems will protect their data. Our approach to the management of emergency information provides first responders with temporary, transient access to sensitive information, and ensures that the information is revoked after the emergency. The following contributions are presented: a systematic analysis of the basic forms of trusted communication supported by the architecture; a comprehensive method for secure, distributed emergency state management; a method to allow a userspace application to securely display data; a multifaceted system analysis of the confinement of emergency information and the secure and complete revocation of access to that information at the closure of an emergency.

Keywords: Information Assurance, Computer Security, Policy Enforcement, Secret Protection (SP), Transient Trust, Emergency Response.

1 Introduction

In a crisis, first-responders can often save lives and limit damage if they have access to certain sensitive or restricted information. Examples of such emergency information are: building floor plans, schematics for infrastructure or transit systems in a city, or medical records of victims. However, government policy makers and third-party data providers lack confidence in the ability of emergency IT systems to protect their data relative to confidentiality, sensitivity, privacy, liability, and other concerns, and are unwilling to release such data, even on a temporary basis, to civilian first responders[1].

L. Chen, C.J. Mitchell, and A. Martin (Eds.): Trust 2009, LNCS 5471, pp. 133–152, 2009.
© Springer-Verlag Berlin Heidelberg 2009

In this paper, we address the essential confidentiality, integrity, access control, revocation and data containment capabilities needed in future emergency response systems. We show how a platform based on commercial off-the-shelf technology can be used for the secure management of emergency information and we detail how it can (1) communicate securely with a trusted authority, first responders, and information providers; (2) manage distributed emergency state with high integrity and assurance; and (3) enable emergency access to sensitive information while strictly maintaining its confinement as well as revoking access with high assurance.

In the sections that follow, we show how a handheld Emergency Device, the *E-Device*, utilizing the latest generation separation kernel technology [2,3] and state-of-the-art hardware security concepts [4], can be a trusted foundation for secure crisis response.

2   Secure Platform Architecture

The secure platform architecture of the E-Device (see Fig. 1) is based on a commercial general-purpose processor (nominally an x86) enhanced with the Authority-Mode Secret Protection (SP) architecture features [4], a Trusted Management Layer (TML) — comprising a least privileged separation kernel [2], and a security services layer that virtualizes certain separation kernel resources — and trusted software programs that run in one of the TML-provided partitions. These hardware/software components, with the addition of a Trusted Software Module (TSM) application supported by SP, form the Trusted Computing Base (TCB) for our E-Device.

2.1   Secure Software Stack

The trusted software for the E-Device utilizes Intel x86 privilege levels to protect the resources in each level from the subjects in less-privileged domains. The two most privileged layers are collectively referred to as the TML, while the next most privileged layers house a trusted executive and the Trusted Path Application (TPA).

The TML provides software-based security enforcement, and is supported by security features of the underlying Intel x86 and SP hardware. While support for many different client OSes is not the focus of this research, the TML is designed to provide to the commodity OS a standard execution environment with respect to platform hardware features.

The TML manages all system hardware resources (e.g., memory, devices, processors, etc.). It reserves some resources for its own use, and exports other resources in the form of processes, memory segments, I/O devices, raw disk volumes, segment volumes, etc. The TML separates all exported resources into distinct *partitions*, governs the flow of information between partitions and between individual exported resources, and protects raw disk volumes by encryption.

The TML creates three types of partitions: *Emergency, Trusted* and *Normal*. A normal partition and an emergency partition each run a commodity

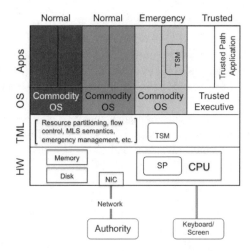

Fig. 1. Security architecture instantiated for an emergency scenario

(untrusted) OS. The Trusted Partition runs an extremely compact trusted executive. Information flow rules and partition definitions provided to the TML define a partial ordering of flows between partitions, indicative of a multilevel security (MLS) policy, and corresponding security labels may be associated with partitions.

The TML manages interactive user sessions through what is referred to as *partition focus*, whereby the user can interact with one partition at a time, via the system keyboard and screen.

For applications in the trusted partition, the trusted executive provides simple OS-like support. The trusted executive manages passwords and provides user authentication services. The TPA is invoked by pressing what is known as the *secure attention key* (SAK), such as Ctrl-Alt-Delete. When the TML detects the SAK, it changes partition focus to the Trusted Partition, which starts the TPA. The TPA provides a variety of other security services to the user, including: setting the security sensitivity label for a session, changing a password, and shutting down the E-Device.

2.2 Trusted Software Protected by SP Hardware

A novel aspect of our architecture is provided by SP's Trusted Software Module (TSM). TSMs have two critical characteristics: they are protected from observation and modification by non-TSM software (including the OS), and they have exclusive access to SP crypto-transforms and to two processor-resident data registers.

A TSM is defined to be code that is executable in a special processor mode called Concealed Execution Mode (CEM) that is entered via the *Begin_CEM* instruction. Once in CEM, special SP instructions can be executed — *SP_derive*, *Secure_Load*, *Secure_Store*, and *End_CEM* — and special SP registers can be used — Device Root Key (DRK) and Storage Root Hash (SRH). Other CEM-only instructions are provided to read and write the SRH register. Also, when in CEM, the processor checks the integrity of each instruction cache line of the TSM with respect to compiled-in signatures based on the DRK.

The *Secure_Load* and *Secure_Store* instructions cause memory locations to be tagged as TSM-only while they reside in on-chip caches, and to be automatically encrypted and hashed when they move to off-chip memory to prevent unauthorized observation or modification. CEM execution is suspended during an interrupt and is automatically resumed upon return, with data in processor registers protected from the OS by the hardware.

The protection of TSM code can be viewed as being independent from the protection of the underlying OS, as follows. The trustworthiness of a program is generally understood to be limited by the trustworthiness of the programs that it depends on. The TSM, which runs in the Emergency Partition "on top of" an untrusted OS, does not make calls to the OS (i.e., and can not, since the OS is not a TSM) and so a TSM is not "functionally" dependent on the OS, and can actually be more trustworthy than the OS itself.

SP stores two master secrets in non-volatile registers on-chip, which provide the roots of trust for the E-Device's operations. The DRK, which never leaves the processor, protects the integrity of TSM code and is also used by *SP_derive* to cryptographically derive new keys for the TSM. The SRH can only be read or written by the TSM, and provides it with a small amount of on-chip storage, which can be used to store the output of crypto-hashing operations for protecting larger persistent data structures such as key chains (a hierarchy of keys) and the policies regarding use of those keys. This allows the TSM to moderate all access to the protected data and enforce the corresponding policies on each access.

The Authority can communicate with the E-Device during operation, providing updates to keys and policies in its persistent secure storage and to send new encrypted data to the E-Device. When establishing a secure communication channel, the parties use derived keys. Therefore, the E-Device's ability to generate those keys and communicate demonstrates that it still has the correct DRK value and signed TSM code, and serves as an implicit authentication, since only the E-Device and the Authority know the DRK.

3   Information Sharing during an Emergency

Our concept for emergency response involves a network of participants (the *Emergency Network*), including a coordinating *Authority*, the expected *first responders*, and *third party data providers* who maintain information that is expected to be useful during an emergency. The Authority manages the distribution of keys and policies via its own secure computing facility, and coordinates emergency response for a given crisis, including alerting all entities on the Emergency Network of the emergency and disseminating emergency data to first responders.

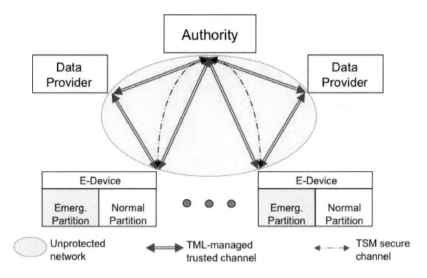

Fig. 2. Emergency Network Architecture

While E-Devices may be owned by various emergency network participants, their correct configuration is the responsibility of the authority, and they will be operated in the field by first responders. Fig. 2 shows the emergency network.

The operation of the Emergency Network is governed by prearranged organizational security policies [5]. These include the lattice-based MLS policy enforced by the TML and the access policy enforced by the TSM in the application domain.

3.1   Emergency Operation

The Authority maintains a binary global emergency state, i.e., ON or OFF, and notifies the authorized E-Devices of any state changes. The E-Devices may grant access to emergency information if the state is ON, and must deny access when OFF. Secure synchronization of the global state is discussed below.

When an emergency is declared, the Authority sends state-change notifications to the E-Devices. Once the TML interprets the message, it prompts the user to access the Emergency Partition, via the TPA.

While the emergency is in effect, the user can access any active partition the user is cleared to see, including the preconfigured Emergency Partition. Within the Emergency Partition, finer granularity application-specific access controls on emergency data may be provided by an application domain Emergency Management TSM.

When the emergency is over, the Authority announces a change to the global emergency state, prompting the TML to start the emergency closure process. It displays an end-of-emergency message which prompts the user to change focus to the Trusted partition (to be completed within a configurable period), revokes access to the Emergency Partition, and restores the Emergency Partition to its original state.

4   New Security Mechanisms

This section presents a systematic analysis of the available secure communication channels and describes mechanisms for completing the trust chain from the remote Authority to the E-device, and to its Emergency Partition and display, including: emergency state management, trustworthy display and mechanisms for revocation of sensitive data.

4.1   Secure Communication Channels

A secure communications protocol protects against message content disclosure and modification, as well as traffic analysis and insertion or deletion of packets.

We consider a channel to be a *secure channel* if it uses a secure protocol, the protocol is implemented correctly, and the channel endpoints are secure against both the modification of their behavior and against unauthorized disclosure of channel and keying information.

The E-Device, while simple, supports several different forms of secure communications channels, which provide emergency systems designers with flexibility in constructing new systems. Three basic channels are shown in Fig. 3: the *Trusted Channel* (A), the *TSM-TSM Channel* (D), and the *Trusted Path* (B).

A Trusted Channel (A) is a secure channel between two TCBs (e.g., a TML or a trusted system) [6]. A TSM-TSM Channel (D) provides cryptographic assurance against message disclosure and modification between application TSMs, e.g., on different machines. A Trusted Path (B) is a secure channel between a user and the TML on the E-Device, implemented by the TPA.

A *Remote Trusted Path* (E) is a secure channel between a remote user (e.g., the Authority) and a TML, which is constructed by combining a Trusted Path with the remote end of a Trusted Channel. An *Extended Trusted Channel* (F)

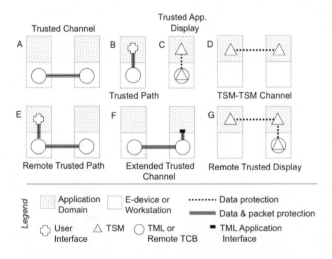

Fig. 3. Types of Channels

is a secure channel created by extending the I/O interface of a Trusted Channel to the TML interface of a given partition, which allows applications to securely interact with a remote TCB.

A *Trusted Application Display* (C), discussed below, enables an application (i.e., the Emergency Partition TSM) executing in the context of an insecure OS to securely write to the screen, which is managed by the TML. A *Remote Trusted Display* (G) connects a TSM-TSM Channel with a Trusted Application Display so a remote system, such as that used by the Authority, can display data to the local user with assurance against message disclosure and modification.

The TML exports to partitions *virtual NICs* (see Fig. 4), which are logical devices, each with an IP address, for use by the OS and applications in a specific partition.

The TML manages the negotiation of session keys and cryptographic algorithms, as well as the cryptographic transformation of data for encrypted channels via the IPsec "security association" paradigm [7], although the entire IPsec suite is not required (e.g., crypto-transforms are statically assigned). An Extended Trusted Channel therefore embodies the mapping of a partition ID to a remote IP address and a security association. Communication channels, display channels and logical devices are configured during E-Device initialization with information such as: each channel's remote TCB address, and security level; various keying material; and the mapping of Extended Trusted Channels to specific partitions. Security levels are also assigned to partitions and physical devices.

An out-of-band distributed "root" secret key that is shared with the TCB at the other end of a trusted channel is the basis for channel session keys [8]. For trusted channels between the E-Device and the Authority, the DRK is used as the root secret. For other trusted channels, such as those with third party data

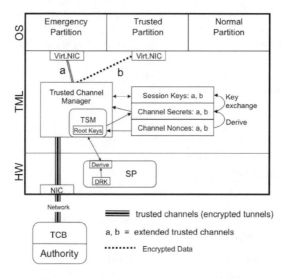

Fig. 4. Networking Support of the TML

providers, a shared secret key is stored by a TSM in the TML's Trusted Channel Manager instead.

Nonces to support generation of session keys are dynamically exchanged or periodically distributed. The TSM hashes the nonce with the root secret to derive a temporary shared secret, with which it can generate a session key using a standard key exchange protocol, such as TLS. Alternatively, the derived value itself could be used as a session key. All communications between endpoints within the emergency network use these channels.

4.2   Emergency State Management

As discussed above, the Authority manages the global emergency state with *emergency state management messages*. State management consists of the following steps: (1) message generation; (2) message transmission; and (3) message processing on the E-Device. Each of these steps needs to be trustworthy to ensure consistent and correct emergency state management.

In addition to the emergency state, the Authority maintains a counter of the number of state changes it has issued; also, it maintains a record of the acknowledged state and counter values for each E-Device, along with its DRK. When the Authority changes the global state, it must securely synchronize with each E-Device. On the individual E-Device, local emergency state and a state transition counter are maintained by a state-management (E-State) TSM in the TML.

When the Authority declares an emergency, it increments its counter associated with the E-Device and generates an emergency state management message for each E-Device that consists of: (a) a command type indicator (indicating a state update message); (b) a payload of the new state and counter, encrypted with an encryption key derived from the DRK; (c) a signature (cryptographic keyed hash) of the encrypted payload and command, using a signing key derived from the DRK; and (d) two nonces to derive the encryption and signing keys.

The emergency state management message is sent to the E-Device through a *Remote Trusted Path* channel. Only the E-Device to which the emergency state management message was intended is able to successfully process the message. The E-State TSM independently [1] verifies the originator of the state management message. For emergency state management, two functions, *Update_State* and *Get_State* are implemented on the E-Device. The Update_State function checks the integrity of the message using the signature, and the counter. It also generates a response to the Authority by generating a signature over the message using a signing key derived from the signing nonce and the DRK. The E-State TSM sends the signature back to the Authority over the trusted channel, but does not need to send the message payload or nonce, since the Authority already has the initial update message.

The TML, via its TSM, uses *Get_State* to retrieve the new state, as discussed in Section 3.1. To ensure that the update of emergency state is trustworthy, only

---

[1] Decoupling the channel authentication from message authentication allows for flexibility to incorporate ad-hoc and/or peer-to-peer transmission of emergency state management messages in the future.

the TML can pass update messages from the trusted channel with the Authority into the E-State TSM; and only the E-State TSM can invoke *Update_State* and *Get_State*.

For high-threat deployment environments, enhanced assurance is provided by a version of SP that includes state management primitives in its ISA. Instead of implementing them in the E-State TSM software, this version, includes registers for a state variable and a state transition counter, as well as instructions for the *Update_State* and *Get_State* functions. With these hardware enhancements, even the TSM does not have the ability to directly modify the emergency state on the device.

4.3   Containment of Emergency Data

The organizational security policy enforced by the E-Device requires that emergency information from the data providers only be accessible to authorized users acting within the emergency partition, and only during a proper emergency declared by the Authority. MAC policy enforcement (by the TML) and DAC policy enforcement (by the Emergency Management TSM) jointly restrict information flows on the E-Device before, during and after the emergency.

Emergency data is installed at the Authority's secure facility or sent to the E-Device from the Authority and data providers over Trusted Channels, and is confined in the Emergency Partition. The data may be further encrypted so that it can only be accessed by the Emergency Management TSM application, which can enforce more granular access policies within the Emergency partition.

The Authority establishes an *Extended Trusted Channel* to the Emergency Partition. The Emergency Partition and the Authority are allocated an "emergency" MLS label that is distinct from that associated with other partitions. The TML attaches the "emergency" label to data it receives over the channel, restricting the data to only this partition of the E-Device. Data flows for emergency management are shown in Fig. 5, as follows: (1) the Authority propagates changes to the global emergency state and receives confirmation from the device; (2) the Authority sends keys, policies, and revocations to the Emergency Management TSM, via an Extended Trusted Channel managed by the Trusted Channel Manager (TCM); (3) the authority sends encrypted emergency data to the Emergency Partition, via an Extended Trusted Channel; (4) data providers provide additional data for the authority to send to the E-Device; (5) when needed, the Emergency Management TSM decrypts the emergency data with keys and policies in its storage.

Trusted channels between the TML and the Authority are protected using freshly negotiated channel secrets for each connection, based on the DRK rather than a stored root key. As a result, only parties with access to the DRK (the Authority and the E-Device) can authorize an Extended Trusted Channel to the Emergency Partition.

Aside from these secure channels, the information cannot flow out of the Emergency Partition, e.g., to any other partition, device or network, ensuring that emergency data cannot be revealed outside of the equivalence class of

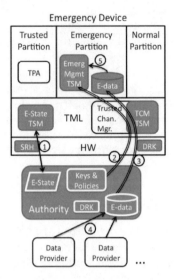

Fig. 5. Data Flow for Emergency Management

components labeled as "Emergency." Additionally, the Emergency Partition itself is only made available to the user by the TML and TPA when an emergency has been declared, as previously described. This temporal restriction limits the threat of malicious insiders, and in combination with the partition's spatial separation, provides defense in depth for the confinement of emergency information.

The Authority provides its own emergency data to the E-Device, and can convey data provided by third party data providers. When the latter data is proxied through the Authority and the third party has no direct communication with the E-Device, the third party does not need and is not given the privileges associated with the "Emergency" label.

If a third party is considered trusted, it can be included in the "Emergency" equivalence class and allowed to establish an Extended Trusted Channel directly to the Emergency Partition. Since the Third Party does not have access to the E-Device's DRK, it and the Emergency Management TSM share an "emergency" key, which is stored locally in the TSM's persistent secure storage. Even when third party data is provided directly, the TSM on the E-Device can still be configured to only accept policies for that data directly from the Authority.

All emergency data sent over the Extended Trusted Channel is encrypted by the Authority or data provider prior to transmission using keys only available (on the E-Device) to the TSM. This enables the TSM to enforce its discretionary access control policy on use of the data by the responder or any software within the Emergency Partition, and audit the use of the data, even though it executes alongside untrusted software in the Emergency Partition.

Within the Emergency Partition, the TSM can release data to untrusted, feature-rich commercial applications for display. However, there is no assurance that untrusted applications will accurately display data when asked. Some information, e.g., that which is critical and easy to manipulate, may require greater protection. For this, we provide the high-integrity *Trusted Application Display* mechanism, which allows an application-TSM to send text-only emergency data directly to a reserved region of the display via a secure call to the TML that bypasses the untrusted software in the Emergency Partition.

The trusted display mechanism provides an unspoofable means for an application domain program to display messages with high integrity such that they cannot be observed or modified by any untrusted software in the system. This mechanism is available to the TSM in the Emergency Partition and the TPA running in the Trusted Partition. Both the TSM and TPA are designed to be evaluated to ensure their correct behavior, which helps to ensure that the correct data is input to the trusted display mechanism.

The TML virtualizes the video graphics card such that it appears to each partition that it has control of the screen. These virtual devices pass input to the TML's secure display driver, which divides the physical display into two regions. One region is restricted for the TML-controlled high-integrity display (for example, the bottom two lines of text on the screen). The remaining region of the screen is exported to the partition with focus as normal.

High integrity data to be displayed is encrypted and either comes directly from the Authority for *Remote Trusted Display* or is chosen to be released by the TSM during its operation for Trusted Application Display. To pass the data securely to the TML, the TSM is divided into two pieces: an application-TSM in the partition and a kernel-TSM in the TML. The former is responsible for preparing the data for display and the latter for passing the plaintext data to the TML securely. SP's CEM protects the data as it is passed between privilege levels through the untrusted software in the Emergency Partition.

The application-TSM first decrypts the data using keys in its storage, and then stores the resulting display text in a memory buffer (at a known location) using *Secure_Store* instructions. This data is now only accessible in plaintext to TSM code. An x86 call-gate is used to transition from the application-TSM to the kernel-TSM without an interrupt. The kernel-TSM uses *Secure_Load* instructions to read from the CEM-protected memory buffer and regular *Store* instructions to write the cleartext data to the TML buffer. It then exits CEM mode and invokes the TML-provided Trusted Screen Handler, which sends the data to the TML's Trusted Screen Driver for display in the restricted display region. Finally, the kernel-TSM code re-enters CEM and returns to the call gate in the application-TSM, with a return value indicating the success or failure of the display operation.

To complete the data lifecycle, access to emergency data must be rescinded once the emergency is over. Data revocation takes place through complementary mechanisms, using both mandatory and discretionary access control.

The coarsest granularity of revocation available to the Authority is to declare the emergency to have ended. As described in Section 4.2, this results in the closing of the Emergency Partition to users and applications, and restores its code and data to the pre-emergency state. Stopping application activity and overwriting the entire partition effectively removes all data generated or released inside the partition.

A finer-granularity of revocation is provided by the Emergency Management TSM itself, as described in [4]. Over and above the TSM-enforced policies restricting access to data based on expiration dates, usage counts, search query restrictions, etc., at its discretion, the Authority can communicate with the TSM and direct it to modify policies, keys, and other emergency restrictions to revoke access to existing data, for example, in preparation for ending the emergency.

Guarantees to the Authority and third parties about revocation and the state of the E-Device depend on connectivity and availability of the TSM. If the E-Device is disconnected temporarily from the network, or an application TSM managing communication with the Authority is subject to a functional denial of service attack, the Authority will be unable to synchronize the local emergency state with its own global state. An emergency expiration timer is provided by the TML, such that if connectivity with the Authority cannot be established within a defined time, the TML can end the emergency on the E-Device. The use of this timer may not be appropriate for all responders and is therefore configurable.

Once communication is restored, the E-Device can attest to the Authority that the requested updates to emergency state, policy, and keys have been made.

5   System Security Analysis

Overall system security can be understood in terms of the threats to which it will be exposed and how the system is capable of counteracting those threats.

5.1   Threat Model and Assumptions

We assume that the E-Device is initialized securely with TML-, TSM- and SP-specific keys. We also assume that the third parties and the Authority securely exchange the required keying material and protect their own keys from exposure.

We assume the standard Dolev-Yao model [9], that arbitrary parties can capture, modify or insert network traffic. Intentional or malicious network-level denial of service — as opposed to prevention of process functionality at the workstation — is outside the threat model. The threat model and analysis for SP, which includes spoofing, splicing and replay of TSM code, intermediate data in registers and memory, and secure persistent storage, are discussed in [4], including the protection of emergency data encrypted with TSM keys. The threat model for the TML is that applications of the TML, including guest OSs other than the trusted executive, are not trusted to conform to its policies, and may in fact be hostile. For example, at runtime, the software executing above the TML may attempt to access keys used by the TML to establish secure channels — and application software or the commodity operating systems may attempt to write emergency data to a location outside the partition or attempt to access high integrity information through low integrity mechanisms. The trusted executive is only trusted to manage its applications in a manner that does not introduce covert channels between applications that are at different security levels. The persistent disk storage is encrypted and signed, and so is protected against, e.g., theft of the E-Device.

TCB software at the Authority, third parties and in the E-Device is assumed to behave correctly and securely. But, application TSMs are subject to inconsistencies in their execution environment, such as denial of access to the processor, as they execute independently from the trusted software that controls physical resources.

5.2 Security Capabilities

The architecture presented in this paper combines the secure execution and key confidentiality provided by SP hardware with information containment assurance provided by the TML. Further, secure boot ensures that the correct TML configuration is loaded on boot and SP's *code integrity checking* (CIC) ensures syntactic runtime integrity of TML code. This ensures that large classes of software attacks that involve code modification are prevented.

The DRK acts as the shared secret between the E-Device and the Authority. On the E-Device, the confidentiality provided by the SP hardware ensures that software never has access to the DRK directly, ensuring this shared secret is always protected with high assurance.

Software is only allowed to use the DRK to derive other keys, which is sufficient for mutual authentication and secure channel establishment. The SP hardware along with the TSM ensures that all computation involving keys derived from the DRK, including intermediate data, never leaves the processor chip in unencrypted form. This avoids the possibility of any software outside the TSM getting access to derived keys. Since this is an invariant of the TSM and SP hardware, keys used for secure channels are always protected. The TML code is protected by the CIC mode of the SP processor, ensuring that the access control polices enforced by the TML cannot be changed by code modification attacks. The privilege levels provided by hardware ensure that subjects with lesser privilege than the TML cannot read or write to objects in the TML. This ensures that the TML always sets up the secure channels between the different endpoints on the E-Device and the Authority/third parties as configured.

A Trusted Path provides bidirectional security: (1) ensuring that user input to the TCB is accurately and securely received by the TCB, via a keyboard-to-TCB data pipeline (where the keyboard is a proxy for the user); and (2) ensuring that output from the TCB is seen by the user, without ambiguity or compromise, via the TCB-to-screen data pipeline (where the screen is a proxy for the user).

The Trusted Path is a secure channel, since it is secure and it provides a direct connection to the TCB endpoint via a secure interface provided by the TML, with no intervening untrusted components. The Trusted Channel is a secure channel, since it is assumed to use secure protocols and the endpoints are secure.

The E-Device has three TSMs: one is an Emergency Partition application, and the other two are TML modules. Since these TSMs provide system security services, they are considered to be part of the TCB and are built to the same level of assurance as the TML. When they communicate, the TSMs on both ends of the TSM-TSM Channel have access to DRK-derived keys as well as CEM-protected memory, so the receiver can validate the integrity of messages and ensure confidentiality. The TSMs on the E-Device similarly share the same DRK-derived keys with the Authority, and two TSMs on different devices can be provided a shared secret by the Authority. We further assume that a TSM-TSM Channel to the Authority or another E-Device utilizes a Trusted Channel, adding another layer of protection over the network.

Any data used, transmitted, or displayed by an application-TSM is still subject to a functional denial of service by the untrusted OS, which may prevent its execution or tamper with its encrypted data — but the tampering will be detected.

In the Extended Trusted Channel, the TML makes Trusted Channels available to partitions as logical I/O devices, which provides a secure channel between the I/O device interface and the trusted component at the other end of the Trusted Channel. The Extended Trusted Channel can provide plain-text or encrypted data to a given partition (where the cryptographic functions are provided by applications in the partition).

In Normal and Emergency Partitions, a commercial OS manages the logical I/O device, and makes it available to *its* applications via an abstraction such as a socket. The security of the Extended Trusted Channel from the perspective of the OS application then depends on the security of the OS and any encryption of the data.

The Trusted Application Display is a uni-directional secure channel between the local application TSM and the user, assuming continuity in execution of the TSM and protection of TSM message data. Continuity of execution depends on the TSM's processing environment, including the ability of the application domain OS to schedule the TSM and other applications consistently and avoidance of attacks on application-TSM code, data buffers, or communications to the TML. While these would constitute a functional denial of service attack on the TSM, they could not compromise the confidentiality or integrity of the display data. Of course, the confidentiality of displayed data is not protected from out of band analog mechanisms, e.g., visual observation of the screen.

Combining a TSM-TSM Channel with the Trusted Application Display channel results in a Remote Trusted Display channel that is a single-direction channel whose security depends on the security of the component channels (i.e., the TSM-TSM Channel and Trusted Application Display channel discussed above).

Emergency state management message generation is a security critical operation. Only the Authority is able to generate valid messages for a given E-Device as they are based on the device-specific DRK, known only to the authority and the E-Device. Since SP hardware ensures software never has access to the DRK and the authority secures its copy of DRK, arbitrary parties cannot generate a valid message. Since the emergency state change generates a response that is also cryptographically signed by a DRK-derived key, the authority can be assured that the emergency state management was correctly processed by the intended E-Device.

There are several layers of protection that detect and prevent replay attacks on emergency state management messages: (a) all messages are transmitted over secure primary channels such that only the subjects with access to the endpoints of the secure channels can see even the encrypted message; (b) the TSM in the TML could also overlay a secure mutual-authentication protocol between the TSM and the Authority to prevent other parts of the TML from accessing the encrypted emergency state management message; (c) since the message is encrypted using keys derived from the DRK, only the TSM on the correct E-Device can decrypt and process the message; (d) the monotonically increasing counter ensures that a given message is never processed twice.

Once the emergency is declared, and the E-Device successfully changes its emergency state, the Emergency Partition is enabled and the user is able to access it. The TML ensures that the Emergency Partition can write only to channels leading to the Authority and to trusted data providers. Further, no other partition on the E-Device can read content in the emergency partition labeled as "Emergency." The TML ensures only known virtual device abstractions of trusted pre-configured physical devices are presented to the OS in the Emergency Partition, thus avoiding the possibility of the user being able to attach a device with unconstrained information flow properties to the partition.

When the emergency data is decrypted and displayed within the Emergency Partition, the untrusted applications or OS may keep parts of the clear text emergency data in memory and/or write it to disk, but the TML's Emergency-partition separation policy ensures that the data remains in the Emergency Partition. While all data in memory is erased or otherwise invalidated on a shutdown of the E-Device, the data on the disk may still be accessible if the Emergency Partition is still present. Any offline attacks on emergency data on disk are prevented as the TML protects all data on disk by encryption with keys derived from the DRK. These encryption keys are derived as needed and are never revealed or stored. These properties ensure emergency data containment during the emergency. When the declaration of emergency is rescinded, the Emergency Partition becomes inaccessible to the user and its contents are encrypted and stored for audit purposes or immediately deleted.

Applications in the Emergency Partition are not expected to display high integrity content, as both the applications and the OS are not trusted. Instead, high integrity information is displayed on the reserved portion of the screen, via the Trusted Application Display, with data that is appropriately encrypted and hashed. Since the TML manages the physical display, no partitions are given direct access to the portion of the screen reserved for high integrity display.

6   Validation

We have implemented an E-Device prototype that provides a worked example of how the coherent integration of complementary hardware and software security mechanisms can enhance security, and validates elements of our overall approach.

6.1 Prototype Implementation

The prototype demonstrates the feasibility of TSM technology as well as key layering and partitioning mechanisms in the TML.

The prototype TML runs on bare hardware on the x86 platform and provides multiple partitions which the user can switch between using the Secure Attention Key. The partitions each run a primitive trusted executive, providing I/O to the user-space application running above it. Authority-mode SP features, which have been independently prototyped [4], are provided here by a trusted kernel module which emulates its behavior and security properties.

Our prototype implementation of the integrated architecture demonstrates the feasibility of: (a) emergency management operations using remote trusted path; (b) the ability for the Authority and data providers to disseminate keys and data to the emergency partition; (c) the use of the trusted display mechanism provided by the TML to applications to securely display high integrity data; (d) protection of the code integrity of TSMs and its secure storage by the SP hardware; (e) prevention of access to TSM secure storage by the untrusted OS or untrusted applications; and (f) detection of simulated attacks on the remote trusted path, key/data usage policies, and confidentiality and integrity of emergency data using standard cryptographic algorithms. For the prototype, it is assumed that the TML-managed trusted channels for secure communication with the Authority and data providers are in place and the key management messages between the E-Device and the Authority/data providers are pre-computed.

7 Related Work

Previous work in processor-based cryptographic support include: SP [4], separation kernels [2], and "least privilege" security architectures [3]. We note that cryptographic coprocessor mechanisms [10,11] do not provide processor-level protection for system software and data, and may be more vulnerable to attack by elements within the platform. Also, while IBM announced an architecture [12] featuring processor-based encryption for protecting data on chip and in transit to remote systems, little information is available regarding system trustworthiness, or the separation of information based on events or mandatory policies.

The Turaya [13,14] and MILS [15,16] architectures are designed to host commercial operating systems and security services as parallel application-domain entities, with certain interactions between those entities controlled by a microkernel (e.g., L4) and a separation kernel, respectively. The security architecture presented here differs from these efforts in that it does not rely on application domain programs for enforcement of the primary underlying security policy, and it provides an interface for the enforcement of intra-OS least privilege policies as well as inter-OS sharing policies. Additionally, the Turaya and MILS efforts do not address the temporal confinement, revocation, and distributed state-change issues inherent to emergency management of information, and they do not provide processor cryptographic transformations or processor protection of critical keying material.

Trusted Channels provide point-to-point encrypted tunnels between a TML and a remote TCB that has at least as much assurance of security enforcement as the TML. Trusted Channels are similar to Virtual Private Networks [17] although VPNs are usually expected to support arbitrary and changing sets of network nodes rather than point-to-point connections.

The "trusted path" has been understood as a requirement for secure computer systems since the early 1970s [18], and has been implemented in many high assurance [19,20] and commercial systems [21,22]. In our work, the Trusted Path Application implements a traditional user interface for trusted interaction between the user and the TCB (TML). The Remote Trusted Path extends the user's ability to communicate, from the local TCB to a remote TCB. Our work differs from previous remote trusted path results (e.g., [23,6]) in that the security of the communication is rooted in a processor-resident secret key, for communication with the Authority.

The Xen "hypervisor" provides support for security policies by way of "domains" that are similar to TML partitions. Security labels can be associated with a domain, and a security policy can be defined to describe resource isolation or controlled inter-domain information flow [24]. However, Xen was built specifically to provide hardware-assisted virtualization of operating systems [25] rather than a more generic operating environment with other services, such as those provided by the TML.

With the Extended Trusted Channel we replace the Trusted Path's *human* interface to the TCB with a direct *programmatic* interface, which allows applications to interact with a remote TCB (via a Trusted Channel). Similarly, for the Trusted Application Display, the TML exports a programmatic interface for submitting data to the TCB for display. A TML-resident TSM subsequently decrypts the data and then the TML displays it on the screen in a reserved area. Securing the computer display against subversion has been reflected in early work on multilevel windowing [26], and subsequent hardware and software-supported development [27,28]. Our work differs from these developments in providing a means for an application executing in the context of an insecure operating system to securely write to the screen.

In its Global Information Grid (GIG), the US Government has recognized that, in emergencies, the need to access information may be more important than the need to protect the information, and has developed extensive technical and policy roadmaps to support that vision [29,30]. Our framework for management of emergency information advances these concepts by providing a theory and concrete realization to confine information made available under extraordinary circumstances and to rescind access after the completion of those circumstances.

OASIS provides the EDXL standard [31] for information exchange during emergencies, such as payload and message encryption. Our architecture provides a trusted context for the management of EDXL data.

8   Conclusions

To address the inability of existing IT systems to support integrated information sharing, temporary emergency data access, and secure revocation of that access, we have developed an architectural solution that integrates hardware-anchored cryptographic protection with a high assurance software architecture that provides data separation and security services. We have proposed a secure hardware-software platform for an E-Device that can provide trustworthy dissemination and revocation of access to sensitive data during an emergency.

We described the architectural support for trusted communication channels, including a *remote trusted path* between the authority and the E-Device, as well as *trusted display channels* in the E-device. We integrated the SP protocols for DRK-based key-generation into the trusted channel mechanism to protect the storage of channel keys and ensure the authentication of parties who will gain access to the Emergency Partition.

We presented a comprehensive design for the management of distributed emergency state, which is critical for effective emergency response. We also described the *Trusted Application Display* to allow user-space applications to securely communicate with the user via direct x86-style call gates to a kernel-TSM. We also described the multifaceted containment of emergency data and reliable revocation of access at the end of the emergency, using a combination of hardware and software mechanisms and trust chains.

Finally, we have built a prototype that validates key concepts of the architecture, indicating the feasibility of using commodity mobile and wearable platforms for secure emergency-response data dissemination. In the future, in-depth usability and performance testing, as well as formal system security verification, will further validate this work.

Acknowledgments. This material is based upon work supported by the National Science Foundation under Grants No. CNS-0430566, CNS-0430487 and CNS-0430598 with support from DARPA ATO. This paper does not necessarily reflect the views of the National Science Foundation or of DARPA ATO.

References

1. Johns Hopkins University, National center for study of preparedness and catastrophic event response. Technical Report,
   http://www.pacercenter.org
2. IAD: U.S. Government Protection Profile for Separation Kernels in Environments Requiring High Robustness. Version 1.021 edn. National Information Assurance Partnership (March 2007)
3. Levin, T.E., Irvine, C.E., Weissman, C., Nguyen, T.D.: Analysis of three multilevel security architectures. In: Proceedings 1st Computer Security Architecture Workshop, Fairfax, VA, 37–46 (November 2007)
4. Dwoskin, J.S., Lee, R.B.: Hardware-rooted trust for secure key management and transient trust. In: Proc. of 14th ACM conference on Computer and communications security, pp. 389–400. ACM, New York (2007)

5. Sterne, D.F.: On the buzzword "security policy". In: Proceedings of the IEEE Symposium on Research on Security and Privacy, Oakland, CA, pp. 219–230. IEEE Computer Society Press, Los Alamitos (1991)
6. CCMB: Common Criteria for Information Technology Security Evaluation, Part 2: Security functional components. 3.1 revision 1 edn. Number CCMB-2006-09-001 in Criteria. Common Criteria Maintenance Board (September 2006)
7. Kent, S., Atkinson, R.: Security Architecture for the Internet Protocol. Number 4301 in Request for Comments. The Internet Society (December 2005)
8. Badra, M., Hajjeh, I.: Key-exchange authentication using shared secrets. Computer 39(3), 58–66 (2006)
9. Dolev, D., Yao, A.C.: On the security of public key protocols. In: Proc. Of 22Th annual symposium on foundations of computer science. IEEE Computer Society press, Los Alamitos (1981)
10. Smith, S., Weingart, S.: Building a high-performance, programmable secure coprocessor. Computer Networks 31, 831–860 (1999)
11. Trusted Computing Group: TCG specification architecture overview. Technical Report Rev 1.2, Trusted Computing Group (April 28, 2004)
12. IBM: Ibm extends enhanced data security to consumer electronics products. Technical Report,
http://www.cio.com/article/20075/
IBM_to_Offer_Chip_Based_Encryption_for_PCs_PDAs
13. Alkassar, A., Scheibel, M., Sadeghi, A.R., Stüble, C., Winandy, M.: Security architecture for device encryption and vpn. In: Proc. of Information Security Solution Europe (ISSE) (2006)
14. Sadeghi, A.R., Stüble, C., Pohlmann, N.: European Multilateral Secure Computing Base - Open Trusted Computing for You and Me. In: Datenschutz und Datensicherheit (DUD), pp. 548–554. Vieweg Verlag (2004)
15. Alves-Foss, J., Taylor, C., Oman, P.: A multi-layered approach to security in high assurance systems. In: Proceedings of the 37th Annual Hawaii International Conference on System Sciences, Big Island, HI (January 2004)
16. Vanfleet, W.M., Beckwith, R.W., Calloni, B., Luke, J.A., Taylor, C., Uchenick, G.: Mils: Architecture for high assurance embedded computing. CrossTalk 18(8), 12–16 (2005)
17. Gleeson, B., Lin, A., Heinanen, J., Armitage, G., Malis, A.: A framework for ip based virtual private networks. Technical Report RFC 2764, IETF (February 2000)
18. Bell, D.E., Fiske, R.S., Gasser, M., Tasker, P.S.: Secure on-line processing technology - final report. Technical Report ESD–TR-74–186, The MITRE Corporation, Bedford, MA (August 1974)
19. Solutions, G.G.: XTS-400, STOP 6.0, User's Manual. Getronics Government Solutions, LLC, Herndon, VA. Xtdoc0005-01 edn. (August 2002)
20. National Computer Security Center: Final Evaluation Report of Gemini Computers, Incorporated Gemini Trusted Network Processor, Version 1.01 (June 28, 1995)
21. Gligor, V., Burch, E., Chandersekaran, G., Chapman, R., Dotterer, L., Hecht, M., Jiang, W., Luckenbaugh, G., Vasudevan, N.: On the design and implementation of secure xenix workstations. In: IEEE Symposium on Security, pp. 102–117 (May 1986)
22. Bickel, R., Cook, M., Haney, J., Kerr, M., Parker, T.: Guide to Securing Microsoft Windows XP. National Security Agency (2002)
23. Burger, W., et al.: Remote trusted path mechanism for telnet. Number 07/150966 in Patent. International Business Machines Corporation, Armonk, NY (May 1989)

24. Xen User's Manual. Xen v3.0 edn. University of Cambridge (2005)
25. Barham, P., et al.: Xen and the art of virtualization. In: Proc. Nineteenth ACM Symposium on Operating System Principles, pp. 164–177 (2003)
26. Epstein, J., et al.: Evolution of a trusted b3 window system prototype. In: Proc. of the 1992 IEEE Symposium on Research in Security and Privacy (May 1992)
27. Anderson, M., North, C., Griffin, J., Milner, R., Yesberg, J., Yiu, K.: Starlight: Interactive link. In: Proceedings 12th Computer Security Applications Conference, San Diego, CA (December 1996)
28. Epstein, J.: Fifteen years after tx: A look back at high assurance multi-level secure windowing. In: Computer Security Applications Conference. ACSAC 22nd Annual, pp. 301–320 (2006)
29. National Security Agency. Executive Summary of the End-to-End IA Component of the GIG Integrated Architecture. Version 1.0 edn. National Security Agency Information Assurance Directorate (April 2005)
30. Wolfowitz, P.: Global Information Grid (GIG) Overarching Policy, directive number 8100.1. U.S. Department of Defense (September 2002)
31. OASIS Emergency Data Exchange Language (EDXL) Distribution Element. v1.0 edn, http://docs.oasis-open.org/emergency/EDXL-DE/V1.0

Trustable Remote Verification of Web Services

John Lyle

Oxford University Computing Laboratory,
Wolfson Building, Parks Road, Oxford, OX1 3QD
john.lyle@comlab.ox.ac.uk

Abstract. Service Oriented Architectures currently provide little or no
evidence that each remote component has been implemented correctly.
This is a problem for businesses hoping to exploit the potential benefits
of SOA. We present a technique called Trustable Remote Verification,
which lets providers create behavioural guarantees of their web services.
Our approach is flexible, using Extended Static Checking for verification
and has the significant advantage of requiring no additional trusted third
party.

1 Introduction

As applications and services move online, we are implicitly expected to place
more trust in the developers and providers of these systems. But how do we
know if a remote service is trustworthy? Bugs and vulnerabilities will continue
to exist, and while dedicated providers might be considered more capable of
administering systems than end users, they also become valuable targets for
attack. As a single point of failure, a poorly implemented service will affect
everyone who relies upon it. We therefore need some way of establishing trust
in remote systems.

There are several issues to overcome before being able to trust an online application. Fundamentally, the users of a web service have no information about the
quality of its implementation. Furthermore, most services only have a WSDL[1]
description, which contains little semantic information, only method names and
basic data types. Without a more detailed behavioural interface, trustworthiness
is difficult to establish. If we do not know how it *should* work, whether or not
it has been programmed correctly becomes irrelevant. Finally, software installed
at a service will frequently be patched and upgraded, usually without warning
or notification. As a result, a relying party will potentially need to reassess it
before every request.

We have developed a solution to some of these problems which uses trusted
computing and tools for specifying and verifying Java programs. A brief overview
of these in given in Section 2. In Sections 3, 4 and 5 we refine the problem,
introduce the idea of Trustable Remote Verification, and present details of our
prototype. It is then evaluated and compared against existing solutions in Section
6. Future work is discussed in Section 7 and in Section 8 we conclude.

L. Chen, C.J. Mitchell, and A. Martin (Eds.): Trust 2009, LNCS 5471, pp. 153–168, 2009.
© Springer-Verlag Berlin Heidelberg 2009

2   Background, Definitions and Related Work

2.1   Remote Attestation

Remote attestation is an authentication technique for trusted computing platforms. It uses the 'TPM Quote' operation to create a signed record of the attesting computer's Platform Configuration Registers (PCRs)[2]. These are intended to be used to record the platform's boot process, including the bios, bootloader, OS and applications. A quote can therefore be considered trustworthy evidence of what software has been run on the attesting platform. This is a valuable piece of information, as it potentially gives a remote user the ability to identify and make a judgement about the software that is running.

In a basic server implementation, PCRs are held on a separate chip, the Trusted Platform Module (TPM), and store a 20 byte SHA-1 hash value. These values can only be modified by software through the extend(..) command. This appends the current PCR value to the supplied input, hashes it, and stores the result in the PCR. A PCR value therefore reflects a chain of individual hashes. The TPM Quote operation takes a number of these PCR values and signs them with the private half of an *Attestation Identity Key* (AIK), which is held within the platform's TPM. This AIK must have a credential, issued by a trusted third party (a 'Privacy CA'), which typically states that the platform has a valid TPM[3]. Upon receiving a quote, therefore, it is necessary to check that the AIK used has been certified by a trustworthy Privacy CA. Quotes can also contain a nonce, set by the challenger, in order to guarantee freshness.

On platforms which support *authenticated boot*, every piece of code executed in the boot process is hashed and extended into a PCR. This is done sequentially (a *chain of trust*), with each preceding step extending a measurement of the next before allowing it to execute. This means that a malicious piece of code cannot be run without its identity first being recorded. So long as every step in the process is trusted to perform measurements faithfully, it is possible to attest that a platform is only running known pieces of software. Remote attestation is therefore about reporting system *integrity measurements*, as the modification of any executable will be noticed. This is obviously attractive from a system security perspective, as it becomes possible to identify a machine which has been infected with a virus or rootkit.

However, attestation does not necessarily give any indication of a platform's *security state* but rather its *execution state*[4]. Sadeghi and Stüble[5] introduce the notion of 'Property-Based Attestation' (PBA) in order to simplify the process. In PBA, platforms provide a list of guaranteed security properties, rather than just a binary integrity measurement. This can be implemented in a number of ways, but generally relies upon at least one party being able to match the PCR values to security properties, and then issuing certificates to this end. PBA is a level of indirection which can take some of the burden from the attestation requester.

2.2   Web Services

Web services are a well-established approach to creating large, component-based applications[6]. Services communicate and describe themselves using standard data formats, such as SOAP[7] and WSDL, and have interoperability as a primary requirement. Each service offers some kind of useful functionality, but the real benefit of SOA is that they can be combined together easily, allowing the rapid creation of new, custom applications. These workflows also have the potential to be very reliable, as services can be chosen and composed together at the last minute. This means that an individual fault can be dynamically avoided by choosing alternative services where necessary.

However, many of the perceived advantages rely upon better specification and assurance of the component services. Without knowing precisely how each will behave, it is difficult to use them in combination with any confidence. Testing web services is also difficult, as they might exist in different administrative domains or operate on live data. This becomes more of an issue when considering services with critical functionality, such as in financial, medical or valuable intellectual property scenarios. Remote verification of web services therefore seems necessary, but few methods of doing so have been developed.

2.3   JML and Design by Contract

The Design by Contract (DbC) approach advocates having a 'precise definition of every module's claim and responsibilities'[8] in order to create reliable and, importantly, *reusable* components. This is exactly what we would like to

```
/*@ requires
  @   accFrom != null && accTo != null && amount > 0;
  @
  @ ensures
  @   ((accFrom.getBalance() == \old(accFrom.getBalance())) &&
  @     (accTo.getBalance() == \old(accTo.getBalance())) ) &&
  @     (errLog.content.theSize == \old(errLog.content.theSize+1))
  @   ||
  @   ((accFrom.getBalance() == (\old(accFrom.getBalance()) - amount)) &&
  @     (accTo.getBalance() == \old(accTo.getBalance()) + amount) &&
  @     (transLog.content.theSize == \old(transLog.content.theSize+1)));
  @*/

public void makeTransfer(Account accFrom, Account accTo, int
amount) {
      ...
}
```

Fig. 1. An example web method, complete with JML annotations. Two outcomes are specified: either the account balances change in the expected way, or both remain the same. An entry is added to the transaction log in the first case, and to the error log in the second.

achieve with web services. Module interfaces are annotated with pre- and post-conditions in the form of `requires` and `ensures` clauses. There are also class invariants, which express 'general consistency constraints that apply to every class instance as a whole'[8]. Several annotation languages exist for the DbC methodology, including Eiffel, Spec# and JML, the Java Modeling Language. JML[9] offers other language features, including specification of exceptions, non-null annotations and class ownership. A simple example of JML can be found in Figure 1.

2.4   ESC/Java2

The annotations introduced by Design by Contract can be used for automatic source-code checking. This is usually performed with a static analyser, which attempts to verify assertions without ever executing the code. One such analyser is ESC/Java2[10], an extended static checker for Java and JML. It translates code and annotations into logical terms, and then runs these through the Simplify theorem prover, producing either a counter example or an 'ok' result.

3   A Basic Web Service Behavioural Attestation Model

For the purposes of this work, we assume a simple scenario where a service requester (R) wants to use a web service (W). Before doing so, R wants to find out two things: what software is being run at W and what that software promises to do. The first part can (in theory) be achieved through remote attestation, but the second is more difficult. The approach we have taken is to add JML annotations to the service end point. This means that each web method can include pre- and post- conditions, as well as other formal properties. Although only Java services are supported, similar methods could be used with Spec# for .Net services, or any other Design by Contract language.

However, we have yet to show that the annotations attached to a service are really implemented. In this basic architecture, a *Trusted Compilation Service (C)* fulfils this role. The source code (W_{src}) of W is compiled and checked against its annotations (W_{ann}) by C, using a method such as model checking. A certificate is then produced by C which contains a hash of the compiled application (W_{bin}), a list of any dependent libraries used in the compilation process and an assertion stating which program properties hold. W can then present this certificate to R, along with a fresh remote attestation[1], and R will have a much greater level of confidence that W has the promised behaviour.

There are a number of assumptions. R must trust that C will do a thorough analysis of the source code at W. W must trust C with all the source code, which may not be possible. More fundamental assumptions include:

---

[1] The fresh attestation must, of course, contain an entry which is identical to W_{bin}. If it does not, then the certificate produced by C cannot be used to validate this service.

- C must be capable of analysing the source code at W. This is not a trivial task, and may depend on the availability of numerous code libraries, operating system features, and so on.
- The middleware and OS running at W must also be trusted by C and R.
- All important configuration settings must be either made available to C or R. This might be undesirable if they contain passwords or confidential settings.
- The middleware and OS must be *attestable*. Each part of the software stack must support integrity measurement. It must be possible for R to receive a remote attestation from W and interpret it. This implies the existence of an integrity management infrastructure, which has a list of 'known-good' pieces of software. Every binary running at W will need to be on this list.

Overall, this is a proposal for using Remote Attestation to establish meaningful properties of a web service. However, there are a number of drawbacks, including the requirement for a trusted third party, C. The rest of this paper introduces Trustable Remote Verification, which allows us to remove C altogether.

4   Trustable Remote Verification

There are generally two approaches to program verification. It can be done by a trusted third party, but they may charge a high price for their services. They are also a target for attack, and should be avoided if at all possible. The alternative is to verify an application locally. If source code can be inspected before compilation, any errors can potentially be spotted before it is run. However, given the size of any complex application, even a highly skilled programmer would struggle to spot potentially erroneous behaviour in source code. This has been improved by Proof Carrying Code[11], where the majority of the effort is carried out by the application distributor. However, this is not a suitable solution for web services, where all applications are running remotely. Users have no idea what source code is being run at the service, and have no way of verifying it. Neither third-party nor local analysis can be considered appropriate and instead we require some way to let the *provider* perform verification, and then prove to users that they have done so.

4.1   Overview

Trustable Remote Verification (TRV) uses TPM attestations as credentials. The service provider performs program analysis using a local machine (the verification platform, V) and then attests the result. To do this, V must be booted into a trustworthy OS, which measures every step of the process and extends each into a PCR. After authenticated boot, the annotations (W_{ann}) which represent the service contract are measured. These will specify some important property of the service which the requester requires (see Figure 1 as an example). Then a program verifier (TV) is measured and loaded, and the source code (W_{src}) is analysed against its annotations. The result of this step (TV_{res}) is also measured

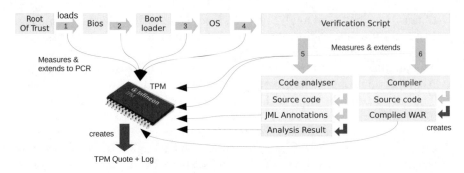

Fig. 2. An overview of the Trustable Remote Verification process, showing the order of execution and all items measured into PCRs

and extended into a PCR. Next, the source code is compiled by a trusted compiler, TC. A hash of it and all the compiled binaries (W_{bin}) are measured and extended. At the end of the verification process, a quote (V_{quote}) is produced which contains two sets of PCRs, holding measurements:

$$V_{quote} = \left\{ \begin{array}{l} PCR\ 0..15 = \{\ [\text{ boot process at } V]\ \} \\ PCR\ 21\quad = \{\ TV, TC, W_{ann}, TV_{res}, W_{bin}\ \} \end{array} \right\}_{AIK_V} \tag{1}$$

This is a credential, which will be used by the provider to show that a program binary, W_{bin}, was compiled from source code which was verified against its annotations, with analysis result TV_{res}. In the ideal case, TV_{res} would state something simple such as 'verified'. The credential can be checked by making sure that TV, TC and the boot process are all trustworthy, checking that TV_{res} does not show any errors and finally verifying that the annotations are sufficiently strong for the program to be trusted.

At runtime, the service provider attests in the normal way, creating another quote:

$$W_{quote} = \left\{ \begin{array}{l} PCR\ 0..15 = \{\ [\text{ boot process at } W]\ \} \\ PCR\ 21\quad = \{\ L_{bin}\ \} \end{array} \right\}_{AIK_W} \tag{2}$$

Where L_{bin} is the measurement of the binary that has been loaded at service runtime and will be accepting requests. In order for the V_{quote} credential to be useful, L_{bin} must be equal to W_{bin}.

4.2   Assumptions

Trustable Remote Verification relies on several assumptions:

- The platform performing verification has a valid TPM which has not been tampered with.
- A PKI infrastructure for issuing AIKs exists and all platforms have valid AIKs and certificates available to them.
- There exists a *verifier*, a piece of software which can read the program contract and source code and automatically decide whether the latter corresponds with the former. This must run without any user interaction, and

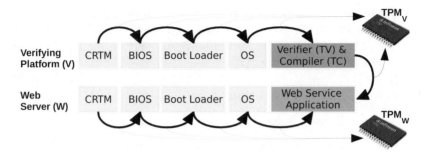

Fig. 3. The chain of trust for Trustable Remote Verification, showing execution order and measurement storage

be trusted to work properly by the client. In our proof-of-concept implementation we have JML annotations as a contract and use ESC/Java2 for verification.

- There is a simple operating system and boot loader, again trusted by the client, which the verifier can run on without interference. This will measure all programs executed on the platform, and is itself measured as part of the boot process.
- The verifier, compiler and operating system have SHA-1 identities known to the client.
- Any third-party libraries that the verified application uses are either annotated and verified with the service, or their identities are published by the server and trusted by the client.
- All configuration files used by the web service or the verifier are made available to the client.

4.3   The New Chain of Trust

TRV decouples the process of certification and application execution. This means that once the web service binary has been verified, it can be run on any service which supports authenticated boot, and the same credential can certify it. This is desirable from an end-user perspective, as the amount of effort required to establish trust in a set of remote services (perhaps implemented for load-balancing reasons) is greatly reduced. The disadvantage is that the chain of trust is now longer, and contains potentially two TPMs, one for the web server (TPM_W) and one for the verifier (TPM_V).

5   Prototype Implementation

We developed two parts of this system: the credential-creation stage on V and requester validation stage at R. In our prototype, services are written in Java, with methods from one class exposed as a web service. This class is annotated with JML assertions, which are the properties that this service promises to fulfil. ESC/Java2 is used as the program verifier (TV) and Ant plus the standard

Sun JDK are used as the compiler (TC). The result of compilation is a WAR[2] file which is run from the Glassfish Application Server. We did not implement authenticated boot for either the verification or web service, but several potential candidates exist for this purpose[12].

5.1 Server Credential Creation Stage

The program verification stage requires the following steps:

1. The service source code and configuration files are placed onto V.
2. An AIK certificate is obtained from a Privacy CA.
3. The trustworthy OS with authenticated boot is started.
4. The OS measures the JVM, and then runs the verifier. This measures the following items into the TPM:
   – The front-end JML annotations of the service.
   – All libraries and files necessary for compilation.
   – The WAR archived created by compiling the service.
   – The output of running ESC/Java2.
5. A quote (V_{quote}) is created, signed by the AIK, containing 2 sets of PCR values. One has the trustworthy OS and application measurements and the other has all the measurements made by the verifier.

Additionally, an archive is created to help the service requester validate the measurements. This includes references to external libraries, ESC/Java2 output, JML annotations and a log of the entire process. This is used by the requester to validate the process later on. References to external libraries should point to where the end user can download the library to verify its identity.

$$V_{arch} = \{ \ V_{quote}, [\text{ libraries }], W_{ann}, TV_{res}, \ \log, [\text{ config files }] \ \} \tag{3}$$

The compilation stage and WAR file creation is complicated by incompatibilities. Java web service annotations are only valid in Java 1.5 and above but ESC/Java2 can only interpret version 1.4 source code. As a result, the service must be written in Java 1.4 and then wrapped by an automatically-generated Java 1.5 front-end class.

5.2 Credential Validation Steps

The service requester, R, must obtain and verify the credential that was created using the steps in Section 5.1. This requires the requester to download V_{arch} and obtain a fresh attestation of the web service's current configuration, W_{quote}, and then do the following:

1. Check that the software running on W, as reported in W_{quote} is trustworthy.
2. Check that the currently-running web service application, L_{bin}, matches the verified service identity W_{bin}, included in V_{arch}.

---

[2] Web application archive `http://java.sun.com/developer/technicalArticles/Servlets/servletapi/`

3. Check the AIK used to sign W_{quote} and V_{quote}.
4. Check the freshness of W_{quote}. V_{quote} is not time dependent, so a freshness check is unnecessary.
5. Check that V's OS and boot process are trustworthy.
6. Check that the verification program (including TV and TC) is trustworthy. We imagine checking against a public list of verifiers (with available source code) which are known to be sound and complete.
7. V_{arch} contains a log of the verification process, which will need to be checked against the PCR values held in V_{quote}.
8. Each individual step described in the log must now be verified. The server must provide any comparison resources that the client does not have access to. This includes:
   - All configuration files used in the verification process.
   - The external libraries used and any assumptions made about them.
   - The verification result itself.
   - The verified service annotations.

Additionally, some useful service properties must be described in the annotations, and the verification result should not show any situation where they do not hold. With our sample implementation, some of the checks described are performed manually, but it would be feasible to create automated tools. Part 1 and 5 require an integrity management infrastructure, such as IMI [13].

5.3   Configuration Files and Compilation with Ant

Because the credential-creation step is complex, involving program compilation and creation of web service artifacts, there are a number of configuration options. These could potentially make the verification process untrustworthy (for example, running ESC/Java2 on one piece of software and then compiling and measuring another). Therefore, we measure the configuration files and include them in V_{arch}.

Program compilation can also be complicated, involving libraries, configuration, and archive creation. As a result, most Java developers use Ant rather than just javac . For the compilation step of our prototype, we have to deal with the same issues, so reusing the Ant build file seems sensible. However, Ant is a powerful tool and it would be possible to write a malicious build file to avoid verification. In order to stop this from happening, the build file must be measured into the quote and included in V_{arch}. It must also be checked by the requester, along with all the libraries and files it references. In our prototype this is done manually.

Another problem arises from runtime configuration. Most applications are designed to work differently at runtime depending on how they are configured. If any of the security properties of a service can be violated by a change of settings file, then they will (correctly) not pass the verification step of our system. The same is true for a service which depends upon a running database or human input. Essentially, any system that can be made to violate its specification *after* compilation will be a problem. The alternative method discussed in Section 7 does not have this limitation.

6   Evaluation

6.1   Benefits of Trustable Remote Verification

In our proposed system it is possible to determine, with a fairly high level of assurance, *something* about what a remote service will do when invoked. This something will range from a complete logical description of the functionality of the service, down to perhaps a simple invariant. In the example given in Figure 1, we gain the knowledge that the method `makeTransfer` will at least revert back to our previous state rather than fail in an unknown way. We also know that the error log is guaranteed to keep track of any failures. In terms of security, we could use assertions about information flow to be sure of confidentiality. JML has been used before for security properties[14].

JML's ability to express useful properties (and ESC/Java2's ability to check them) is a significant consideration when evaluating the prototype. There are properties that cannot be expressed or checked, and the properties that the service provider has asserted may not be important to the requester. Because ESC/Java2 requires a significant amount of supporting JML, time must be spent annotating the source code for each particular property. However, this time can be justified by considering some of the other benefits of Design by Contract, such as improving documentation and overall code robustness. Furthermore, we must also assume that the requester will correctly understand the given properties, and not misinterpret a set of conditions or invariants which may be complex. More research is needed to find out where Trustable Remote Verification would be most beneficial, but it is likely to be services which have simple properties to assert, such as the conditions in which an exception will be thrown, or the correct implementation of simple mathematical functions.

No additional third party is required to create the service credentials, beyond a Privacy CA which may exist already. However, as noted in Section 5.2, an integrity measurement infrastructure will be needed for verifying the trusted software components, such as TC and TV. This may require a trusted third party. The client and server-side code needed to implement these features is fairly small (the prototype is under 3000 lines of code), with the only significant extra requirement being an operating system that supports authenticated boot. Furthermore, this system allows for software update, as each new version of a service can be re-verified and a new credential produced. This can be part of the standard build-cycle for a project. Another key benefit to this system over the basic architecture is that the source code of the service never needs to be revealed, not even to a third party. This would be attractive to a company with valuable or confidential code.

6.2   Trustworthiness of the Architecture

The strength of TRV can be measured by how difficult it is for a provider to *falsely* claim that a service has certain properties. Any system can be broken through weaknesses in its trusted components, so we will now assess ours. We rely upon one (or more) TPMs, a verification OS, verification tool, compiler and the software stack running at the web service. TPMs are designed to be immune to software attack, and hardware attacks are non-trivial. They are therefore unlikely to be the weakest point in the system.

The verification environment also needs to be a trusted component. However, the verification OS can be small and simple and only needs to be able to run a program verifier and compiler. It does not need network access, or the ability to accept user input at runtime. Future CPUs which run bytecode might be a good way of avoiding vulnerabilities, as might a microkernel-based OS. The verifier and compiler, on the other hand, are a bigger issue. They are necessarily complex systems, which accept input in the form of program code and configuration files. Arguably, however, we must already trust the compilers we use, and there are several open source compilers which have gone through considerable scrutiny. A weakness in the verifier would be a problem. If it produced false negatives, it could then potentially certify a system which does not maintain its properties. We offer no solution to this problem, but expect that creating one acceptable verifier or compiler is likely to be easier than creating many perfect applications.

Perhaps the most significant trusted element is the rest of the software running at the web service. If a bug or vulnerability causes it to behave in an unexpected manner, then the properties guaranteed by the web service application are irrelevant. This is likely to happen, as the amount of code running which has not been formally checked greatly outweighs the small amount that has. It includes the service middleware, operating system, and any libraries that the service relies upon. This 'middleware problem' has been discussed in a grid scenario by Cooper and Martin[15], and solutions involving virtualization sound promising. This problem is true of almost all trusted computing systems involving legacy applications, and ours is no exception.

Overall, TRV is clearly limited in the level of trust it can establish, and is not appropriate for extremely high assurance systems. Instead, it would work best as an additional check for service providers who are attempting to improve their perceived reliability in the marketplace. In such a scenario, one threat is that a company with normally good intentions tries to subvert the system for a new version of their service. They might try to rush a new feature, at the expense of verification. TRV would make this much more difficult to do, and so the provider would be more likely to spend the extra effort on verification instead.

6.3   Related Work

Haldar et al. [16] introduce Semantic Remote Attestation, a technique for verifying the remote behaviour of a platform. They use a Trusted Virtual Machine

(TVM) to attest to high-level properties of the running code. The presence of the TVM is attested first using normal methods, then the TVM can report on properties such as class hierarchies, Java VM security constraints and run-time dynamic state. Arbitrary properties can also be tested by requesting the TVM accept and run code written by the requester. This is a powerful technique, offering remote users the ability to make better trust decisions. However, the focus of this work is on dynamic feedback and testing rather than showing formal properties. We feel that our work compliments this by proving different semantic properties. Our approach is also significantly different, not relying on a runtime virtual machine, thus removing any potential performance issues.

Yoshihama et al. [17] and Monetoh et al. [13] have created and extended a web service attestation architecture called WS-Attestation. It uses a third party Validation Service (VS), which maintains an integrity database, linking software hash values to known application identities. The VS also has access to a vulnerability database. The idea is that the attesting platform reports its integrity measurement to the requester along with a certificate issued by the VS. This certificate can state a more easily interpreted property, such as the number of known vulnerabilities. However, this system is best suited to verifying the integrity of the OS and middleware of a platform, rather than of a custom application, which is unlikely to have any entries in the vulnerability database. It is also not clear how properties beyond vulnerability counts might be established.

Betin-Can et al. [18] use a design for verification approach to verify services. They introduce the 'Peer Controller Pattern' which separates out the message exchange from the logic, simplifying the verification process. An explicit behavioural interface is also generated. Assertions that are known to hold in individual services are then combined and the behaviour of the whole system can be checked with regard to synchronizability. Individual implementations are considered to conform with their interfaces if their call-sequences are acceptable to its state machine. This is verified using the JavaPathFinder model checker. It seems an excellent approach when considering concurrency issues, but does depend on all source code being available to the verifier, with trust in remote parties being less of an issue.

Tsai et al. [19] describe a framework ('WebStrar') for web service assurance. Services are registered and a series of tests are performed on it. Each service has a specification written in OWL-S and this is checked via 'Completeness and Consistency' analysis and model checking of the specification and verification patterns. There is also a step involving positive and negative test cases, which all go towards ranking the services in terms of reliability. This approach is a logical way of gaining assurance, but does have some issues. Testing is not appropriate in a situation where the service operates on live data, and it is also not clear whether the tested services have any obligation to re-register in the case of a change to their implementation.

7   Observations and Future Work

7.1   Runtime Checking and Compile-Time Translation

A similar but alternative approach to the one taken in our prototype is to use the JML compiler[9], `jmlc`, as opposed to the Java compiler. `Jmlc` adds runtime assertion checks into the program bytecode in addition to normal compilation. These will raise an exception if any of the preconditions, postconditions or invariants fail. Except for a small performance hit, this behaviour is transparent unless one of the assertions is violated.

The advantage of this scheme is that we no longer need to perform static analysis. This was one of the issues identified in Section 6.2. As a result, runtime components such as configuration files and databases can be accessed without breaking the assertions. However, the major downside is that an untrustworthy service can make promises, and then break when they are not fulfilled. This might result in lost data and an unreliable system. The best this would be able to say is that *if* the service does not fail, it will work as expected. However, despite these limitations it may be worth investigating in the future. This approach is similar to earlier work by Haldar et al. [16].

7.2   Multiple Verifications and the New Chain of Trust

One useful property of our system is that the credential-creation process is entirely separate from the runtime attestation. As a result, we can extend our prototype to offer multiple, potentially independent verifications and certificates for the same service. For example, one service provider could first verify their source code with ESC/Java2, producing a certificate, and then do the same with an alternative program analyser. This might satisfy users who will only trust a particular analysis program.

We can go even further, and let multiple organisations verify the same service. Assuming they are given the source code, they can all independently run a verifier and produce a certificate. This significantly strengthens the chain of trust, as it is no longer 'anchored' by just one TPM. Figure 3 is no longer as big a problem, as the top chain can be put in parallel with several others. This might be useful for high-assurance systems, such as e-voting.

7.3   Using a Dynamic Root of Trust

One way in which we could optimise our proposed TRV system, with respect of the number of integrity measurements, would be to use a dynamic root of trust. Rather than measuring every part of the boot process, including the BIOS, we could use either AMD's Secure Virtual Machine (SVM) architecture or Intel's Trusted Execution Technology (TXT) to dynamically load and measure ('late launch') a trustworthy operating system. McCune et al. [20] provide a good summary of these technologies. This would reduce the number of measurements that the service requester needs to verify, and therefore make the overall system

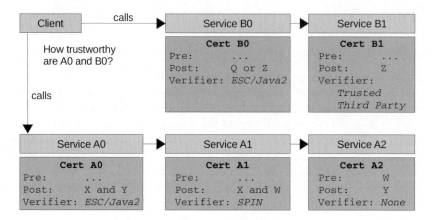

Fig. 4. The challenge of verifying service workflows

trustworthiness easier to quantify. With the recent development of a suitable bootloader[21] this would be a sensible future improvement.

7.4   Verifying Multiple Services

We have not considered verifying web services which themselves contact other services. This is quite a common scenario, and a significant limitation of our prototype. However, there do not seem to be any obvious reasons why any services which have also followed this scheme could not be incorporated. These 'sub services' could be wrapped by a stub object, which asserts the same annotated properties. This would not be verified, and instead all the certificates could be presented to the user. Implementing this in a user friendly and secure manner would be a challenge.

Presenting multiple service certificates presents another set of problems. Firstly, what happens if one of the sub services is not considered trustworthy? This could be for a number of reasons, for example the verification tool might be out of date, or the AIK certificate could have expired. The implications of this may affect all or part of the overall combined service. Secondly, do we still trust a system with so many trusted components? If a TPM was successfully attacked on any of the sub services it might compromise the whole process. Finally, it is possible that we will be contacting services which do not use this certification system. They may have a different trust mechanism, or none at all. How to weight the trustworthiness of this service is an open question.

8   Conclusion

We have introduced the idea of Trustable Remote Verification, a technique which allows a service provider to verify its own software and create a trustworthy guarantee of the result. The main advantages are that no new third parties are needed, and providers can easily create a new verification result whenever necessary. Furthermore, one verification can be used as a credential for many platforms. We have also identified the key shortcomings and limitations to our work, including the large amount of necessarily trusted code, and the need for an annotated, verifiable service. However, our prototype implementation uncovered few additional issues, and we feel justified in persuing these ideas further. Overall, this technique has great potential, and could be a viable way of adding assurance to Service Oriented Architectures. Future work will concentrate on finding where the best applications of this idea are, what properties it can guarantee, and whether architectural approaches can be used to reduce the trusted computing base of verified services.

Acknowledgements

Special thanks go to Andrew Martin and Jun Ho Huh for several helpful discussions while writing this paper and developing the concepts. I am also grateful to Joe Loughry, Andrew Cooper, Shamal Faily and Cornelius Namiluko for their comments. Finally, I thank the reviewers for their useful and positive feedback.

References

1. Christensen, E., Curbera, F., Meredith, G., Weerawarana, S.: Web Services Description Language (WSDL) 1.1. Technical report, W3C (March 2001),
   http://www.w3.org/TR/2001/NOTE-wsdl-20010315
2. The Trusted Computing Group: TCG Specification Architecture Overview, Revision 1.4 (August 2007), https://www.trustedcomputinggroup.org/groups/
   TCG_1_4_Architecture_Overview.pdf
3. The Trusted Computing Group: TCG Glossary of Technical Terms (2008),
   https://www.trustedcomputinggroup.org/groups/glossary/
4. Poritz, J.A.: Trust[ed | in] Computing, Signed Code and the Heat Death of the Internet. In: SAC 2006: Proceedings of the 2006 ACM Symposium on Applied Computing, pp. 1855–1859. ACM Press, New York (2006)
5. Sadeghi, A.R., Stüble, C.: Property-based Attestation for Computing Platforms: Caring About Properties, Not Mechanisms. In: NSPW 2004: Proceedings of the 2004 Workshop on New Security Paradigms, pp. 67–77. ACM Press, New York (2004)
6. Papazoglou, M.P., Dubray, J.j.: A Survey of Web Service Technologies. Technical Report DIT-04-058, Informatica e Telecomunicazioni, University of Trento (June 2004)
7. The W3C: Simple Object Access Protocol (SOAP) (April 2007),
   http://www.w3.org/TR/soap/
8. Meyer, B.: Design by Contract: Building Reliable Software. In: Object-Oriented Software Construction, pp. 331–341. Prentice Hall, Englewood Cliffs (1997)
9. Leavens, G., Cheon, Y.: Design by Contract with JML (2003),
   http://citeseer.ist.psu.edu/leavens04design.html
10. Cok, D.R., Kiniry, J.R.: ESC/Java2: Uniting eSC/Java and JML. In: Barthe, G., Burdy, L., Huisman, M., Lanet, J.-L., Muntean, T. (eds.) CASSIS 2004. LNCS, vol. 3362, pp. 108–128. Springer, Heidelberg (2005)

11. Necula, G.: Proof-Carrying Code. Website (July 2002),
    http://raw.cs.berkeley.edu/pcc.html
12. Jaeger, T., Sailer, R., Shankar, U.: PRIMA: Policy-Reduced Integrity Measurement
    Architecture. In: SACMAT, pp. 19–28 (2006)
13. Munetoh, S., Nakamura, M., Yoshihama, S., Kudo, M.: Integrity Management In-
    frastructure for Trusted Computing. IEICE Transactions on Information and Sys-
    tems E91-D(5), 1242–1251 (2008)
14. Pavlova, M., Barthe, G., Burdy, L., Huisman, M., Lanet, J.L.: Enforcing High-Level
    Security Properties for Applets (2004)
15. Cooper, A., Martin, A.: Towards a secure, tamper-proof grid platform. In: CCGRID
    2006. Sixth IEEE International Symposium on Cluster Computing and the Grid,
    2006, vol. 1, p. 8 (May 2006)
16. Haldar, V., Chandra, D., Franz, M.: Semantic Remote Attestation - Virtual Ma-
    chine Directed Approach to Trusted Computing. In: Virtual Machine Research and
    Technology Symposium, USENIX, pp. 29–41 (2004)
17. Yoshihama, S., Ebringer, T., Nakamura, M., Munetoh, S., Maruyama, H.: WS-
    attestation: efficient and fine-grained remote attestation on Web services. In: ICWS
    2005. Proceedings. 2005 IEEE International Conference on Web Services, pp. 743–
    750 (July 2005)
18. Betin-Can, A., Bultan, T.: Verifiable Web services with Hierarchical Interfaces. In:
    ICWS 2005. Proceedings. 2005 IEEE International Conference on Web Services,
    vol.1, pp. 85–94 (July 2005)
19. Tsai, W., Wei, X., Chen, Y., Xiao, B., Paul, R., Huang, H.: Developing and assuring
    trustworthy Web services. In: Autonomous Decentralized Systems, 2005. ISADS
    2005. Proceedings, pp. 43–50 (April 2005)
20. McCune, J.M., Parno, B.J., Perrig, A., Reiter, M.K., Isozaki, H.: Flicker: an ex-
    ecution infrastructure for tcb minimization. In: Eurosys 2008: Proceedings of the
    3rd ACM SIGOPS/EuroSys European Conference on Computer Systems 2008, pp.
    315–328. ACM, New York (2008)
21. Wei, J., Cihula, J., Wang, S.: Trusted Boot Sourceforge Project Website (2008),
    http://sourceforge.net/projects/tboot/

Trustworthy Log Reconciliation for Distributed Virtual Organisations

Jun Ho Huh and John Lyle

Oxford University Computing Laboratory
Wolfson Building, Parks Road
Oxford, OX1 3QD
{jun.ho.huh,john.lyle}@comlab.ox.ac.uk

Abstract. Secure management of logs in an organisational grid environment is often considered a task of low priority. However, it must be rapidly upgraded when the logs have security properties in their own right. We present several use cases where log integrity and confidentiality are essential, and propose a log reconciliation architecture in which both are ensured. We use a combination of trusted computing and virtualization to enable *blind log analysis*, allowing users to see the results of legitimate queries, while still withholding access to privileged raw data.

1 Introduction

The notion of a *Virtual Organisation* (VO) runs commonly through many definitions of what constitutes a grid: "many disparate logical and physical entities that span *multiple administrative domains* are orchestrated together as a single logical entity" [15]. The rise of many types of organisational grid systems, and associated security threats, makes the provision of trustworthy audit-based monitoring services necessary; for instance, to monitor and report violation of service-level agreements [18], or to detect events of dubious user behaviour across multiple domains and take retrospective actions [17].

In reality, a lot of these audit-based controls are prone to be compromised due to the lack of verification mechanisms for checking the correctness and the integrity of logs collected from different sites; and also because some of these logs are highly sensitive, and without the necessary confidentiality guarantees, neither trusts the other to see the raw data. Many log anonymisation techniques have been proposed [9,12,19] to solve the latter issue; however, adapting such techniques and assuring that these anonymisation policies will be correctly enforced at a remote site, is a whole new security issue. The problem with existing solutions is that they provide only weak protection (or none) for such security properties upon distributed log collection and reconciliation (Section 3).

In our previous work [8] we have proposed a logging infrastructure using the driver virtualization in Xen that enables trustworthy generation and storage of the log data. In this paper, we take a step further and describe a log reconciliation method for guaranteeing their integrity and confidentiality.

L. Chen, C.J. Mitchell, and A. Martin (Eds.): Trust 2009, LNCS 5471, pp. 169–182, 2009.
© Springer-Verlag Berlin Heidelberg 2009

The rest of the paper is organised as follows. In Section 2, we present a number of motivational examples and highlight distinct security challenges with processing distributed log data. Section 3 discusses the security gaps of existing solutions. Then, in Section 4, we present the trustworthy log reconciliation requirements which address these security gaps. Mindful of such requirements, we describe a reconciliation infrastructure for a VO in Sections 5 and 6. Finally, in Section 7 we discuss the contribution of this paper and the remaining work.

2   Motivational Examples

2.1   Healthcare Grids and Dynamic Access Control

The first example application arises in the context of a healthcare grid. In 'e-Health', many data grids are being constructed and interconnected in order to facilitate the better provision of clinical information. Each clinic (an independent legal entity) participating in the grid owns and manages physical databases which together form the virtualized clinical data and log stores. To motivate the use cases described later in this section we use an abstract view of the VO (see Figure 1): each node consists of external and internal services where the virtualization of data sources takes place; it also has its own local data and logs; a standard external service enables communication between different nodes.

Consider the following example in the context of Figure 1. A simplified healthcare grid consists of two nodes, a GP Practice (GP) and a Specialist Clinic (SC). A patient in GP is often referred to SC to see a specialist. We shall assume that a single table at each clinic (T_1, T_2) is made accessible to a researcher R, and that the National Health Index (NHI) uniquely identifies a patient across the grid to enable the linking of data. R is carrying out a study that looks at association between smoking status (T_1) and development of lung cancer (T_2) in the population of Oxfordshire.

R has originally been granted full access to both T_1 (at GP) and T_2 (at SC) to conduct this research. By joining the data across two clinics, R would have access to potential identifiable information about patients: for example, R could

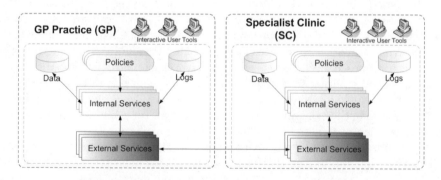

Fig. 1. Abstract View of the Virtual Organisation

find out that patient 1, born on the 20/05/88 and living in OX2 5PS who has Dr. Anderson as their GP, is a smoker and has a lung cancer.

GP Practice (GP) T_1				
NHI	DOB	GP	Smoke	Risks
1	20/05/88	Dr. Anderson	yes	overweight
2	30/07/88	Dr. Anderson	no	allergies

Specialist Clinic (SC) T_2		
NHI	Postcode	LungCancer
1	OX2 5PS	yes
2	OX2 6QA	no

In a secure VO, as soon as R finds out from querying T_2 that patient 1 has lung cancer, R's access on T_1 for patient 1 needs to be restricted to, for example, only the NHI and Smoke fields. For GP to have restricted R's access rights to information pertaining to patient 1 on T_1, would have required GP to collect *data access logs* from SC to build up a picture of what R already knows, and to update its own access control policies to prevent R from collecting potential identifiable information. Although, in general, SC would never give out patients' lung cancer status in the form of audit logs to an untrusted GP.

This type of distributed audit approach has been suggested [17] to detect patterns of behaviour across multiple administrative domains by combining their audit logs. However, the problem arises from the fact that log owners do not trust other sites to see their privileged raw logs. This approach will only work if log owners can be assured of *confidentiality* during transit and reconciliation.

2.2 The Monitorability of Service-Level Agreements (SLAs)

The provision of Service-Level Agreements (SLAs) and ensuring their *monitorability* is another example use for trustworthy log reconciliation.

A SLA is a contract between customers and their service provider which specifies the levels of various attributes of a service like its availability, performance and the associated penalties in the case of violation of these agreements. Consider a case where the client receives no response for a service (for which they have entered into a SLA) within the agreed interval of time, complains to the provider that a timely response was not received and requests financial compensation. The provider argues that no service request was received, and produces a log of requests in their defense. There is no way for the client to find out the truth: the provider could have delivered tampered evidence regarding this event. The problem with this type of SLA is that it is defined in terms of events that the client cannot directly monitor, and they must take the word of the provider with respect to the service availability.

Skene et al [18] suggest a way of achieving the monitorability with trusted computing. This involves generating trustworthy logs, ensuring that unmodified logs have been reported by both parties and that these logs have been used for monitoring SLAs. For instance, if the client is able to verify with remote attestation that trustworthy logging and reporting services operate at a remote site, then the client may place conditions on any event of their interest and construct more useful SLAs. This approach needs to guarantee the *integrity* of all service request/response logs to an evidential standard (i.e. to a standard acceptable for judicial usages) upon distributed reconciliation and analysis. A monitoring service would then be able to generate a reliable SLA report for the client to make claims.

Logs often contain sufficient information to be used as evidence in a variety of context. However, the inability of a site to verify the integrity of logs collected from other sites and the lack of guarantees that their own logs are being used unmodified at remote sites, make it extremely challenging for one to adapt the usual audit-based monitoring method to the VO.

3   Relevant Work and a Gap Analysis

Having identified the security challenges of imposing audit-based controls, we are now in a position to present a gap analysis on existing solutions.

DiLoS (Distributed General Logging Architecture for Grid Environments) [5] provides general logging facilities in service oriented grid environments to enable tracking of the whole system. One of its application models is to facilitate accounting for resource-providing services: to measure and annotate who has used which services, and to bill usage prices. In this accounting domain, however, DiLoS does not consider the log integrity issues and the possible threats that have been covered in Section 2.2. Without security mechanisms to protect log integrity, their architecture cannot be relied upon to perform calculating and billing functions.

Piro et al [14] have developed a more secure and reliable data grid accounting system based on metering resource usage. All communications are encrypted [13]; but a privileged user may still configure the Home Location Register (HLR), a component that collects remote usage records for accounting, to disclose sensitive usage records. A rogue resource owner may modify the Computing Element (CE), which measures the exact resource usage, in order to fabricate records and prices for profit.

The NetLogger Toolkit [20] provides client application libraries (C, Java, Python APIs) that enable one to generate log messages in a common format. It also includes monitoring tools for log collection and analysis at a central point. Again, the log integrity and confidentiality threats discussed in the previous section undermine their approach: access requests are processed without any authorisation policy enforcement, and the logs are transferred across the network in an unencrypted and unsigned format. No attempt is made to safeguard the logs while they are being collected and processed at the reconciliation point.

Similar security problems undermine other existing grid monitoring tools such as APEL (Accounting Processor for Event Logs) [3], which builds accounting records from system and gatekeeper logs generated by a site; and GMS (Grid Monitoring System) [11], a system that captures and stores job information in a relational database, and supports resource usage monitoring and visualising.

4   Trustworthy Log Reconciliation Requirements

To fill the security gaps identified above, we provide a high-level overview of the key requirements with respect to our motivational examples.

Log Migration Service. Due to the number of potential security vulnerabilities, complex grid middleware services can not be relied upon to perform trusted operations [4]. Instead the security controls required for safe log data transfer need to operate within a more secure migration service. This implies data flow encryption and signing requirements upon log access and transfer requests. These are integral in preventing intruders from sniffing the logs processed through insecure grid middleware, and from launching man-in-the-middle type of attacks. It is also possible for a log owner to deliver fabricated logs, as the service provider might do in the SLA example. To provide a safeguard against such a threat, the migration service needs to access the signed logs (and the original logs) directly from the protected log storage. This would give sufficient information for an end user to verify the log integrity.

Log Reconciliation Service. Our examples have a common set of requirements for a trustworthy reconciliation service. They require each site to negotiate with others and grant permissions to view their logs. These sites (before granting permissions) need to be assured that their logs will not be compromised and will be used without modification. The integrity and the confidentiality of the collected logs as well as the processed results (e.g. summaries on SLA violation) need to be protected to prevent a malicious user from modifying or stealing them.

To make it harder for insiders to gain unauthorised access and modify the reconciled logs, this service needs to run in a strongly isolated compartment with robust memory protection. It should also be a small and simple code to minimise the number of security holes that might be exploited.

Blind Analysis of the Logs. Returning to our healthcare example, imagine that SC has agreed to share their logs with GP for dynamic access control. But at the same time they are unwilling to let the system administrator at GP see the actual contents of the logs; or only let part of the data be seen as a summary information. For example, "R's access rights on T_1 for a patient with NHI 1, aged 20 and living in OX2 area, have been restricted to NHI and $Smoke$ fields.". Such anonymisation of end results ensures that the administrator cannot find out about a patient's lung cancer status, and yet, still know exactly how the access control policy has been changed for R.

Log owners need to be assured that any sensitive information contained in their logs will only be revealed to an extent that has been agreed and stated in anonymisation policies: this requires a mechanism, possibly within the reconcil-iation service, to carry out a blind analysis of the collected logs so that a user only sees the running application and the end results, which are just sufficient for them to carry out post log analysis or to know about the important system updates.

5   Trustworthy Logging Architecture

In our previous work [8], we have developed a logging architecture based on Virtual Machine (VM) isolation and remote attestation (see Figure 2). Upon installation of this architecture, each VO participant will be capable of generating and storing log data, and proving to other sites that these logs are trustworthy.

The Trusted Computing Group (TCG) [1] has developed a series of technolo-gies based around a Trusted Platform Module (TPM) which helps to provide two novel capabilities [7]: a cryptographically strong identity and reporting mecha-nism for the platform, and a means to *measure* reliably a hash of the software loaded and run on the platform (from the BIOS upwards); such measurements are stored and retrieved from Platform Configuration Registers (PCRs) in the TPM. These provide the means to *seal* data so that it is available only to a par-ticular platform state, and to undertake *remote attestation*: proving to a third party that a remote device is in a particular software state. TPM-generated Attestation Identity Keys (AIKs) are used to sign PCR values and to prevent tracking of platforms. These trusted computing capabilities can be used in a vir-tualized environment where a physical host is segmented into strongly isolated compartments to make attestation feasible (with robust memory protection), and to limit the impact of any vulnerability in attested code. Our architecture uses the Xen Virtual Machine Monitor (VMM) [2] to achieve this isolation: a thin layer of software operating on top of the hardware to enable VM abstraction and control the way a VM accesses the hardware and peripherals.

All log security functions are enforced by the *log security manager* VM, a small amount of code running inside *back-end driver* VMs and the *log analysis manager* VM; each of which has been designed to perform a small number of simple operations so that it can be compartmented with a high degree of assurance.

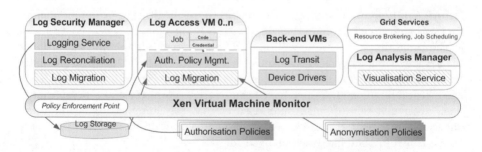

Fig. 2. Abstract View of Trusted Logging Services

Attestation of these compartments, the Policy Enforcement Point (PEP) and the VMM is sufficient for one to establish trust with a VO platform, and to be assured that its log security functions have not been subverted; this is our Trusted Computing Base (TCB).

A small number of trusted back-end driver VMs are responsible for generating all logging requests upon use of device drivers. All other VMs must communicate with one of these driver VMs to access the physical hardware. Inside these VMs, the *log transit* component collects important I/O details and submits requests to the log security manager. Applications and middleware services running in other compartments are no longer relied upon to generate trustworthy log data.

The log security manager performs a range of security functions through the following services:

- The *logging service* ensures that no adversaries can access or modify the log data dispatched from log transits. It filters out untrustworthy logging requests and verifies their integrity before storing them.
- The *reconciliation service* facilitates trustworthy reconciliation and transformation of the collected logs. It enables blind analysis of the logs by enforcing anonymisation policies.
- The *migration service* is an external service which facilitates secure communication between VMs in one or more sites by enforcing security controls required for safe log transfer.

End-user applications only have access to the externally facing *visualisation service* running inside the log analysis manager, which provides the minimal interface necessary for user applications to interactively analyse the processed log information. A compartment manager within the PEP executes a job in a per-user log access VM configured with trustworthy services. The grid services compartment isolates the middleware stack and is untrusted; it performs resource brokering and job scheduling.

6   Trustworthy Log Reconciliation

Based on the work in previous section and the requirements analysed in Section 4, we present a trustworthy reconciliation infrastructure.

6.1   The Configuration Resolver

We expand our abstract view of the VO to include a Configuration Resolver (CR) that manages metrics about the available sites in the VO and their current software configurations. To become part of the VO a site needs to first register itself with the CR by submitting the PCR representations of its TCB and log access VM image files, and a credential containing its public key for which the private-half has been sealed to both PCR values. The CR then creates a Configuration Token (CT) from this information:

$$CT = (PCR_{AIKS(N)}(TCB), PCR_{AIKS(N)}(LA), cred_{AIKS(N)}(P_K))$$

A trustworthy $PCR(TCB)$ value proves that secure logging VMs have been responsible for generating and protecting the log data; this allows a participant to have high confidence in the correctness of the logs stored in node N. Furthermore, a trustworthy $PCR(LA)$ value guarantees the security configurations of a log access VM. A value of $PCR(LA)$ is stored in a *resettable* PCR 23 because these VM image files will be remeasured and verified by the PEP at run-time before being launched.

The CR acts as a token repository in our system and offers no other complex functionality. The burden of verifying tokens is left to the participant. This is attractive from a security perspective, as the CR can remain an untrusted component. The worst that a malicious CR can do is affect the availability of the infrastructure. However, the simple CR does increase the management overhead on each node. They will all need the ability to check tokens. This involves maintaining a list of trustworthy software (a white-list), and keeping a revocation list of compromised TPMs and platforms. The security of our system depends on the proper management of this information. We suggest that a suitable compromise might be to devolve some of this functionality to local proxy-CRs, which would perform the token filtering for one specific administrative domain. This keeps control local to one site, but would decrease the effort at each individual node.

To conform to existing standards, we imagine that CR would be implemented as a WS-ServiceGroup [10]. Each node would then be a member of this CR's group, and have a ServiceEntry in its list. The membership constraints would be simple, requiring only a valid token and identity. We assume that there is a public key infrastructure available to verify their identity. As a result, the levels of indirection introduced by the TCG to prevent any loss of anonymity are unnecessary. We would suggest that the Privacy CA is not a key component of the system, and a publically-available one could be used. AIKs can be created as soon as the platform is first installed, and should very rarely need updating.

6.2   Trustworthy Log Reconciliation Infrastructure

With the resolver in place, security procedures of the reconciliation infrastructure have been carefully designed. Our healthcare example in Section 2.1 has been revisited to explain these procedures.

Creation and Distribution of a Log Access Grid Job. All end user interactions with a clinic node are made via the visualisation service. It provides the minimal interface (APIs) necessary for development of grid-enabled applications. An analysis tool should be designed to allow a user to select acceptable host configurations and user credentials, and enter the log access code/query (**1**, numbers refer to Figure 3).

A system administrator at GP, using one of these tools, requests for dynamic updates on the local access control policies. The visualisation service requests for the list of available configuration tokens (CTs) (**2**, **3**, Figure 3); the list is

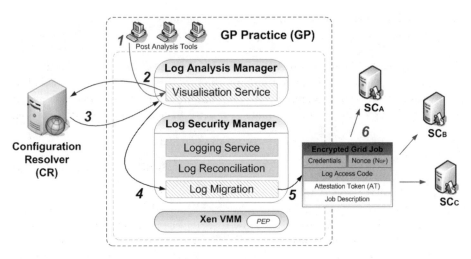

Fig. 3. Creation and Distribution of a Log Access Grid Job

forwarded to the log migration service running inside the log security manager (**4**, Figure 3). The migration service makes a list of acceptable hosts by comparing each CT against a user-specified white-list. It then creates a set of grid jobs, each of which contains the administrator's credential, log access code, job description, a nonce (N_{GP}) and an Attestation Token (AT) that can be used by any SCs to verify the security state of the system running at GP (**5**, Figure 3); AT consists of the following information:

$$AT = (PCR_{AIKS(GP)}(TCB_{GP}), cred_{AIKS(GP)}(P_K))$$

$cred_{AIK(GP)}(P_K)$ is GP's P_K credential which identifies the corresponding S_K as being sealed to $PCR(TCB_{GP})$.

For each job, the credential, the code and N_{GP} are encrypted with a $P_K(SC)$ obtained from a CT to prevent an adversary from modifying the code and to ensure that the credential is only revealed to a trustworthy SC. The use of the nonce, N_{GP}, is explained further on in this section. After encryption, these jobs are sent across the network via an untrusted grid middleware compartment which can only read the job description to identify the target SC; jobs are submitted to the PEPs of their target nodes that handle job submission (**6**, Figure 3).

Operations of a Trusted Log Access VM. In Figure 4 we take a closer look at how a job gets processed at one of the target nodes, SC_A. Any security processing required before becoming ready to be deployed in a per-user log access VM is done through the PEP: it compares $PCR_{AIKS(GP)}$ (from AT) with its set of known-good values stated in a policy to verify that the job has been created and dispatched from a correctly configured log security manager; this is how the job is authenticated at SC_A (**1**, Figure 4). Upon successful attestation, the PEP first measures the local copy of log access VM image (and a configuration

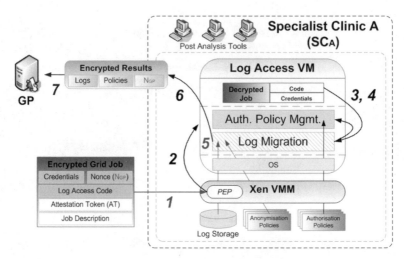

Fig. 4. Submission of a Grid Job, Creation and Operations of a Log Access VM

file), and resets PCR 23 with the new measurement, $PCR(LA_A)$; this image consists of the guest OS and the trusted middleware stack (authorisation policy management and migration services) which provides a common interface for a job to access the logs. The PEP then attempts to unseal the decryption key, $S_K(SC_A)$ (bound to $PCR(TCB_A)$ and $PCR(LA_A)$), in order to decrypt the job. Note that $S_K(SC_A)$ will only be available if SC_A is still running with trustworthy configurations *and* the VM image files have not been subverted. This is intended to guarantee that only a trusted VM has access to the decrypted credential, code and N_{GP}.

If these security checks pass, the compartment manager launches a trusted VM from the verified VM image files, and deploys the decrypted job on top of the middleware stack (**2**, Figure 4). The migration service first requests the policy management service to decide whether the administrator is authorised to view the requested logs (**3, 4**, Figure 4). If the conditions are satisfied, the code gets executed. A log anonymisation policy (*Pols*) specified by the log owner, which states what part of the requested log data should be available to the administrator at GP, is also selected (**5**, Figure 4): in this scenario *Pols* would restrict disclosure of *LungCancer* status (see T_2). Existing log anonymisation techniques such as FLAIM [19] can be used in specifying these policies, in order to sanitise the sensitive data while pertaining sufficient information for analysis.

The migration service then generates a secure message containing these results (**6**, Figure 4):

$$R = \{Logs, Pols, N_{GP}\}_{P_K(GP)}$$

GP's nonce, N_{GP}, is sufficient to verify that this message has been generated from a trusted VM and unmodified code has been executed. The entire message is encrypted with $P_K(GP)$ so that it can only be decrypted if the system

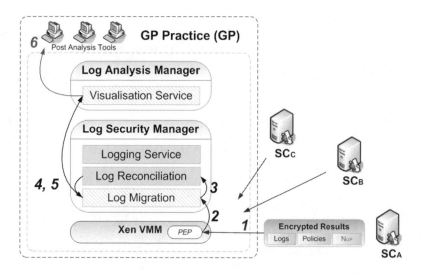

Fig. 5. Reconciliation of Collected Logs

at GP is still configured to match $PCR(TCB_{GP})$ (from AT); a compromised system will not be able to decrypt this message. An attacker will not be able to tamper with it since the private-half, $S_K(GP)$, is strongly protected inside the TPM.

Reconciliation of Collected Logs. This message arrives at the PEP of GP's system where it is decrypted using $S_K(GP)$ (**1**, Figure 5). The decrypted message is then forwarded to the migration service which compares the returned N_{GP} with the original nonce (**2**, Figure 5). A matching value verifies the correctness and the integrity of the collected $Logs$.

The internal reconciliation service reconciles the logs collected from SC_A, SC_B and SC_C and updates the access control policies according to what users have previously seen from these three specialist clinics (**3**, Figure 5). During this process $Pols$ are enforced to fully anonymise the log data. Attestation of GP's log security manager (**1**, back in Figure 4) is sufficient to establish that these anonymisation policies will be imposed correctly during reconciliation. VM isolation and its robust memory protection prevent an attacker from accessing the memory space of the log security manager to steal the raw data.

A summary of the policy updates is then generated using the anonymised data and forwarded to the original requestor, the visualisation service (**4, 5**, Figure 5). The administrator only sees this summary information on how the policies for their patient data have been updated for different users, and performs blind log analysis (**6**, Figure 5). VM Policy Attestation [6] may be used on the log analysis VM to verify that it does not permit the summary to be exported to an unauthorised device.

Table 1. Trustworthy Log Reconciliation Features

Security Goals	Trustworthy Log Reconciliation Features
Logs need to be protected from the grid middleware services	Isolation of untrusted grid middleware services; the log migration service encrypts logs using a log owner's public key for which the private-half is strongly protected inside log owner's TPM.
A log requester needs to be able to verify the integrity of the collected logs	Trustworthy log-generating sites are selected from configuration token verification; only a trusted log access VM is able to decrypt the grid job and return the logs from a remote site.
A log owner needs to be assured that their logs will be safeguarded from compromise and used unmodified at remote sites	Attestation token (part of the grid job) is used to verify the trustworthiness of a log requester's platform and its reconciliation services; the logs are encrypted using requester's public key for which the private-half is sealed to a trustworthy configuration.
Blind log analysis	Log anonymisation policies are enforced by the reconciliation service and the raw data never leaves the log security manager; an end user only sees the fully anonymised data.

6.3   Observations

Configuration Token Verification. The trustworthiness of our architecture is dependent on the ability for each participant to make the right decision about the security provided by software at other nodes. The identity of this software is reported in the PCR values contained in the CTs. We imagine that these values will then be compared to a white-list of acceptable software. However, this assumes prior knowledge of all trusted node configurations, which may not be the case if the VO is particularly large. Such a scalability issue is magnified when considering settings files, many of which will have the same semantic meaning but different measured values. It is difficult to assess how big a problem this is, but future work may look at using Property-Based Attestation [16] as a potential solution.

Node Upgrades. The most significant overhead of our system is the cost of upgrading existing nodes to support the new infrastructure. This involves installing the Xen VMM and various logging VMs. While this is a large change, the advantage of our architecture is that legacy operating systems and middleware can still be used in their own VMs. The overall administration task is therefore not so large. Furthermore, virtualization is increasing in popularity, and it seems likely that the scalability and management advantages will persuade VO participants into upgrading to a suitable system anyway.

7   Conclusions and Future Work

In this paper, we have described a trustworthy log reconciliation infrastructure to facilitate audit-based monitoring in distributed virtual organisations with strong guarantees of the log integrity and confidentiality. Table 1 summarises how our infrastructure satisfies the security requirements analysed in Section 4.

Prototype implementations of some of these features will be constructed and their inherent security and practicality will be carefully evaluated.

We intend to extend and generalise this work into a Digital Rights Management (DRM) framework in the future. Our reconciliation and migration VMs, as the root of trust, will enforce DRM policies to protected data and ensure that they are safeguarded wherever they move in a virtual organisation.

Acknowledgements

The work described is supported by a studentship from QinetiQ. Andrew Martin reviewed an early draft of this paper and provided constructive comments and suggestions. David Power and Peter Lee provided help with the healthcare grid example.

The authors would also like to thank the anonymous reviewers for their careful attention and insightful comments.

References

1. Trusted computing group backgrounder (October 2006), https://www.trustedcomputinggroup.org/about/
2. Barham, P., Dragovic, B., Fraser, K., Hand, S., Harris, T.: Xen and the art of virtualization. Technical report, University of Cambridge, Computer Laboratory (2003)
3. Byrom, R., Cordenonsi, R., Cornwall, L., Craig, M., Djaoui, A., Duncan, A., Fisher, S.: Apel: An implementation of grid accounting using r-gma. Technical report, CCLRC - Rutherford Appleton Laboratory, Queen Mary - University of London (2005)
4. Cooper, A., Martin, A.: Trusted delegation for grid computing. In: The Second Workshop on Advances in Trusted Computing (2006)
5. de Alfonso, C., Caballer, M., Carrión, J.V., Hernández, V.: Distributed general logging architecture for grid environments. In: Daydé, M., Palma, J.M.L.M., Coutinho, Á.L.G.A., Pacitti, E., Lopes, J.C. (eds.) VECPAR 2006. LNCS, vol. 4395, pp. 589–600. Springer, Heidelberg (2007)
6. England, P.: Practical techniques for operating system attestation. In: Lipp, P., Sadeghi, A.-R., Koch, K.-M. (eds.) Trust 2008. LNCS, vol. 4968, pp. 1–13. Springer, Heidelberg (2008)
7. Grawrock, D.: The Intel Safer Computing Initiative, pp. 3–31. Intel Press (2006)
8. Huh, J.H., Martin, A.: Trusted logging for grid computing. In: 3rd Asia-Pacific Trusted Infrastructure Technologies Conference, China (2008)
9. Lincoln, P., Porras, P., Shmatikov, V.: Privacy-preserving sharing and correction of security alerts. In: 13th conference on USENIX Security Symposium, p. 17 (2004)
10. Maguire, T., Snelling, D.: Web services service group 1.2 (ws-servicegroup). Technical report, OASIS Open (June 2004)

11. Ng, H.-K., Ho, Q.-T., Lee, B.-S., Lim, D., Ong, Y.-S., Cai, W.: Nanyang campus inter-organization grid monitoring system. Technical report, Grid Operation and Training Center, School of Computer Engineering - Nanyang Technological University (2005)
12. Pang, R.: A high-level programming environment for packet trace anonymization and transformation. In: ACM SIGCOMM Conference, Germany (2003)
13. Piro, R.M.: Datagrid accounting system - basic concepts and current status. Workshop on e-Infrastructures (May 2005)
14. Piro, R.M., Guarise, A., Werbrouck, A.: An economy-based accounting infrastructure for the datagrid. In: Fourth International Workshop on Grid Computing (2003)
15. Power, D.J., Politou, E.A., Slaymaker, M.A., Simpson, A.C.: Towards secure grid-enabled healthcare. Software Practice And Experience (2002)
16. Sadeghi, A.-R., Stüble, C.: Property-based attestation for computing platforms: Caring about properties, not mechanisms. In: NSPW 2004: Proceedings of the 2004 workshop on New security paradigms. ACM Press, New York (2004)
17. Simpson, A., Power, D., Slaymaker, M.: On tracker attacks in health grids. In: 2006 ACM Symposium on Applied Computing, pp. 209–216 (2006)
18. Skene, J., Skene, A., Crampton, J., Emmerich, W.: The monitorability of service-level agreements for application-service provision. In: 6th International Workshop on Software and Performance, pp. 3–14 (2007)
19. Slagell, A., Lakkaraju, K., Luo, K.: Flaim: A multi-level anonymization framework for computer and network logs. In: 20th Large Installation System Administration Conference (2006)
20. Tierney, B., Gunter, D.: Netlogger: A toolkit for distributed system performance tuning and debugging. Technical report, Lawrence Berkeley National Laboratory (December 2002)

Attacking the BitLocker Boot Process

Sven Türpe, Andreas Poller, Jan Steffan,
Jan-Peter Stotz, and Jan Trukenmüller

Fraunhofer Institute for Secure Information Technology (SIT),
Rheinstrasse 75, 64295 Darmstadt, Germany
{sven.tuerpe,andreas.poller,jan.steffan,jan-peter.stotz,
jan.trukenmueller}@sit.fraunhofer.de
http://testlab.sit.fraunhofer.de

Abstract. We discuss five attack strategies against BitLocker, which target the way BitLocker is using the TPM sealing mechanism. BitLocker is a disk encryption feature included in some versions of Microsoft Windows. It represents a state-of-the-art design, enhanced with TPM support for improved security. We show that, under certain assumptions, a dedicated attacker can circumvent the protection and break confidentiality with limited effort. Our attacks neither exploit vulnerabilities in the encryption itself nor do they directly attack the TPM. They rather exploit sequences of actions that Trusted Computing fails to prevent, demonstrating limitations of the technology.

1 Introduction

One promise of Trusted Computing is better protection of system integrity. Various applications can profit from mechanisms that protect software on a computer from being tampered with. To this end, a v1.2 TPM supports authenticated boot, keeping track of the boot process and eventually basing operations such as sealing and attestation upon the result. This is one step short of what theory suggests for best security: stopping the boot process of fixing the issue as soon as a manipulation has been detected [1,2].

This leads to the question what the implications of this difference are in practice. We explore this question for one particular software design and application: BitLocker. Included with some editions of Microsoft Windows Vista and Windows Server, BitLocker encrypts volumes on disk and uses the sealing function of a v1.2 TPM for part of its key management. We devise several scenarios for targeted attacks that break the confidentiality BitLocker is supposed to protect.

Note that there are two distinct attack strategies against which BitLocker should ideally protect. *Opportunistic* attacks use only what is easily obtained under common real-world conditions. An example is recovering data on a disk or computer that has been bought in used condition from somebody else, or stolen somewhere. A *targeted* attack is different in that the attacker attempts to get access to data on a specific, predetermined disk or machine, usually within some time and resource constraints. According to Microsoft, BitLocker is designed

L. Chen, C.J. Mitchell, and A. Martin (Eds.): Trust 2009, LNCS 5471, pp. 183–196, 2009.
© Springer-Verlag Berlin Heidelberg 2009

to withstand at least opportunistic attacks. Considering targeted attacks as we are doing here may be beyond its specification. However, disk encryption along with TPM-based key management might be expected and perceived to be more powerful than what the manufacturer is willing to promise, and we deem it useful to explore the actual security properties and limitations regardless of claims and cautionary notes.

The remainder of this paper is organized as follows. Section 2 briefly describes the design of BitLocker, focusing on its key management and how it is using the TPM. Our adversary model and security considerations are outlined in section 3. Section 4 describes attack scenarios that seem feasible and either yield secret key or data or achieve some important steps towards a successful attack. Causes and contributing factors are discussed in section 5. Section 6 outlines our practical implementation of the attack, followed by the conclusions in section 7. Related literature is referenced where appropriate but not specifically discussed.

2   An Overview of BitLocker

This section only mentions facts about BitLocker that we will use in this paper. For further details refer to the documentation available from the manufacturer [3,4] and from unofficial sources [5].

2.1   Integrity Model and Design Constraints

BitLocker works, at boot time, as a component of the boot loader and later as a driver of the operating system kernel. Its design assumes that the kernel boots from a BitLocker-protected volume, that BitLocker sufficiently protects the integrity of data on this volume, and that anything that happens after initiating the OS boot process is sufficiently controlled by other security mechanisms. We do not challenge these assumptions here; see [6,7,8] for two known attacks against the running system.

According to these assumptions, BitLocker has to protect the integrity of the boot loader and its execution environment up to the point where the kernel can be read from the locked volume. This code is read from an unencrypted part of the disk and needs to be supplied with a secret key for the AES algorithm. This is where the TPM is being used in. BitLocker uses the *sealing* function to store all or part of its key material in such a way that it becomes accessible only if the platform configuration as represented by the PCR values is in line with the reference configuration. The reference configuration is determined by the administrator accepting the current system configuration at some point in time. This adoption of a reference configuration is initially done during BitLocker activation but can be repeated at any time from the running Windows system.

2.2   Key Management and Recovery Mechanisms

Apart from special cases—BitLocker can also be operated without a TPM or with all key material being managed by the TPM—key material is divided. One part is managed by the TPM and released only if the platform is in the trusted state, the other is supplied by the user as a password and/or key file on a USB memory stick.

If the TPM works as desired, there is no way according to the design to gain access to all required key material if the platform state measured is different from the reference state. This is intended if the platform state is modified by an attack, it is not, if state is modified for a legitimate reason and the change can not be reverted easily, e.g. after BIOS update or hardware repair. BitLocker therefore offers two recovery mechanisms, the recovery password and the recovery key. Both are designed to circumvent the TPM and supply BitLocker with its secret key independent of the current platform state. The recovery mechanisms don't correct the problem, though. This is left to the administrator who, after the recovery boot, may set a new reference state from the running system.

The actual encryption key does not change during the recovery process.

2.3 User Experience

The user experience hides most of the details. When switching on their PC, users will see a text-mode prompt for their PIN and/or USB stick. If the platform is not in reference state they will next be prompted for their recovery key or password. Otherwise the boot process will resume after the PIN or USB key have been provided. Depending on how the computer is being used, users may experience a recovery prompt from time to time, e.g. after accidentally leaving a bootable CD or DVD in the drive or when a bootable USB stick is plugged into their computer.

3   Security Considerations

3.1 Security Objectives

The primary security objective is confidentiality of any data stored on the encrypted volume. Encryption alone, however, cannot guarantee confidentiality as a system security property. Its scope has—at least—two intrinsic limitations. First, disk encryption is not expected to protect cleartext data before en- or after decryption. The system must provide further security mechanisms to provide such protection. Second, encryption does not solve confidentiality problems but rather shifts them: from the data to the key(s). Encryption therefore cannot be more secure than its key management allows it to be.

A secondary objective is integrity of the data stored on disk. We consider integrity here only insofar as it is a prerequisite for protecting cleartext data and keys.

3.2 Attack Success Conditions

There are several distinct conditions that, if achieved by an attacker, would violate the primary security objective:

- The attacker obtains all or some ciphertext and breaks the encryption.
- The attacker obtains the cleartext from place or situation where cleartext is normally handled. The attacker works outside the scope of the encryption in this case and exploits a vulnerability elsewhere.
- The attacker obtains all or some ciphertext as well as sufficient key material, and decrypts the ciphertext.

An attack may achieve everything at once, or it may comprise a sequence of steps, each of which brings the attacker closer to success. We assume that steps can be arranged in arbitrary sequence. But we require that no step except the last one may spoil continuation, e.g. by preventing necessary subsequent steps or by clearly alerting the user to the ongoing attack before it is finished.

3.3   Attack Situations

When accessing the system, the attacker may encounter one of several different situations. Situations can be thought of as a set of parameters that the attacker does not control. The situation found, together with capabilities, determine what the attacker can achieve during the visit. Though not being able to control the situation, in a targeted attack the attacker can wait for the right moment. Some parameters, however, may have a very low probability of changing. An example is the configuration of a disk encryption scheme once it has been installed. Situational parameters are:

- The time and channel available for undetected interaction with the target system. This is really a continuum but we can roughly distinguish three classes of physical access: brief visits (up to few minutes), temporary control of the device (up to a few days), and permanent possession. Another channel is remote communication. We assume that the attacker must successfully install software on the target machine to gain such a channel, and the channel is available only while this software is running.
- The boot state of the target computer. The system may be powered on and fully booted, or it may be powered off. When it is running, encryption keys are present in RAM. The attacker can power it down at the risk of the change being noticed by the user. If the system is powered off, the attacker is not able to fully boot the system without the user-managed secrets. He may boot his own software, however; this is indeed one of the actions that using a TPM should protect against.
- System configuration. There is a vast amount of system configurations that an unprepared attacker may encounter. For a particular target system, however, the configuration rarely changes. If it does, and the system has a TPM and uses it, expected or deliberate changes are likely to be accepted, changing the reference configuration.

If the attacker encounters the system running and has enough time available, the attack is successful immediately: keys can be read from memory using one of the known online attack techniques, and used to decrypt disk contents.

3.4   Adversary Capabilities

With physical access to the target system the attacker can perform one or multiple actions depending on the time available, the state of the system and whether (later) detection is acceptable or not. We are thinking along the lines of [9] here but do not attempt to establish a comprehensive model. Our lists below are likely incomplete.

Brief visits During a brief visit the attacker could:

Power off or on the system, depending on its current state. Powering off implies that the original state cannot be restored if the attacker does not know the secrets requested at boot time. Although the change is noticeable, the attacker may get away with it if the change is plausible to the user. If the system is originally powered off, the attacker can revert to the original state at any time. The attacker will not be able to boot into the regular system without knowing the boot-time secrets.

Modify boot code if the system is powered off or can plausibly be left in this condition. Whether and when such a modification might be detected by the user depends on various side conditions, particularly on the use of a TPM and the actions the code performs. We can expect such code to be executed at least once.

Steal the system, turning a brief visit into permanent possession of the machine. Theft will usually be detected. The attacker may or may not be able to preserve the boot state of the machine, depending on whether it has a sufficiently charged battery or not.

Replace the machine with one that looks exactly the same. This requires some preparation and investment but seems feasible. In addition to getting hands on the target machine permanently the attacker retains the ability of interacting with the target user. The attack will be noticed as soon as the copy behaves differently than the target would, or any other distinguishing feature becomes visible and noticed.

Copy small amounts of data from the disk but not an entire volume or disk. This leaves no traces if the system is powered off, or changes its state if it was powered on. (We assume the software running on the machine cannot be exploited to this end.) Copying entire disks fails not because of any security mechanism but due to the amount of time required.

Possibly copy small amounts of RAM contents if a DMA-capable interface is available and supported, and the system is up and running.

Temporary control. If the attacker can spend more, but sill limited time with the system, additional actions become available:

Install a concealed hardware extension such as a key logger. Whether the system has to be powered down if encountered running depends on the type of extension and various details of the hardware design.

Copy the entire disk or an entire volume of data. This leaves no traces if the system is powered off, or may change its power state if it was powered on. However, given sufficient time the attacker may be able to disconnect the disk from the system without resetting the machine, connect it to another machine, copy all data, and reconnect the drive to the target machine.

Non-destructive attacks against a TPM or other hardware components such as a TPM reset attack [10,11]. Such attacks may have specific prerequisites. A reset attack against a TPM, for instance, requires that the attacker knows the proper sequence of PCR values during regular boot. One way of obtaining this sequence would be to record it during such a boot process, which requires the ability to boot the unmodified system to the point where the TPM is used.

Permanent access. An attacker in permanent possession of the target system has all the capabilities described above. The difference from temporary control is that the attacker does not have to hide anything from the user. Destructive attacks become an option.

Communication. Communication with the attacker is possible whenever the attacker manages to run his own software on the target system or controls existing software with communication capabilities. There are different modes of communication. The most common are: storing data locally where they can be picked up later; transmitting data through a network interface card to the local wired or wireless network; or using an IP network if the computer is connected to one. None of these options requires that the attacker uses the operating system installed on the target system.

4   Attack Strategies

4.1   Plausible Recovery

The attacker modifies the BitLocker code on disk, adding a backdoor. Such a backdoor could be as simple as saving a clear key in some location on disk or elsewhere in the system from where it can be retrieved later. This modification will of course be detected the next time the system is started by a legitimate user. However, the attacker hopes that the user applies one of the TPM-independent recovery mechanisms to overcome the problem. The attacker later visits the system again to collect the key. Encrypted volume data could be copied during each visit to the target system as the actual encryption key does not usually change.

Requirements This attack requires:

- that recovery mechanisms are used at all, and
- that the attacker can physically access the target machine at just the right time without taking it away permanently, and
- that the reported platform validation error seems plausible for the victim.

One obvious implementation of this attack would be to wait for a situation that plausibly changes the state of the platform, such as a repair. It may also be possible to provoke such a situation. The attacker will then have to sneak into the process somewhere before the user accepts the seemingly legitimate modification. This would mask the malicious change with the legitimate one.

Result. If the attack succeeds, the attacker has successfully planted a backdoor into the system in such a way that *all* software-based security features could be circumvented. The attack is unlikely to be noticed by the victim. In order to get both the encrypted data and the secret key the attacker will have to visit the target system at least twice. However, the backdoor may also use other channels to leak cleartext data, possible increasing the risk of detection.

4.2   Spoofed Prompt

Similar to the plausible recovery attack, the attacker modifies BitLocker on the target system and lives with the fact that the TPM will detect this modification. The attacker adds code that spoofs the user interface of BitLocker up to the point where the user has given up his secrets. The malicious code may spoof either the normal-operations UI or the prompt for a recovery key.

Requirements. This attack requires that the attacker can physically access the target system. It is not necessary that the attacker takes the system away permanently.

Result. The attack is easily detected as soon as secrets have been provided to the spoofed prompt. After detection it is generally possible to prevent the attacker from interacting with the compromised system again. Also, the TPM will refuse to unseal its part of the key material while the platform is in this modified state. If a recovery prompt is successfully spoofed and operated by the user, the attack will yield sufficient key material for decryption of a volume.

Extensions. Although it may work under some circumstances, this attack does not appear very critical. However, the next subsection describes a more critical extension.

4.3   Tamper and Revert

The tamper and revert attack extends the spoofed prompt attack. Instead of simply accepting that platform modifications can be detected, the attacker attempts to exploit tampering yet hiding it. This becomes surprisingly easy if one additional boot cycle is possible. The attacker could make a temporary modification to TPM-verified code. If we stick to the spoofed prompt example, this means to add a cleanup function to the malicious code, whose purpose it is to restore the former platform state. After a reboot—which might be initiated by the malicious code after showing a bogus error message—the platform state as measured will be compliant with the reference PCR values again.

Requirements. Requirements are similar to those of the *spoofed prompt* attack. In addition the attacker needs to get away with a boot cycle after platform integrity failure without disturbing the victim so much as to spoil further steps of the attack. Depending on how the credentials or keys obtained are transmitted to the attacker, a further visit to the system may or may not be required.

Results. This attack yields copies of keys controlled by the user. In a simple implementation these keys will end up in clear somewhere on the target system itself but more sophisticated approaches can be imagined, for instance sending the key somewhere using a built-in WLAN interface. Additional effort is required on the attacker's part to gain access to TPM-managed key material.

4.4   Replace and Relay

This is a hardware-level phishing attack. The attacker replaces the entire target machine with another computer prepared for the attack. The replacement, when turned on, produces all the messages and prompts that the original machine would have produced. Up to the point where BitLocker would start, it takes all user inputs (via keyboard or USB) and relays them to the attacker, e.g. using radio. The attacker, being in possession of the unmodified original system, uses this information to start up the stolen computer.

Requirements. This attack requires that:

- the attacker is capable of replacing the BitLocker-protected machine altogether with an identically-looking copy, and
- the machine is plausibly turned off or in suspend-to-disk mode when the legitimate user returns, and
- the replacement device is capable of relaying user input to the attacker.

The attacker will have to remain—or leave some device—in proximity to the target until the next boot is initiated by the victim. The attacker will also need some prior knowledge of non-secret facts, specifically everything that might be needed to perfectly reproduce the user experience.

Result. As a result of this attack, the attacker receives the user-controlled secrets. Depending on the mode in which BitLocker is deployed on the target system, the result is either key material or authentication credentials or both. Either one can be used in conjunction with the unmodified system to start up the operating system. Security mechanisms of the operating system remain intact; another attack will be required to actually access any encrypted data. Such attacks exist [8,7]. The attack will likely be noticed right after the victim provided credentials or keys to the spoofed machine. This attack may be combined with any attack that yields the TPM-managed portion of the key material.

Extensions and Variants. A more sophisticated version of this attack involves two-way communications, turning the replacement into a terminal of the stolen target machine. This would probably require quite some additional effort but might extend the time span between success and detection of the attack. All variants of this attack may also be attempted against recovery mechanisms, which yields sufficient key material to decrypt disk contents immediately.

4.5 Preemptive Modification

This attack is similar to the plausible recovery attack, but at a different point in time. The recovery attack targets systems on which BitLocker has already been activated. Preemptive modification attacks earlier, before BitLocker has been activated at all.

When defining the reference state for future booting, the operator has no choice other than using the current platform state. BitLocker does not provide the user with any means of verifying that this current state has or hasn't any particular property. If an attacker manages to modify critical parts of the platform before BitLocker is activated, this modification therefore goes unnoticed and will be incorporated into the trusted (but not trustworthy) platform state.

Requirements. Preemptive modification requires that the attacker gets physical access to the target system *before* BitLocker is activated. Arbitrary modifications are possible at that time that would weaken the security of the BitLocker instance affected forever. Another physical visit may be required later to retrieve a disk image for decryption or leaked cleartext. However, the system may also be modified in such a way that it leaks data at runtime. Everyone who gets physical access to the machine or OS installation media before BitLocker setup is a potential attacker.

Results. The attacker potentially gains read and write access to all data handled on the system throughout its lifetime. This attack is hard to detect unless there are additional means of verifying the integrity of executable code against external references.

5   Causes and Contributing Factors

This section identifies factors that make the overall system—a PC with BitLocker and Trusted Computing technology—vulnerable to the attacks described above. Factors include fundamental properties of the security mechanisms involved as well as features in the design and implementation of BitLocker and the Trusted Computing platform.

Authenticated boot. Theory states that secure booting requires an appropriate action if the measured state deviates from the reference. The boot process could be stopped or it may be possible to fix the issue once it had been detected [2]. So far, however, we have only authenticated boot. The TPM does not enforce a trusted platform state, it only refuses to unseal a key if the state is currently not trusted. This leaves loopholes for attacks, but also makes it easier to provide recovery mechanisms if they are desired.

No trusted path to the user. BitLocker uses secrets to authenticate the user: the PIN and key material. The channel between the legitimate user and the system in a trusted state is prone to spoofing and man-in-the-middle attacks (replace and relay; spoofed prompt; and tamper and revert). or specifically, the system lacks context-awareness and the user is unable of authenticating the system. Similar problems exist elsewhere, e.g. ATM skimming. Both directions of authentication can be discussed separately:

> *No context-awareness.* The BitLocker has no means of determining whether the computer is under control of a legitimate user or somebody else. It simply assumes that whoever provides the correct key or credential is a legitimate user. Although requesting a PIN or key may be interpreted as authentication, it is not a very strong one, and adding stronger authentication may be difficult.

> *Lack of system authentication.* While BitLocker is capable of authenticating its user at least in the weak sense described above, the user has no means of verifying authenticity and integrity of the device. Keys and passwords are to be entered into an unauthenticated computer.

History-bounded platform validation. The Trusted Computing platform detects and reports platform modifications only within the scope of the current boot cycle. BitLocker uses this feature through the sealing function of the TPM and does not add anything. The system is therefore unable to detect, and react to, any tampering in the past that has not left permanent traces in the system.

Incomplete diagnostic information. If current and reference state are out of sync, it is difficult or even impossible for the user or administrator to determine the exact cause(s). This leaves the user with a difficult choice: to use recovery mechanisms blindly, or not to use them at all. The lack of diagnostic information contributes to the plausible recovery attack. Note that detailed diagnostic information may not be required where a trusted state can be enforced, e.g. by re-installing software from trusted sources.

Lack of external reference. This is another issue that has already been discussed in the literature. BitLocker is capable only of using any current platform state as a reference for future boot cycles. There are no means of verifying that this reference state is trustworthy, opening the road to preemptive modification attacks.

Recovery mechanisms that circumvent the TPM altogether. Except for TPM reset and preemptive modification, all attacks described above do or may profit from the recovery mechanisms built into BitLocker. These mechanisms pose a particularly attractive target as they yield a key that is independent from the TPM and thus can be used more flexibly. The plausible recovery attack would not even be possible without recovery mechanisms.

Online attacks. Disk encryption does not protect from online attacks [6,7,8] and is not expected to do so. They must be considered, however, as they offer a straightforward way of finishing the attack once the attacker has obtained the target system along with sufficient secrets to complete the boot process.

Table 1. Attack scenarios and contributing factors

	Replace and relay	Plausible Recovery	Spoofed prompt	Tamper and revert	Preemptive modification
Authenticated boot			•	•	
No trusted path to user	•		•	•	
No context awareness	•				
Lack of system authentication			•	•	
History-bounded platform validation				•	
Incomplete diagnostic information		•			
Lack of external reference		•			•
Online attacks	•		•	•	
Recovery mechanisms circumventing TPM	•	•	•	•	
Unprotected disk space		•	•	•	
Confidentiality as security objective	•	•	•	•	•

Large amount of unprotected disk space. This is a secondary contributing factor to attacks involving purposeful, detectable modification of the platform (plausible recovery; spoofed prompt; tamper and revert). Large amounts of disk space are available for the attacker to install software or data in. This may be difficult to avoid, though.

Confidentiality as the security objective. The security objective of disk encryption also has an impact on attacks. In order to achieve this objective, the attacker has to obtain a small amount of protected data—the key—along with a larger amount of unprotected data—the ciphertext—or a functioning decryption device. This entails a great deal of flexibility on the attacker's part: individual steps of the attack can be executed in almost arbitrary sequence, and there is little the victim can do to restore secrecy once it has been lost. The latter is what Whitten and Tygar call the *barn door property* [12].

Table 1 shows how these causes and factors contribute to the attacks described before. Each column represents an attack, each line a cause or factor. If a factor contributes to an attack—makes it possible, makes it easier, or makes the result more useful for the attacker—the respective cell is marked with an X. The last two lines contain question marks in all cells: the authors do not fully understand the impact of these factors yet.

Fig. 1. Spoofed BitLocker PIN-entry screen

6   Proof-of-concept Implementation

We have fully implemented the *tamper and revert* attack described in section 4.3, in order to show its practical feasibility.

The attacker installs the BitLocker PIN Trojan on the victim's computer by starting it from a specially prepared USB drive which contains a stripped down Linux system. This takes less than two minutes and requires no interaction.

The BitLocker PIN Trojan consists of a boot loader installed into the MBR and a second stage that is loaded from an unencrypted NTFS partition which is part of every BitLocker installation. An installation tool is responsible for storing the second stage along with the old MBR as a normal file into a continuous area of the unencrypted NTFS partition. The LBA address of the beginning of the file is written into the MBR.

At the next boot, the MBR boot loader loads this file and transfers control to it. A fake BitLocker prompt is displayed (see figure 1); the entered PIN is stored in the NTFS partition, the original MBR is restored and the system rebooted. Later, the entered PIN can be read from the NTFS partition.

7   Conclusion

We outlined five strategies for targeted attacks against BitLocker, a TPM-supported, software-based disk encryption system. All five strategies require and exploit physical interaction of the attacker with the target computer. While Trusted Computing is expected to help protect against such attacks, our research shows this is not necessarily the case. Using a TPM for key management in a straightforward way provides only very limited protection against a dedicated attacker. None of our attack strategies targets the TPM as such. They all exploit the way it is being used by one particular implementation of disk encryption.

Designers as well as users of disk encryption solutions should be aware of these attack strategies in order to realistically assess how much security they get out of trusted computing. The most important lesson to be learned is that even with Trusted Computing a system needs additional physical protection for good security. This has been known for the *running* system [7]; our research shows that it is true as well if the attacker gains physical access only when the system is powered off. Even if direct physical attacks are excluded from consideration, Trusted Computing does not offer the same level of protection as conventional measures of physical security [13,14]

Out of the contributing factors discussed above, three seem crucial. First, Trusted Computing as of today is limited to authenticated boot. The technology cannot enforce any policy for a program, malicious or not, that does not require any support from the TPM to run. Second, to successfully attack an encryption scheme one needs to find just one way to obtain a small secret, the key. The TPM helps protect keys but only during part of their life cycle. Third, the user is forced to trust the computer with his secrets, regardless of its state. There is no way for the user to detect skillful tampering and man-in-the-middle attacks.

A proof-of-concept implementation of the tamper and revert attack shows that malicious manipulation of boot code is not only a theoretical issue.

Our work leads to several questions for further research:

- Design standards and evaluation criteria for TPM-supported disk encryption. The point of this paper is not to dismiss Trusted Computing as useless but rather to get a better idea how it should be used in particular applications to achieve the security properties desired.
- More generally, it seems that the exact role of Trusted Computing technology within applications is still unclear. Like any technology, Trusted Computing provides primitives and building blocks that need to be employed and arranged in meaningful ways. We hope that a set of patterns will emerge over time to show developers how to apply Trusted Computing properly.
- Solutions to particular problems, such as establishing trusted channels between the user and the TPM, or providing useful diagnostic and reference information for users and operators to help them in making their security decisions.
- Modeling of attacker capabilities. We have not found a practical method that would have allowed us to model and analyze in a systematic way what an attacker might do to a system. An easy way of describing a system and analyzing what could or could not be done to it would be helpful.

References

1. Mitchell, C.J. (ed.): Research workshop on future TPM functionality: Final report, http://www.softeng.ox.ac.uk/etiss/trusted/research/TPM.pdf
2. Arbaugh, W.A., Farbert, D.J., Smith, J.M.: A secure and reliable bootstrap architecture. In: Proceedings of the IEEE Symposium on Security and Privacy, pp. 65–71. IEEE Computer Society, Los Alamitos (1997)
3. Fergusson, N.: AES-CBC + Elephant diffuser: A disk encryption algorithm for windows vista. Tech. rep., Microsoft (2006)
4. Microsoft TechNet. BitLocker Drive Encryption Technical Overview (May 8, 2008), http://technet.microsoft.com/en-us/library/cc732774.aspx
5. NVlabs: NVbit: Accessing bitlocker volumes from linux. Web page (2008), http://www.nvlabs.in/node/9
6. Hendricks, J., van Doorn, L.: Secure bootstrap is not enough: Shoring up the trusted computing base. In: Proceedings of the Eleventh SIGOPS European Workshop, ACM SIGOPS. ACM Press, New York (2004)
7. Halderman, J.A., Schoen, S.D., Heninger, N., Clarkson, W., Paul, W., Calandrino, J.A., Feldman, A.J., Appelbaum, J., Felten, E.W.: Lest we remember: Cold boot attacks on encryption keys. Tech. rep., Princeton University (2008)
8. Becher, M., Dornseif, M., Klein, C.N.: Firewire: all your memory are belong to us. Slides, http://md.hudora.de/presentations/#firewire-cansecwest
9. Templeton, S.J., Levitt, K.: A requires/provides model for computer attacks. In: Proceedings of New Security Paradigms Workshop, pp. 31–38. ACM Press, New York (2000)
10. Sparks, E.R.: Security assessment of trusted platform modules. Tech. rep., Dartmouth College (2007)
11. Sparks, E.R.: TPM reset attack. Web page, http://www.cs.dartmouth.edu/~pkilab/sparks/
12. Whitten, A., Tygar, J.D.: Why Johnny can't encrypt. In: Proceedings of the 8th USENIX Security Symposium (1999)
13. Weingart, S.H.: Physical security devices for computer subsystems: A survey of attacks and defenses. In: Paar, C., Koç, Ç.K. (eds.) CHES 2000. LNCS, vol. 1965, pp. 302–317. Springer, Heidelberg (2000)
14. Weingart, S.: Physical Security Devices for Computer Subsystems: A Survey of Attacks and Defenses 2008, updated from the ches 2000 version (2008), http://www.atsec.com/downloads/pdf/phy_sec_dev.pdf
15. Drimer, S., Murdoch, S.J.: Keep your enemies close: Distance bounding against smartcard relay attacks. In: USENIX Security 2007 (2007)
16. Tygar, J.D., Yee, B.: Dyad: A system for using physically secure coprocessors. In: Tech. rep., Proceedings of the Joint Harvard-MIT Workshop on Technological Strategies for the Protection of Intellectual Property in the Network Multimedia Environment (1991)
17. Grawrock, D.: The Intel Safer Computing Initiative: Building Blocks for Trusted Computing. Intel Press (2006)
18. Hargreaves, C., Chivers, H.: Recovery of encryption keys from memory using a linear scan. In: Proceedings of Third International Conference on Availability, Reliability and Security, ARES 2008, pp. 1369–1376 (2008), doi:10.1109/ARES.2008.109

Secure VPNs for Trusted Computing Environments

Steffen Schulz and Ahmad-Reza Sadeghi

Horst-Görtz Institute and Chair for System Security, Ruhr-University Bochum
{steffen.schulz,ahmad.sadeghi}@trust.rub.de

Abstract. Virtual Private Networks are a popular mechanism for building complex network infrastructures. Such infrastructures are usually accompanied by strict administrative restrictions on all VPN endpoints to protect the perimeter of the VPN. However, enforcement of such restrictions becomes difficult if these endpoints are personal computers used for remote VPN access. Commonly employed measures like anti-virus or software agents fail to defend against unanticipated attacks. The Trusted Computing Group invested significant work into platforms that are capable of secure integrity reporting. However, trusted boot and remote attestation also require a redesign of critical software components to achieve their full potential.

In this work, we design and implement a VPN architecture for trusted platforms. We solve the conflict between security and flexibility by implementing a self-contained VPN service that resides in an isolated area, outside the operating system environment visible to the user. We develop a hardened version of the IPsec architecture and protocols by addressing known security issues and reducing the overall complexity of IPsec and IKEv2. The resulting prototype provides access control and secure channels for arbitrary local compartments and is also compatible with typical IPsec configurations. We expect our focus on security and reduced complexity to result in much more stable and thus also more trustworthy software.

1 Introduction

VPNs are a simple and cost effective way to manage and control complex networks. With increasing user mobility however, the VPN perimeter also becomes increasingly complex. Mobile systems are expected to serve as secure VPN gateways, workstations and personal devices at the same time. As a result, it becomes increasingly difficult to assure the security of such systems. Allowing them to connect to a VPN potentially undermines perimeter security and may expose the network to outside attacks. Vendors try to solve this conflict with proprietary security software and software agents, but such solutions increase complexity of the software stack while decreasing interoperability with other software solutions.

With trusted computing, the state of a system can be measured at boot time. A hardware anchor is used to vouch for the correctness of measurement reports, so that the integrity of a system can be verified by remote parties before granting any kind of access. The measurement itself however is not sufficient to trust the system. The integrity of a software configuration is only useful if the software itself can be trusted to fulfill the security requirements. This implies a resistance to attacks and misconfiguration that

L. Chen, C.J. Mitchell, and A. Martin (Eds.): Trust 2009, LNCS 5471, pp. 197–216, 2009.
© Springer-Verlag Berlin Heidelberg 2009

current commodity systems do not achieve. We follow architecture proposed in [1] to separate volatile userspace environments from components that are critical to system security and to allow strong isolation of userspaces for the different roles assumed by the user.

An architecture similar to ours is described in in [2]. However, their work does not consider integration with trusted computing technologies. and proved unsuitable for our work to build up on.

1.1   Contribution

This work adapts the IPsec security architecture for a robust and reliable VPN service for trusted platforms. In our design, critical functionality is externalized into isolated, self-contained security services in a trusted hypervisor environment. We use a central security policy from trusted storage to establish secure channels between isolated userspace environments and to connect them to other IPsec networks. As a result, our architecture enables coexistence of arbitrary userspace environments with restricted workspaces while reliably enforcing the platform owner's network access policy.

To harden our VPN security service, we investigate a simplified IPsec architecture supporting only tunnel mode with ESP[1] protection [3] and IKEv2[2] key negotiation [4]. By removing unnecessary functionality and features that allow insecure IPsec operation modes, we resolve known security issues in IPsec and significantly reduce the complexity of architecture and implementation.

We have implemented a prototype based on the L4 microkernel to verify the feasibility of our solution, to evaluate its interoperability with commodity IPsec implementations, and to measure the complexity in terms of code size. Finally, we discuss compatibility and security of our architecture and suggest feature improvements.

1.2   Applications

Our architecture has significant security-benefits for users that assume different roles during their work. The typical example for home users is online banking, where the sVPN architecture allows to setup a fully isolated userspace environment with strong administrative restrictions to secure banking sessions. Similar use-cases can be found in corporate environments, where access to critical network resources is often restricted to machines with specific software configurations. In such setups, the sVPN service resolves the conflict between flexibility and security by moving all critical functionality out of the userspace environment. Once we finish our integration with trusted storage and remote attestation, our architecture also allows to verify the state of a peer's security subsystem, enforce arbitrary security requirements on connected userspaces. Additionally, our design also delivers a very simple and usable way to deploy secure and IPsec-compatible VPNs. Since our design also focuses on minimal complexity for the critical components, environments with high security demands may also benefit from the possibility of formal code-reviews of the critical components of their VPN. Finally,

---

[1] Encapsulated Security Payload.
[2] Internet Key Exchange version 2.

our implementation also provides virtualized IPsec gateways that can be used to consolidate hardware resources in more complex VPN setups.

1.3   Outline

We present the general idea of our architecture in section 2, followed by a requirements analysis in section 3. In section 4, we investigate related VPN designs and security architectures for microkernel environments. Section 5 reviews the security of the IPsec architecture we leverage on. Based on these results, we design a secure compartmentalized VPN service in in section 6. Section 7 presents our prototype implementation and compares its code-complexity with standard implementations. In sections 8 and 9, we discusses how our modifications influence compatibility and security. We conclude with summary of results and suggestions for future work.

2   High-Level Architecture

Figure 1 shows the VPN architecture of two platforms connected through a wide area network (WAN). The right system shows a commodity IPsec implementation, while the left system shows the design proposed in this work.

In commodity systems, IPsec packet processing is typically implemented as part of the network stack in the kernel. An *IPsec boundary* enforces the IPsec security policy (BYPASS, DISCARD, PROTECT) on all traffic that passes through it, dividing the system into a "protected" and "unprotected" area. Userspace environments (compartments) in the "protected" area use the VPN service by specifying the PROTECT-target on specific

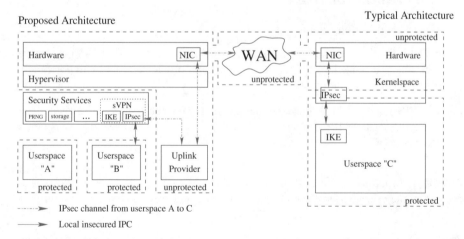

Fig. 1. Overview of the sVPN architecture interfacing with a commodity IPsec implementation through WAN/Internet. The sVPN security service processes all data passing through a local channel between "B" and the "Uplink Provider", according its IPsec policy. By applying IPsec protection to some of the data streams, local channels are logically extended into secure remote channels that reach through the unprotected area to a peer IPsec gateway.

traffic flows. The IPsec boundary then provides a secure channel through the "unprotected" area. The channel ends at a peer IPsec boundary, which decapsulates the data and forwards it to its local "protected" area. In such systems, key negotiation is typically handled by the "protected" endpoints of the channel. With only a single IPsec boundary, such systems also support only a single "protected" area that must be shared between all userspace applications.

The left-hand system in contrast provides multiple isolated userspace environments by design. Virtualization of legacy operating systems and basic operating system functionality is provided by a trusted hypervisor, which is accompanied by an environment of system and security services. Since the different userspace environments have potentially conflicting security requirements, they build separate "protected" areas in IPsec that require a dedicated logical IPsec boundary for policy enforcement. Similarly, the key negotiation component is not part of any particular userspace environment anymore but must be implemented as a neutral security service of the system. Both components are thus implemented as self-contained security services in the trusted hypervisor environment. They are configured by the platform owner and do not rely on any untrusted components to maintain their security. Once packets are processed, the "unprotected" area has the non-critical task of delivering the data to the destination IPsec gateway. Figure 1 thus only shows a single common *uplink provider* for post-processing and uplink management.

The proposed compartmentalized architecture is called *sVPN architecture* throughout this paper, our prototype implementation of it is called *sVPN service* or just *sVPN*. In includes the two mentioned security services in the hypervisor environment and some untrusted applications for pre- and post-processing.

3   Requirement Analysis

3.1   Functional Requirements

IPsec Virtualization. In contrast to typical IPsec implementations, the sVPN service has to be able to provide its VPN service for multiple "protected" areas with potentially conflicting security requirements.

/R1/ sVPN must establish bidirectional channels between local compartments and manage a separate IPsec security policy database (SPD) and security association database (SAD) for each channel.

Usability. To let users to benefit from the enhanced security of our design, it is necessary that the user interface provides high usability and prevents typical configuration errors.

/R2/ sVPN must provide a usable VPN configuration interface that is able to define and deploy secure VPNs and prevents accidental use of insecure cryptographic primitives, operation modes or authentication schemes.

/R3/ sVPN must depend on as few components as possible to implement its security. These dependencies must be specified and easy to understand.

Compatibility. Interoperability with other IPsec-based VPN solutions is strongly desired, as long as it does not conflict with the security of the VPN service.

/R4/ sVPN must be compatible with IPsec in typical VPN configuration.
/R5/ sVPN must provide basic support for the canonical key exchange protocol for IPsec VPNs (i.e., IKEv2).

Security Subsystem. We optimize our VPN service for low internal complexity to facilitate formal security analysis and to reduce the possibility of security flaws in the implementation.

/R6/ The sVPN architecture must isolate components that must be trusted to meet the security requirements.
/R7/ All critical subcomponents and the services they depend on must be of manageable internal complexity with simple communication interfaces.

3.2 Security Requirements

Adversary Model. To simulate the susceptibility of complex applications to local and remote attacks, we assume an adversary to have full access to all userspaces a legal user of the platform has access to. In contrast to legal users however, adversaries are assumed to have no physical access to the platform. An adversary is considered successful if he manages to extract secret key material from the sVPN security service or if he is able to violate the sVPN security policy, for example by creating additional channels between local compartments. In addition, when attacking only from "unprotected" compartments or networks, i.e. without implicit knowledge of transmitted data, he is also considered successful if he manages to extract data that is labeled with PROTECT in the sVPN security policy.

The attack model for the sVPN security service is stronger than that of traditional IPsec-based VPN solutions. The main difference is that local compartments which interface with sVPN are assumed to be compromised, thus providing an attacker with reliable access to data transfers and statistics about resource usage to launch side-channel attacks (e.g. timing attacks, traffic pattern analysis). We assume however that isolation provided by the hypervisor also protects against side-channel attacks based on shared resources[5,6]. Therefore, we only considers side-channel attacks in form of traffic pattern analysis.

Further, we assume that the IPsec architecture has no security flaws aside from those mentioned in section 5.1, i.e. that the core IKEv2 protocol, the ESP protocol and the IPsec architecture itself are sound. Based on these assumptions, we identify the following requirements for the sVPN architecture to remain secure in the described attack model.

Virtualization Security. sVPN has to provide a logically isolated IPsec boundary for every compartment that uses the service, thus isolating every connected userspace environment into a separate "protected" area.

/S1/ sVPN must be able to identify endpoints of a local channel and must enforce the corresponding IPsec policy for that channel.

/S2/ Communication channels between local compartments that are not directed through sVPN must be restricted by the hypervisor such that they can not be used to circumvent the security enforced by sVPN.

/S3/ Although acting as a common endpoint for multiple local channels, sVPN must not break isolation between compartments that are not allowed to establish a channel between each other.

IPsec Security. sVPN must provide a secure VPN service through secure authentication, key management and secure channels.

/S4/ The sVPN architecture must provide a secure channel for deploying IPsec policy and authentication secrets to the sVPN service.

/S5/ sVPN must never disclose any key data to untrusted components. Accessibility of key material must be minimized to the necessary sub-components of sVPN.

/S6/ sVPN must be able to directly authenticate the user of a "protected" area when required so by IPsec policy.

/S7/ The IPsec compatible remote channels provided by sVPN must be secure.

/S8/ sVPN must be able to enforce restrictions on the configuration of compartments that request a particular VPN access.

Since non-critical functionality of sVPN, including receiving and sending of data, is externalized to the connecting "protected" and "unprotected" compartments which are expected to be compromised, it is not possible to protect against DoS in the adversary model described above. If a DoS resistance similar to commodity IPsec implementations is desired, it can thus be implemented in the traffic pre-processing in untrusted compartments.

4   Related Work

Hypervisor-based operating systems environments with userspaces on multiple virtual machines have recently been reconsidered as a base for increased security. The idea to externalize security subsystems into a hypervisor environment resulted in several new architectures like sHype, Terra, EROS, Nizza and Perseus [7,8,9,10,1,11].

A conceptionally similar setup can be found in many microkernel operating systems, but their current IPsec implementations do not exploit the features of their environment for additional security. They exist only in form of adapted versions from monolithic systems or university classes [3].

With μSINA, the authors of [2] present a comparable redesign of IPsec for Nizza. In their architecture, a "network hub" is added to the operating system environment of a Fiasco/L4 microkernel. It processes traffic between two paravirtualized Linux compartments that run on top of the microkernel (L4Linux compartments), enforcing IPsec policies and traffic protection. μSINA aims for enhanced reliability and security by minimizing the attack surface of critical components. An implementation of the IPsec packet processing component is provided with the *Viaduct* security service.

---

[3] See for example www.cis.syr.edu/~wedu/seed/Labs/IPSec/, where simple IPsec processing is regularly implemented on Minix 3.

μSINA was later supplemented by a key negotiation component [12]. To manage the high complexity of the IKEv1 protocol, this component was implemented as a port of the *isakmpd* server from the OpenBSD project. Two adapter components for translation to Unix sockets and the servers native management interface PF_KEYv2 [13] where added to simplify the port.

However, the Viaduct source code is difficult to read, poorly documented and contains considerable amount of non-critical code, for example to route packets between compartments. We were also unable to test it since the development was discontinued and does not work with the current DROPS environment. From the descriptions of the IKEv1 implementation in [12], it is also obvious that μSINA suffers from the high complexity of the IKEv1 standard.

In contrast to μSINA, we do not aim for a generic IPsec implementation. As detailed in the following sections, we propose a more abstract VPN service instead that implements only a reduced set of the IPsec functionalities and exploits the potential of secure virtualization and trusted computing architecture. The resulting design solves many common security issues of VPN endpoints and maximizes the leverage on policy enforcement available through remote attestation.

5   IPsec Security

The IPsec security standard was first specified in 1995 [14]. It is a collection of Internet standards that provide access control, integrity protection and authentication, confidentiality and partial protection against packet replay.

The Internet Engineering Task Force (IETF) published the latest version of the architecture in [15], featuring mainly a simplified design and description. The associated Internet Key Exchange (IKE) protocol was subject to a major redesign and published as version 2 (IKEv2) in [4]. IPsec uses two protocols to implement its security services on a per packet basis, Authenticated Header (AH) and Encapsulated Security Payload (ESP). While the latest version of AH was published without major modifications [16], the current revision of ESP [3] was enhanced with extended Traffic Flow Confidentiality (TFC) and Combined Cipher Modes. The term *IPsec* is used throughout this work to refer to this latest revision of architecture and protocols.

The reader is referred to [17] for an introduction to IPsec or [18] for a review that focuses on cryptographic aspects. For a discussion of the IKE protocol design and alternatives see [19].

5.1   Security Issues

One of the early known security evaluation of IPsec is the comprehensive analysis in [20]. Its authors criticize the complexity of the architecture, point out several design weaknesses and also demonstrate some simple attacks. Their concerns have been confirmed when systematic design flaws where found in IPsec operation modes that use ESP without integrity protection[21,22]. In addition, concerns about information leakage due to traffic analysis led to the advanced TFC scheme introduced in [23]. This criticism from the academic community found only limited recognition in the IETF, with the result that insecure configurations are still part of the standard and thus also still in operation. Based on these works and our own review of the latest revision of the IPsec standards and implementations, we identify the following security issues in the current specifications.

/P1/ Encryption-only ESP. While previous attacks on ESP encryption without authentication or with AH-based authentication have been blamed on implementations, [22] shows that it is indeed a flaw in the standard to allow encrypted traffic to be unauthenticated or make use of other layers to authenticate the traffic.

/P2/ Traffic Flow Confidentiality. To prevent information leakage via traffic flow analysis, the authors of [23] propose a combination of payload padding, injection of dummy packets and recombination of payloads. But although the problem is acknowledged, only a small subset of the proposed traffic obfuscation mechanisms was standardized in the latest version of ESP. In addition, even these simplified TFC measures are not yet implemented in commodity operating systems like Linux and OpenBSD.

/P3/ Manual Keying. Manual keying poses a serious security threat. It provides no forward or backward secrecy and enables attacks through observation of ciphertext block collisions. IPsec however demands explicit support for manual keying for IPsec packet processing [15], even though any secure key provisioning could be adapted to use the automated keying interface. As a result, popular IPsec instruction guides[4] tend to discuss manual keying in great detail and it must be assumed that such configurations are in widespread use.

/P4/ Pre-Shared Key (PSK) Authentication. The IKEv2 specification [4] describes authentication based on pre-shared keys, a feature that is also much appreciated in IPsec configuration guides[5] and likely in broad use. As also pointed out in the specification, PSK authentication is only secure when keys with high entropy are used. However, although such an assumption does typically not hold when keys are chosen or transmitted by humans, the specification requires ("MUST") PSK support for scenarios where the initiator uses a shared key and the responder uses public-key authentication, clearly a scheme that addresses password-based user authentication. The specification also fails to mention any rate limit behavior to counter brute force attacks on short PSKs.

/P5/ Pseudo User Authentication. The IKEv2 authentication mechanisms themselves are not aware of the type of entity that provides authentication data. The two most common authentication mechanisms, public-key authentication based on X.509 certificates (PKIX) and pre-shared keys, are both often used to authenticate users. However, none of the major IKEv2 implementations currently support "direct" user authentication. Instead, the shared key or secret key is typically stored on the local disk, in files that are assumed to be accessible only to the platform administrator. Authentication secrets are thus actually used as tokens, allowing simple attacks like theft or use of the access in absence of the user.

/P6/ Complexity. The complexity of IPsec and particularly IKEv1 has often been subject to criticism, for example in [20] and [24]. Subsequent versions of the

---

[4] http://www.ipsec-howto.org/
[5] http://wiki.bsdforen.de/howto/ipsec-vpn

architecture and particularly IKE include some improvements. However, the complexity of the IPsec architecture and IKEv1 still leads to insecure deployments and
even incompatibilities in the key exchange. This complexity is not necessary however. It was noted in [20] already that transport mode is a subset of tunnel mode and
that security features provided AH can by large be replaced by a corresponding configuration and application of the ESP protocol. The IKEv2 is much more simple in
design than IKEv1, but still has considerable complexity, e.g. in the SA negotiation
payloads and the general payload design (wire format). Simpler key negotiation
schemes like SKIP [25] and JFK [19] have been proposed, but not accepted for the
standard.

/P7/ Miscellaneous Issues. Both versions of IKE employ hash-cookies, simple challenges to efficiently filter spoofed initialization requests, thus mitigating DoS attacks [26]. More advanced protection against DoS is possible by forcing initiators
to invest computation resources, but such proposals have been discarded by the
IETF due to unclear patent encumbrance[6]. Also, since timeout lengths, retransmis-
sion counts and session keep-alive behavior for UDP packet transfer in IKE is not
specified, it is trivial to fingerprint IKE servers by observing such behavior [27].

To achieve the security requirements, sVPN has to implement measures against the
mentioned problems. Section 6.6 presents measures taken to mitigate /P1/ to /P6/.
/P7/ is not covered in this work however, since any information leaked this way is not
considered sensitive. As already mentioned in 3, DoS protection is not necessarily a
task of the sVPN service and shall be discussed separately in section 6.2.

6 sVPN Design

The IPsec architecture uses secure channels essentially to bind transferred data to cryptographic identities. This mapping is used to enforce a security policy for each transferred data packet and provides the secure access control and secure channels needed in
sVPN. In this section we describes how the sVPN architecture was designed to comply
with our requirements and how the IPsec issues discussed in 5.1 are resolved.

6.1 IPsec Virtualization

As described in requirement /R1/, sVPN must be able to implement an isolated IPsec
boundary for each "protected" area. For a secure IPsec virtualization as defined in requirements /S1/ to /S3/, sVPN must also be able to identify endpoints of a requested
channel and locate the corresponding IPsec policy.

We therefore extend the IPsec policy for sVPN with fields for the source and destination identity of local channels. These identities can be arbitrary labels that are provided
to sVPN by other security services. To establish remote channels with other IPsec gateways it must be possible to unambiguously address and authenticate the destination
of a channel. In particular, a standard IPsec implementation must be able to request a

---

[6] http://www.ietf.org/mail-archive/web/ipsec/current/msg02606.html

channel to a specific compartment "protected" by sVPN. To achieve this level of inter-operability, existing methods for identification and authentication of peers must be used, which is why sVPN behaves like *multiple* VPN gateways. It uses separate IP addresses for identification on the network layer and separate cryptographic identities for unam-biguous authentication during key exchange. If multiple IPs for a single host are not available, NAT (Net Address Translation) can be used to map them to a single address. This limitation is inherent to the IPsec architecture.

6.2   Critical Components

Requirement /R6/ is achieved by aggressively delegating functionality into the un-trusted "protected" and "unprotected" endpoints of each local channel. This process is restricted by /R7/, which requires all critical functionality to reside in trusted compo-nents, i.e. in the security service in the hypervisor environment. Based on our security requirements, we identify the following functions as critical.

- The virtualized policy enforcement described in /S1/ requires that identification, classification and policy matching algorithms are implemented in trusted compo-nents.
- /S3/ requires that any component that is connected to multiple local channels that should remain isolated must be trusted.
- To meet requirement /S5/, authentication and key exchange via IKEv2 and IPsec traffic processing must be trusted. Availability of key material is reduced by divid-ing the trusted sVPN security service into two separate modules, the IKEv2 server *iked* and the *ipsec* traffic processing component. As a result, the bulk traffic pro-cessing component is isolated from any kind of long-term authentication keys or key negotiation internals.
- /S6/ and /S7/ require the complete IKEv2 key negotiation and IKE SA manage-ment to be trusted, as well as the traffic processing components for ESP encapsu-lation, TFC padding, replay-protection and lifetime management of sessions and keys.

Any remaining functionality is not critical and should be provided by other compart-ments. Examples are IP routing, packet fragmentation, hardware drivers and NAT traversal. Since the protected and unprotected compartments need to function correctly to establish a connection, DoS protection is only relevant if these are not compromised. Therefore, this feature can be delegated to untrusted components as well.

The rather generic analysis of critical subcomponents is sufficient since our choices in interfaces and components are limited by complexity limitation /R7/.

6.3   Usability

We address our usability requirements /R2/ and /R3/ by providing a more abstract VPN service instead of a universal IPsec implementation. This allows us to ignore spe-cial use cases of IPsec and make additional assumptions about the user's intentions. As a result, we can ignore the IPsec transport mode as well as AH encapsulation and enforce secure usage of ESP encapsulation. This reduces the complexity of our key negotiation and traffic processing components and facilitates the design of a usable configuration interface. We solve the deployment issue mentioned in /R2/ and /S4/ by leveraging trusted storage, a basic trusted computing service that allows secure transport and storage of information by sealing data to known-good system states. [28]

6.4   Compatibility

As described in /R4/ and /R5/, sVPN is required to provide basic interoperability with other IPsec-based VPNs. We implement this by staying compatible with certain operation modes of IPsec, namely authenticated ESP encryption in tunnel mode, and by providing a IKEv2 implementation that is sufficiently compatible with standard implementations to negotiate this particular configuration. We leverage the flexibility of the IKEv2 negotiation to activate additional non-standard features if supported by the peer. A more detailed discussion of interoperability issues follows in section 8.

6.5   Remote Users

Since VPN access for remote users is one of the main use cases of VPN technology, requirement /R4/ implies support for this scenario in sVPN. Apart from direct user authentication required by /S6/, IP configuration of the remote "protected" compartment is also desirable in this use case. For sVPN, we currently rely on higher level protocols like the Layer 2 Tunneling Protocol (L2TP, see [29]) to provide dynamic IP configuration.[7]

For direct user authentication, we aim to leverage trusted user I/O paths of the operating system to protect the user's login credentials when unsealing the IPsec authentication key from trusted storage. The actual authentication keys are always asymmetric and either imported from an existing PKI or automatically generated by the configuration frontend, which also provides secure deployment. For more complex authentication mechanisms, remote attestation of the peer's TCB will allow to delegate critical functionality to other security services which then vouch for successful authentication of the correct user.

6.6   IPsec Hardening

Section 5.1 discussed several issues in IPsec that need to be resolved to meet our requirements for sVPN. Unfortunately, the manipulation of IPsec internals is limited by our compatibility requirements /R4/ and /R5/, with the result that our IKEv2 implementation still suffers from high complexity when compared to our processing component. Nevertheless, our modifications address all identified problems except for fingerprinting and DoS, which we declared minor.

---

[7] Native IKEv2 support through IKE configuration payloads and traffic selector narrowing is still under investigation. Although simpler in design, these would also add non-critical functionality to the security service.

/M1/ ESP protection. To prevent attacks based on /P1/, sVPN enforces ESP encapsulation with encrypted authentication for all traffic that is labeled PROTECT in the security policy. Weak ciphers are not supported.

/M2/ Advanced TFC. To mitigate /P2/, ESP processing supports Traffic Flow Confidentiality (TFC) padding as specified in [4] as well as advanced TFC features described in [23]. Both are negotiated if supported by the peer or enforced by policy.

/M3/ Manual Keying and PSKs. To prevent weak keys and exploitable key management as mentioned in /P3/ and /P4/, our processing component exposes only a low-level interface for automated configuration of keys and policies. To resolve problems with weak PSKs, PSK authentication is not supported in sVPN.

/M4/ User Authentication. As described in 6.5, sVPN authenticates users either through direct user authentication or by leveraging other security services and trusted storage. We expect these mechanisms to supersede the often weak and complex authentication schemes provided by EAP or PSK and to discourage the behavior described in /P5/.

/M5/ Reduced Complexity. To mitigate the complexity issues described in /P6/, transport mode and AH protection are not supported in sVPN. It implements only the minimal set of functionalities of the IKEv2 specification, which additionally was stripped of authentication in X.509 certificate-based public key infrastructures (PKIX). Instead, sVPN currently authenticates peers based on raw RSA keys and key fingerprint whitelists. Leveraging remote attestation, sVPN may also delegate authentication to trusted remote security services.

7   Implementation

We implemented a prototype as a proof-of-concept, to identify interoperability issues and to estimate complexity of the solution. It encompasses the two critical sVPN components ipsec and iked as well as simple adapters named *tun2ipc* and *udp2ipc* for connectivity with userspace compartments.

Turaya was chosen as the operating system environment. It is open source and implements the PERSEUS security framework based on the L4/Fiasco microkernel and microkernel environment of the DROPS project [30,31]. With L4Linux, a paravirtualized version of the Linux kernel, L4/Fiasco is also able run Linux systems as guest VMs. Access control for inter-process communication (IPC) and secure identification of compartments through the compartment manager is not yet implemented in Turaya. Our prototype currently simulates this functionality through a local name registration service.

7.1   sVPN Architecture

Figure 2 provides a more detailed view of the sVPN architecture. It shows a platform with two virtualized L4Linux compartments running on top of the Fiasco hypervisor and its environment. The two critical sVPN components reside in the hypervisor environment, next to other security services like trusted storage and the *randservice* random

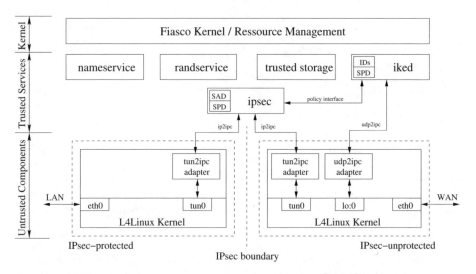

Fig. 2. Detailed architecture of sVPN. A single platform acts as a VPN gateway with two physical network interfaces. The "protected" compartment routes plaintext traffic between the LAN and sVPN. The "unprotected" compartment is responsible for routing the secured data streams into the WAN.

number generator. The two L4Linux compartments have established a local channel through the ipsec module and each also connect to a physical network interface. By configuring the sVPN security policy such that one compartment is in the "protected" and one in the "unprotected" area, the platform is transformed into a VPN gateway, processing traffic between its two interfaces.

Traffic Processing. The tun2ipc adapters establish a local point-to-point IP connection between the "protected" and "unprotected" compartments. The connection is set up by connecting to the ipsec module and requesting a forwarding to the destination compartment. The adapters then translate between the socket interface expected by the Linux userspace and the *ip2ipc* IPC interface of the sVPN service. The ipsec module accepts the local connection request only if corresponding policy entries exist in the SPD. In that case, a dedicated *filter thread* is spawned to handles the actual traffic processing for this channel. The filter thread then finalizes the local ip2ipc connection by establishing the second part to the actual destination of the channel. Once the connection is established, each thread is responsible for enforcing the locally relevant subset of the security policy. Interface and implementation are further simplified by making all ip2ipc channels unidirectional. The destination tun2ipc adapter is responsible for establishing the ip2ipc connection in the other direction, provoking another filter thread to be spawned with corresponding subset of SPD and SAD.

To identify relevant subsets of SPD and SAD, each SPD entry in sVPN also contains two labels identifying source and destination of the ip2ipc channel they apply to, and each SAD entry is linked to an SPD entry. With the relevant parts of SPD, SAD and a unidirectional channel, traffic processing is straight forward. The filter threads have to enforce one of the policy targets (DISCARD, BYPASS, PROTECT) on all traffic they

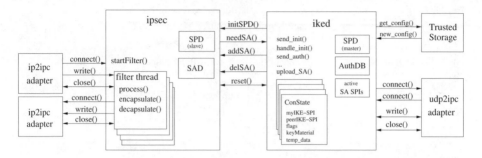

Fig. 3. Schematic overview of the iked and ipsec security modules and IPC channels. Arrows indicate the possible direction of a call, order of calls represents a possible session flow for that interface. The iked component creates a *ConState* structure for each handshake attempt and maintains a list of active SPIs.

receive, which is trivial to achieve for the first two targets. If PROTECT is specified or an encapsulated package is encountered, the packet must be de- or encapsulated with ESP. All required information for ESP processing is contained in the SAD entries available to the thread. If the required SAD entry is not available, the packet is discarded. In case of encapsulation, missing SAD entries additionally trigger a request to the iked module to establish the required SAs. In case of decapsulation, the frames are once more parsed and matched against the SPD to check if the protected environment is allowed to receive this packet. At this point, the SPD would typically specify BYPASS or DISCARD as the target, but re-encapsulation with a different SA is also possible.

Successfully processed IP frames are forwarded to the adapter of the destination compartment. An ip2ipc adapter or its environment may implement additional uncritical pre- and post-processing of received traffic, like IP (de-)fragmentation, NAT or bandwidth management. Our prototypes simply forward all IP frames between the ip2ipc channel and the L4Linux socket interface.

Key and Protocol Negotiation. The key negotiation component iked is a simplified IKEv2 implementation. On startup, it retrieves SPD and long-term authentication keys from trusted storage and establishes the local *policy* and udp2ipc connections to the ipsec and udp2ipc components. The udp2ipc adapter essentially provides a UDP socket to iked, allowing it to send and receive IKEv2 UDP traffic. As can be seen in figure 3, the possible calls for ip2ipc and udp2ipc are very similar, the main difference is that udp2ipc attaches to a UDP socket and that the incoming IPC connection comes from the same iked thread. Like the ip2ipc adapter, it may implement uncritical traffic transformations like defragmentation or even handle IKEv2 protocol features like DoS protection cookies and NAT traversal support. The policy interface between ipsec and iked is used preliminary by iked to initialize the ipsec SPD at startup and manage the ipsec SAD at runtime. The ipsec component only uses it to request a refresh for expired or not yet negotiated SAD entries. Both ends are also able to submit a reset command in case database inconsistencies are detected, e.g. when one component was manually restarted.

As IPsec key negotiation does not require high throughput, iked is implemented as a simple single-threaded application. SA negotiation requests from ipsec or remote

IKEv2 servers trigger a simple IKEv2 negotiation and that negotiates authenticated encryption with tunnel mode ESP encapsulation and the strongest available cipher suite. Features like NAT detection, DoS protection, endpoint configuration or renegotiation of SAs are not supported. If desired, these should be implement in the untrusted compartments. On success, the resulting SAs pair is uploaded to the ipsec SAD, possibly replacing previous instances for that SPD entry.

7.2 Complexity

We estimate the complexity of the prototype by counting lines of source code (LoC) with SLOCCount[8], which excludes comments from the measurements. As it is custom, our measurements do not include external libraries and cryptographic primitives. However, the two critical components do not make use of use any complex libraries and the cryptographic primitives are comparatively easy to verify. Although the Mikro-SINA project did not document how LoC were measured, their reports for the Viaduct component do not substantially deviate from our own measurement of it with SLOC-Count (3,575 LoC). Our prototype has a total code-complexity of 5,187 LoC including adapter components. The critical subcomponents iked and ipsec have a complexity of only 2,919 and 839 LoC, respectively, plus 917 LoC for common SPD and SAD management. Although our prototype still misses some important features, the difference to standard IPsec implementations is impressive. The Mikro-SINA adaption of the isakmpd IKEv1 server in [12] has an estimated 22,800 critical LoC if unnecessary components were to be removed. We counted 46,600 and 30,800 LoC for the IKEv1 and IKEv2 implementations of the strongSwan project, plus 30,000 lines of IKE specific libraries. Our ipsec module is significantly less complex than the Mikro-SINA Viaduct (839+917 vs. 3,575 LoC), since we exclude transport mode and AH encapsulation. For comparison, a sample of obviously IPsec related files in Linux 2.6.26[9] results in a similar figure of about 3,500 LoC.

7.3 Current Status

Our prototype successfully establishes ESP tunnels with a standard IPsec implementation and the strongSwan IKEv2 server. The connection was established with PSK authentication however, since raw public key authentication is not yet implemented in iked and strongSwan. The negotiated SAs for IKEv2 and ESP use AES-128, SHA-1 and the standard Diffie-Hellman groups from [4]. The current implementation still misses some necessary functionality like timeout handling and public key authentication for iked and advanced TFC for ipsec. Still, we do not expect their complexity to rise anywhere near the size of standard implementations.

8 Interoperability Issues

The IPsec modifications /M1/ to /M5/ and the untypical compartmentalized architecture potentially result in interoperability problems with standard IPsec implementations. As

---

[8] SLOCCount by David A. Wheeler: http://www.dwheeler.com/sloccount/

[9] include/net/{ip.h,ah.h,esp.h,xfrm.h,ipcomp.h} net/ipv4/{esp4.c,ah4.c,xfrm4*,ipcomp.c}.

will be seen in this section however, most modifications are simply a matter of appropriate configuration of the IPsec peer. We shall also discuss some optional features like IPComp and NAT detection that conflict with our compartmentalized design approach.

IPsec Modifications. To reduce implementation complexity and improve security, section 6.6 specified modifications to the IPsec implementation in sVPN. As described below however, most of these modifications are only a question of correct configuration so that interoperation with standard IPsec implementations is still possible.

/M1/ Authenticated Encryption and Primitives. Employed cryptographic algorithms and their combination are by design negotiated during key exchange and subject to SPD configuration. Standard IPsec implementations tend to include as many strong and required suites as possible, increasing the chance to find a common cipher suite.

/M2/ Advanced TFC Padding. Similarly to the extended TFC, support for advanced TFC padding can be negotiated during IKEv2 key exchange. It thus does not interfere with standard implementations except when enforced by sVPN policy.

/M3/ Manual Keying and PSK. Manual key provisioning and pre-shared key authentication are alternative key distribution models supported by IPsec, along with public key authentication and others. sVPN in contrast supports only public key authentication. However, any resulting interoperability problems are an intended trade off for complexity and security. If desired, it is possible to use alternative key management systems instead and directly interface with the policy IPC interface of the ipsec module.

/M4/ No direct User Authentication. Although identity types are supported in the IKEv2 protocol, the authentication mechanism is ignorant of the type of entity that is authenticated. However, direct user authentication can obviously not be enforced on IPsec implementations that do not support remote attestation or direct user authentication. The enhanced user authentication can only be beneficial to the platform that supports it, possibly decreasing the security of the overall network security.

/M5/ Transport Mode, AH, raw RSA Keys. Missing support for transport mode and the AH protocol should not result in unsolvable interoperability issues since their use is a matter of policy configuration and negotiated via IKE. The same applies for raw RSA key authentication, although this authentication mode is less commonly supported by other IKEv2 implementations.

Automated NAT Traversal. IPsec uses UDP encapsulation of ESP payloads for compatibility with NAT, adding 8 bytes of overhead per packet to traverse NAT routers [32,33]. In IKEv2, existence of NAT is automatically detected during SA negotiation and UDP encapsulation is activated. In sVPN however, udp2ipc abstracts from the UDP socket interface and currently just provides a channel ID instead of ports and addresses, relieving iked from any layer 3 protocol handling. Additionally, NAT detection is not a critical feature and should ideally be implemented in untrusted components.

From a security perspective, the best solution may be to add fake NAT detection pay-loads into the IKEv2 exchange and thus transform the automated detection into a manual configuration option controlled by the adapters. Alternatively, the udp2ipc adapters could provide network layer information to iked when establishing a new udp2ipc channel, thus enabling iked to implement NAT detection.

IP Fragmentation. As discussed in section 7 of the specification in [15], the IPsec architecture has systematic issues with fragmentation. For sVPN, the relevant places where fragmentation may be encountered are ESP encapsulation and decapsulation, where header information may be missing for correct policy matching of packets or authentication of ESP fragments may fail. Additionally, the ip2ipc channel also imposes a limitation to the size of packets that may have been defragmented to larger frames in the untrusted compartment.

Our approach is similar to the suggestions in [15]. At startup, our ipsec processing thread searches their sub-SPD for any entries that require knowledge of higher layer protocols. If such entries are not encountered, any kind of packet can be parsed according to policy. Otherwise, it will drop any fragmented packets and leave defragmentation to the sending adapter or its environment. For successful decapsulation, the security service has no choice but to rely on the sending compartment to defragment the ESP frames. Fragmented frames are dropped based on IP header information, since they will always fail to authenticate. The behavior is optimized by setting the Don't Fragment bit in the IP header of outgoing ESP frames. The Maximum Transmission Unit (MTU) of the ip2ipc IPC channel is also handled in the adapter components. They must watch the size of defragmented ESP frames or other payloads and inform the sender on the limited maximum segment size if required.

IP Compression. The IP compression standard IPComp specified in [34] compresses IP payloads, inserting itself as a logical protocol layer between the payload and the IP layer before encryption of the packet. While it should be implemented in the tun2ipc adapters, IPComp changes the information available to ipsec. The protocol type is changed to indicate a compressed payload and the transport layer information is not directly available to the ipsec module. Therefore, IPComp has to be applied between processing steps in the ipsec component and can not be delegated to untrusted components.

9   Security Considerations

In this section, we re-evaluate our design based on our security requirements in 3.2 to show that all demands are met.

/S1/ For local IPC channels, identification of the endpoints is an implementation detail that should be solved by the operating system's IPC mechanisms. We also extended the standard SPD entries by two fields to specify source and destination identity each rule applies to. Even without OS support, this already allows us to implement secure identification by providing random unique identification labels to the untrusted compartments at startup time. Requirement /S1/ is thus fulfilled.

/S2/ We fulfill this requirement since we assume that the hypervisor enforces isolation between all local compartments and channels. It follows directly that any interconnection of compartments is thus be routed through sVPN or other trusted services.

/S3/ This requirement is fulfilled by a correct implementation of the trusted service, i.e. logically isolated processing of channels in the service. We implemented this by launching a separate processing thread for each local channel. The threads do not share any writeable resources; they could even be encapsulated in separate L4 tasks so that the memory isolation is enforced by the kernel.

/S4/ This requirement is fulfilled since sVPN is designed to retrieve its IPsec policy and authentication secrets directly from trusted storage. The sealing functionality of trusted computing systems protects the configuration data using public key cryptography and local attestation of the environment that requests accesses to the data.

/S5/ As discussed in section 6.2, we implement all critical functionality, including all functionality that requires long-term authentication secrets or session keys, in the sVPN security service. Keys are only transmitted inside this module or in a local isolated channel between sVPN and trusted storage. The interfaces exposed by sVPN are equivalent to those exposed by standard IPsec implementations. Based on the security of the IKEv2 and ESP protocols, it follows that no covert channels exist to retrieve key material. Additionally, we reduced the availability of short- and long-term keys to the required subcomponents.

/S6/ As a trusted component in the security services layer, our service is able to directly connect to other trusted security services. These in turn are able to establish physical presence of a user or to enforce arbitrary authentication schemes. Although not yet implemented in our prototype, our design thus fulfills /S6/.

/S7/ We hardened our traffic processing based on our review of IPsec security issues in section 5.1. Additionally, we aim to provide optional advanced protection against traffic flow analysis (advanced TFC). Except for possibly weak authentication modes, which we addressed through direct user authentication in section 6.5, there are no relevant security issues with IKEv2. There are thus no known problems with the secure channels provided by sVPN.

10   Conclusion

We proposed an adaption of the IPsec architecture for VPNs in trusted computing environments. In accordance with the PERSEUS security concepts, we isolated critical functionality into self-contained subcomponents of minimal complexity. We solved several security issues of IPsec by reducing the framework to a simple VPN service and discussed how additional features can be integrated in a compatible fashion.

The result is a high-security VPN service that should provide a high usability. The architecture solves the conflict of interest between owner and user in the remote user use case, allowing companies to deploy machines that are highly secure regarding access to the company VPN and applications, but use flexible compartments to suite the needs of the employees. Its small code-size and modular design make sVPN an ideal target for future research on secure channels in trusted environments.

11   Further Work

As noted in section 7.3, our implementation is far from complete. We also postponed investigation of IKE mobility extensions [35] , resistance against timing-based side-channel attacks and detailed performance optimizations.

For remote attestation, the Trusted Network Group (TNG) proposes an extensive framework in [36]. However, these specifications seem to add significant overhead to sVPN. It remains an open question if similar flexibility can be achieved through other means or if this level of flexibility is even required.

References

1. Sadeghi, A.R., Stüble, C.: Bridging the Gap between TCPA/Palladium and Personal Security (2003), citeseer.ist.psu.edu/575430.html
2. Helmuth, C., Warg, A., Feske, N.: Mikro-SINA - Hands-on Experiences with the Nizza Security Architecture. In: Proceedings of the D.A.CH Security (March 2005)
3. Kent, S.: IP Encapsulating Security Payload (ESP). RFC 4303, Internet Engineering Task Force (December 2005)
4. Kaufman, C.: Internet Key Exchange (IKEv2) Protocol. RFC 4306, Internet Engineering Task Force (December 2005)
5. Kocher, P.C.: Timing attacks on implementations of diffie-hellman, rsa, dss, and other systems. In: Koblitz, N. (ed.) CRYPTO 1996. LNCS, vol. 1109, pp. 104–113. Springer, Heidelberg (1996)
6. Percival, C.: Cache missing for fun and profit. In: Proceedings of BSDCan 2005 (2005)
7. Sailer, R., Valdez, E., Jaeger, T., Perez, R., van Doorn, L., Griffin, J.L., Berger, S.: sHype: Secure Hypervisor Approach to Trusted Virtualized Systems. Research Report RC23511, IBM Research (February 2005)
8. Garfinkel, T., Pfaff, B., Chow, J., Rosenblum, M., Boneh, D.: Terra: A Virtual Machine-Based Platform for Trusted Computing. In: Proceedings of the 9th ACM Synopsium on Operating System Principles, pp. 193–206 (2003)
9. Shapiro, J., Hardy, N.: EROS: A Principle-Driven Operating System from the Ground Up. IEEE Software, 26–33 (January 2002)
10. Härtig, H., Hohmuth, M., Feske, N., Helmuth, C., Lackorzynski, A., Mehnert, F., Peter, M.: The Nizza Secure-System Architecture. In: Proceedings of IEEE CollaborateCom 2005, p. 10. IEEE Press, Los Alamitos (2005)
11. Heiser, G., Elphinstone, K., Kuz, I., Klein, G., Petters, S.M.: Towards Trustworthy Computing Systems: Taking Microkernels to the Next Level. ACM Operating Systems Review 41(4), 3–11 (2007)
12. Syckor, J.: IPSec Infrastruktur für Mikro-SINA, Diplomarbeit, Technische Universität Dresden (November 2004), os.inf.tu-dresden.de/papers_ps/syckor-diplom.pdf
13. McDonald, D., Metz, C., Phan, B.: PF_KEY Key Management API, Version 2. RFC 2367, Internet Engineering Task Force (July 1998)
14. Atkinson, R.: Security Architecture for the Internet Protocol. RFC 1825, Internet Engineering Task Force (August 1995)
15. Kent, S., Seo, K.: Security Architecture for the Internet Protocol. RFC 4301, Internet Engineering Task Force (2005)
16. Kent, S.: IP Authentication Header. RFC 4302, Internet Engineering Task Force (December 2005)

17. Doraswamy, N., Harkins, D.: IPsec: The new Security Standard for the Internet, Intranets and Virtual Private Networks, 2nd edn. Prentice Hall PTR, Englewood Cliffs (2003)
18. Paterson, K.G.: A Cryptographic Tour of the IPsec Standards, citeseer.ist.psu.edu/737404.html
19. Aiello, W., Bellovin, S.M., Blaze, M., Ioannidis, J., Reingold, O., Canetti, R., Keromytis, A.D.: Efficient, DoS-resistant, secure key exchange for internet protocols. In: CCS 2002: Proceedings of the 9th ACM conference on Computer and communications security, pp. 48–58. ACM, New York (2002)
20. Ferguson, N., Schneier, B.: A Cryptographic Evaluation of IPsec (2000), www.schneier.com/paper-ipsec.html
21. Bellovin, S.: Problem Areas for the IP Security Protocols. In: Proceedings of the Sixth Usenix Security Symposium (July 1996)
22. Degabriele, J.P., Paterson, K.G.: Attacking the IPsec Standards in Encryption-only Configurations (2007), eprint.iacr.org/2007/125
23. Kiraly, C., Bianchi, G., Formisano, F., Teofili, S., Lo Cigno, R.: Traffic masking in IPsec: architecture and implementation. In: Mobile and Wireless Communications Summit, 16th IST, pp. 1–5 (2007)
24. Simpson, W.A.: IKE/ISAKMP Considered Harmful. Usenix, login 24(6) (December 1999)
25. Aziz, A., Patterson, M.: Design and Implementation of SKIP. In: INET 1995 Hypermedia Proceedings (1995)
26. Kaufman, C., Perlman, R., Sommerfeld, B.: DoS protection for UDP-based protocols. In: CCS 2003: Proceedings of the 10th ACM conference on Computer and communications security, pp. 2–7. ACM, New York (2003)
27. Izadinia, V.D., Kourie, D., Eloff, J.: Uncovering identities: A study into VPN tunnel fingerprinting. Computers & Security 25(2), 97–105 (2006)
28. Storage Work Group. Tcg storage architecture core specification. Technical report, Trusted Computing Group (May 2007)
29. Lau, J., Townsley, M., Goyret, I.: Layer Two Tunneling Protocol - Version 3 (L2TPv3). RFC 3931, Internet Engineering Task Force (2005)
30. Alkassar, A., Stüble, C.: Die Sicherheitsplattform Turaya. In: Trusted Computing, pp. 86–96. Vieweg+Teubner (May 2008)
31. Härtig, H., Roitzsch, M.: Ten years of research on l4-based real-time systems. In: Proceedings of the Eighth Real-Time Linux Workshop (2006)
32. Aboba, B., Dixon, W.: IPsec-Network Address Translation (NAT) Compatibility Requirements. RFC 3715, Internet Engineering Task Force (2004)
33. Huttunen, A., Swander, B., Volpe, V., DiBurro, L., Stenberg, M.: UDP Encapsulation of IPsec ESP Packets. RFC 3948, Internet Engineering Task Force (2005)
34. Shacham, A., Monsour, R., Pereira, R., Thomas, M.: IP Payload Compression Protocol (IPComp). RFC 2393, Internet Engineering Task Force (December 1998)
35. Eronen, P.: IKEv2 Mobility and Multihoming Protocol (MOBIKE). RFC 4555, Internet Engineering Task Force (June 2006)
36. TNC Work Group. Architecture for interoperability. Specification, Trusted Computing Group (April 2008)

Merx: Secure and Privacy Preserving Delegated Payments

Christopher Soghoian[1] and Imad Aad[2]

[1] Berkman Center for Internet and Society, Harvard University, USA
csoghoian@gmail.com
[2] DOCOMO Euro-Labs, Germany
aad@docomolab-euro.com

Abstract. In this paper we present Merx, a secure payment system that enables a user to delegate a transaction to a third party while protecting the user's privacy from a variety of threats. We assume that the user does not trust the delegated person nor the merchant and wishes to minimize the information transmitted to the user's bank. Our system protects the user from fraud perpetrated by the delegated party or by the merchant. The scheme has a number of other applications such as delegating the withdrawal of cash from Automated Teller Machines (ATM) and allowing companies to restrict an employee's expenses during business trips. Merx is designed to be used with mobile phones and mobile computing devices, especially in situations where end-users do not have access to the Internet. We evaluate the performance of the proposed mechanism and show that it requires negligible overhead and can be gradually deployed as it is able to piggyback on existing payment-network infrastructures.

1 Introduction

A new form of mobile electronic payments is on the horizon and is already being used in a few advanced markets. This technology, based on Near Field Communications (NFC), allows people to use their mobile phones to pay for tickets, goods and services in a practical and fast way. Users simply wave their mobile phone over a pad and they're done [1]. Mobile phones with e-wallet and credit card capabilities will soon replace our wallets and the paper currency within as the means of paying for shopping, a restaurant bill or even as a way to give "virtual pocket money" to your children before they go on holiday.

While these NFC-based mobile payment systems are ideal for in-person transactions, they do not (yet) allow users to *delegate* purchases. Mobile systems are not alone in failing to address this need, as most other existing electronic payment schemes also fail to provide usable delegated payment functionality.

Traditional payment methods require that users place significant trust in those to whom they delegate tasks. Parents cannot prevent their teenage children, away on holiday, from spending food money on alcohol and other unapproved products. Servants and cooks may opt to purchase lower quality food with the week's

L. Chen, C.J. Mitchell, and A. Martin (Eds.): Trust 2009, LNCS 5471, pp. 217–239, 2009.
© Springer-Verlag Berlin Heidelberg 2009

budget and keep the money that they saved for themselves. Companies cannot be sure how their traveling employees are spending their per diem budget. Many people in remote areas of developing countries without banking services nearby must give their ATM card and Personal Identification Number (PIN) to friends or family who are themselves making the journey to the ATM several hours away [2]. While these individuals only wish to have a moderate sum withdrawn, they must trust their friends not to completely drain their account.

We present a system for securely delegating a payment or withdrawal task to a third party (e.g. the concierge, in an example setting involving a customer, a concierge, a merchant and a bank). We provide a means for restricting the items that can be purchased. Our system is privacy preserving, in that the account holder does not reveal her shopping list to the bank, yet it provides a means for the bank and merchant to communicate in order to prevent un-approved items from being purchased. Our scheme does not suffer from the problems of double spending. Furthermore, merchants do not learn the customer's name or bank account details. The scheme allows for a shopping list to be partially fulfilled by multiple merchants, without requiring that the consumer specify them ahead of time. The scheme also enables the consumer to restrict which delegated parties may retrieve the items, as well as restricting, should she wish, which merchants are permitted to sell the selected items.

Our proposed payment system provides privacy preserving transaction delegation to users with mobile phones and portable computing devices. Our scheme is not dependent on mobile Internet access or NFC capabilities. As we will show in the following sections, our system can also be used by fixed computers with or without Internet service. However, the most likely usage scenario involves a user delegating payments with her smart-phone, PDA or laptop.

When considering the problem of payment delegation in the real-life scenarios that we have described, it is easy to see that the existing payment methods, such as cash, credit cards and even some digital payment schemes, simply do not provide the needed functionality. As we show below, existing schemes that permit payment delegation are simple and prone to abuse. Later, in the related work section, we show why the Internet-based solutions lack the features required for real-world mobile commerce.

The Problems of Delegation Using Cash: The simplest of the traditional delegation methods involves giving someone cash and telling them what they can and cannot purchase. The security of this system relies completely on trust. The payer has no way of knowing if the delegated party will run off with the money or attempt to purchase inferior-quality goods and pass them off as the genuine article.

The Problems of Delegation Using Credit Cards: Many businesses give their employees corporate credit cards. This method of delegation also involves a fairly significant amount of trust. Information on the individual items purchased is not provided to the credit card company by the merchants but rather the merchant

ID only. Thus, the business has no reliable method of knowing which items an employee has purchased.

Another significant problem which credit cards introduce is that of insider theft, or a data loss incident by the merchant. For a credit card transaction to process successfully, the customer, or concierge must provide her credit card details to the merchant during the sale. A malicious merchant, a corrupt employee, or an intrusion by hackers and subsequent theft of data from the merchant's database can result in the theft of a customer's credit card information. While most credit card companies place minimal, if any liability on the customer in cases of credit card fraud, the very act of disputing invalid charges, canceling a credit card and requesting a new one can be time consuming and disruptive. Any scheme which prevents the merchant from gaining access to the customer's credit card information will avoid these problems.

The Problems of Delegation Using Reimbursement. Another delegation scheme commonly used by businesses requires that employees pay for all expenses with their own funds, collect receipts, and then submit expense reports afterwards. This system has a number of downsides. Employees often resent the loan they are essentially making to their employer. Prolonged business travel or legitimate large purchases can result in financial difficulties for employees. Employees can also forge false receipts.

The rest of the paper is organized as follows: In Sec. 2 we discuss related work in the field of electronic payment systems. In Sec. 3 we present the system model and the proposed solution. In Sec. 4 we evaluate the privacy protections provided by our solution and the processing and communication overhead. Section 5 shows example applications of our payment delegation method., and Sec. 6 concludes the paper.

2   Related Work

There has been a considerable amount of research into electronic payment systems over the past few years. [3] lists several of these payment schemes. The underlying characteristic of all of the proposed systems is obviously "security." Other desirable properties include scalability, anonymity, non-repudiation, delegability, and various others that are specific to certain applications. We can split most of the electronic payment techniques into two groups: macro and micro-payments. While macro-payments are typically used to exchange high value sums, micro-payment techniques [4,5,6,7,8,9,10,11] involve far smaller amounts of money that are typically used to pay for Internet-based services such as streaming multi-media, software downloads, VoIP etc. The major features that differentiate our scheme from existing payment systems are: delegability and the ability to function offline. Other differences are cited in the later sections, after introducing the technical details of our approach.

Anonymity is an appealing feature for numerous applications. The challenging problem with anonymity is that it typically contradicts non-repudiation, an essential property in payment systems. The iKP scheme [4], one of the first papers to tackle this issue, is also quite similar to our system. iKP (where i=1, 2, or 3) is a set of protocols where the security and complexity of the system increase with i. The protocols implement credit card based transactions between a customer, a merchant, and a bank while using the existing payment networks for gradual deployment. A requirement of the 1KP protocol is that the bank must create an asymmetric encryption key pair and publish its public key. Customers and merchants must have a copy of the bank's public key in order to engage in commerce. While the bank's communications can be authenticated through the use of public key based signatures, a customer can only authenticate herself in 1KP by using her credit card number and PIN which she then encrypts with the bank's public key. The 2KP protocol is similar, although both the merchant and bank are required to have asymmetric cryptographic keys. 3KP further requires that the customer also have a public and private encryption key pair. Unlike our system, the iKP protocols do not support delegation[1]. As a result, our goals of attempting to control which items can be purchased and a desire to keep them secret from the bank are both not possible with the iKP protocols.

Until recently, research into payment delegation was almost completely absent from the literature. The projects most relevant to our work is the research done by Patil et al. [12,13,14,15]. In [12,13] the authors propose a micro-payment system called e-coupons. Their system is secure, like most payment schemes. However, they also provide transaction delegation in such a way that users do not have to obtain an authorization from the bank before each payment. An e-coupons user wishing to delegate payments first requests a "PayWord" [8] chain from the bank, which enables them to pre-register multiple transaction delegations for a single vendor. The user must sync with each vendor before a PayWord chain can be used. The user can also delegate control of a portion of a PayWord chain to other agents. For Internet-based commerce, it is perfectly reasonable to require users to synchronize with the bank and vendor before any actual exchange of goods. However, this requirement can be a significant problem for real life scenarios in which users might not have regular Internet access. Furthermore, the e-coupons scheme requires that the delegating person know the identity of the merchants ahead of time, which is almost impossible in many situations. Finally, the e-coupons system does not allow the customer to remain anonymous with respect to the merchant.

Our delegation solution applies to the real-life scenarios discussed above without the need for any apriori customer contact with the bank or the merchants. It is secure, preserves the anonymity of the user, and can involve one or several merchants without extra preparation overhead. In fact, our solution keeps the apriori contacts between all involved parties to an absolute minimum: without contacting the bank or the merchant(s), the user passes the "token" to the concierge at the same time as the shopping list. The concierge passes the token to the merchant as she purchases at the checkout. The merchant contacts the

---

[1] More precisely, iKP assumes that the issuer and inquirer (the customer and concierge in our protocol) share some level of trust, an assumption that runs contrary to one of the central design requirements for our system.

bank only during the payment. We believe that reducing the number of apriori contacts is vital for a system to succeed in real-life scenarios.

In addition to keeping the number of contacts to a minimum, our technique preserves the privacy of the user foremost. The concierge obviously has no access to the user account number or PIN (similar to e-coupons), and the user's identity is kept hidden from the vendor, and even optionally from the concierge, unlike e-coupons. The shopping items are kept hidden from the bank, while still giving it control over what is allowed to be purchased. The e-coupons system can hide the purchased items from the bank, however, it is not possible to control what can be bought from a given vendor. For these reasons, we believe that e-coupons and the other payment schemes are not suited to real-world delegated payments.

One of the key standards for securing electronic payments is SET [11], originally developed by VISA and MasterCard. In spite of the strong industry backing, SET failed to gain market share due to a number of reasons, one of which was the logistics of client-side certificate distribution, i.e. requiring every user to have an asymmetric key pair. Merx leverages the level of trust that customers usually share with their banks, to keep the "default requirements" for the customers to a minimal level, and therefore increase the chance of rapid market penetration.

Finally, mobile-banking (commonly known as m-banking) [16] is a rapidly growing industry, that aims to bring financial services to the world's under-banked via the millions of deployed mobile phone handsets. M-banking schemes are similar to Merx, in that they function primarily using the customer's phone. However, the m-banking products already on the market do not allow for delegation of payments, controlled purchases are limited to specific products, nor do they function when the customers are in areas without cellular connectivity.

3   System Model

We will first introduce the actors who interact using Merx[2], their goals, and what they will hope to get out of the scheme. We then provide the technical description of the whole system.

3.1   The Actors

Without loss of generality, we consider an example scenario in which a *customer* delegates a *concierge* to purchase goods from a *merchant*, where the payment is processed by the customer's *bank*.

The Customer: This person would like to have a third party, the concierge, purchase one or more items for her. She wants to be sure that the concierge can only buy the items that she has specified, within the price constraints she has dictated. She also requires that the merchant does not know who she is, that the bank does not know what she bought, and that neither the concierge nor merchant should be able to learn her credit card or bank account information.

---

[2] From Latin, "merchandise, goods".

The Concierge: This person is hired by the customer to visit one or more merchants and purchase items listed on a supplied shopping list. Depending on how the list is transmitted to the concierge (possible methods include Bluetooth, Multimedia Messaging Service (MMS), email and a paper print out) and how items are delivered to the customer, it is quite possible that the concierge may never learn the customer's identity. The concierge will not learn the customer's financial details, including her bank or credit card account numbers.

The Merchant: The merchant is a business with goods or services to sell. It wants to be sure that the customer's banking information provided by the concierge is valid and that the items are authorized (by the user, then the bank) before it permits the transaction. The merchant will not learn the identity nor the financial details of the customer.

The Bank: The customer has a pre-existing relationship with the bank. This can be a more traditional bank account, a debit card, or a credit card. The bank will never learn which items the customer has purchased. It will, however, learn the maximum price specified for each item as well as a maximum value for the entire shopping list. The bank will enforce these limits by refusing to allow transactions with a total price higher than the customer specified maximum value. Working with the merchant, the bank will also ensure that only those items described in the shopping list will be approved for purchase by the customer. In other use cases, the bank can be substituted by a mobile phone operator charging its susbscribers using their monthly bills.

Unlike most of the various existing techniques cited before, we reduce the number of interactions between the different actors to an absolute minimum: Neither the customer nor the concierge need to contact the bank and/or merchant prior to the actual sale of goods. Reducing the requirements for contact between the actors is of high practical relevance since we are primarily focusing on in-person retail experiences, rather than online purchases. Furthermore, this is essential to permit the creation of tokens when the customer and concierge do not have Internet access.

3.2   Secure and Privacy-Preserving Delegation System

The customer creates a shopping list (Fig. 1(a)) and the corresponding *token* (Fig. 1(b)). She transmits them both to the concierge, who acts as the delegated party. The concierge then passes the token and the list of items to be purchased to the merchant, which validates the purchases with the bank. This process will be described in detail below.

Creating The Token: We now gradually present our solution, along with the motivation for each added component.

- *Motivation:* The customer wishes to securely communicate her account information to the bank, while keeping her account number ($Acct\#$) and PIN secret from the merchant and concierge.

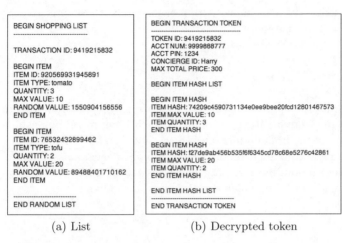

| (a) List | (b) Decrypted token | (c) Token QR code |

Fig. 1. A sample Merx shopping list, with the decrypted contents of the corresponding token and its QR code

Solution: Encrypt the token using the bank's public key and require that the user enter her PIN each time a token is created.[3]

$(\dots Acct\#, PIN \dots)_{BankPubK}$

Advantages:

- If the concierge's mobile phone is stolen, a printed copy of the token is lost or if the concierge is malicious, the customer's $Acct\#$ and PIN are not revealed.
- If the merchant accidentally loses a copy of the transaction data or suffers from a data breach, the customer's $Acct\#$ and PIN are kept safe.
- The merchant does not learn the customer's identity.
- If enough customers delegate the same concierge, it is possible to gain some level of anonymity with respect to the merchant. As the number of customers delegating any one concierge grows, the anonymity set also increases. One example of this is a grocery delivery service used by several customers.
- If customers transmit their data to the concierge via Bluetooth, MMS, fax or the Internet, it is even possible to be anonymous with regard to the concierge (using some kind of drop-box for the delivery of goods afterwards).

---

[3] To validate the PIN locally, and avoid giving the concierge a token with an invalid PIN, a hash of the PIN concatenated to a salt value $(h(PIN\|salt))$ can be encrypted and stored on the phone. This data will be encrypted with the phone's PIN, which the user will be required to enter (along with her bank PIN) each time a token is created.

– *Motivation:* Restrict the concierge to purchasing only those pre-selected items specified by the customer.
  Solution: Include the list of items in the token.

$$(\dots item_0 \dots item_i \dots)_{BankPubK}$$

– *Motivation:* Prevent the bank from learning which items are to be purchased.
  Solution: Compute a unique item identifier for each item, made by hashing the concatenation of the item number and the transaction ID. Then, create a 256-bit unique random number for each item. Finally, concatenate the item identifier and the random number, and hash this result. This will act as a privacy-preserving item hash, which can be given to the bank.

$$(\dots h(item_0 || TransactionID || r_0) \dots h(item_i || TransactionID || r_i) \dots)_{BankPubK}$$

When items are purchased by the concierge, the merchant will calculate the hash of the item and its associated random number, and send the hash to the bank to validate the purchase.
Advantages:
  • The transaction can be split into n sub-transactions[4].

– *Motivation:* Restrict the concierge role to a specific individual.
  Solution: Include the Concierge's ID in the token and/or require a transaction PIN at time of purchase.

$$(\dots ConciergeID, TransactionPIN \dots)_{BankPubK}$$

– *Motivation:* Forbid double spending.
  Solution: Include a transaction identifier in the token, e.g. a timestamp and a unique, randomly generated transaction ID:

$$(\dots TimeStamp, TransactionID \dots)_{BankPubK}$$

– *Motivation:* Set a maximum total price for all transactions authorized by a token.
  Solution: Include a maximum total price field in the token, which the bank will verify before permitting a transaction.

$$(\dots TransTotal \dots)_{BankPubK}$$

– *Motivation:* Include open options in the token to enable future features, e.g. disallow specific merchants.

---

[4] From a brute-force attack computation point of view, $h(item || TransactionID || r)$ is equivalent to $h(item || r^*)$ where r^* is orders of magnitude larger than r. $h(item || TransactionID || r)$ is used instead to save storage space.

$(\ldots options \ldots)_{BankPubK}$

- *Motivation:* Protect the transaction token from tampering by malicious persons.
  Solution: Use a Keyed-Hash Message Authentication Code (HMAC) to make the token tamper evident. This is done by including a 256-bit randomly generated key, $MacKey$ in the token, which is used to compute the HMAC of the encrypted token. Both the HMAC and encrypted token will be given to the concierge, merchant and bank.
  $(\ldots MacKey \ldots)_{BankPubK}$

The resulting token format therefore is:

$TransToken = Acct\#, PIN, h(item_0||TransactionID||r_0) \ldots$
$h(item_i||TransactionID||r_i), TransTotal, ConciergeID, TimeStamp, \ldots$
$TransactionID, MacKey, options)_{BankPubK}$

With an associated Transaction HMAC calculated by[5]:

$Trans_H MAC = HMAC_{MacKey}(TransToken)$

A sample Merx shopping list with the corresponding token and its QR code are shown in Fig. 1. The customer transmits the token, its HMAC, along with the list of items $item_0 \ldots item_i$ and the associated random numbers $r_0 \ldots r_i$ (in clear text) to the concierge by one of many mediums including using MMS, Bluetooth, Infrared, Display on Mobile, or a paper print-out.

From Concierge to Merchant: Once at the place of business, the concierge transmits the token (using MMS, Bluetooth, infrared, reader/camera/OCR) and the list of *only* those items that will be purchased to the merchant. Giving the merchant the complete shopping list $(item_0 \ldots item_i)$ with each item's random number $(r_0 \ldots r_i)$ will enable a malicious merchant to submit charges to the bank for authorized but not as yet purchased items. In order to ensure that the concierge maintains control over the items for which the merchant can request payment, the concierge gives the merchant using any of the communication methods mentioned above:

- the token,
- $item_i$ of each item purchased from this merchant,
- r_i of each item purchased from this merchant,
- ConciergeID or transaction PIN, if specified by the customer at time of token creation,

---

[5] Computing an HMAC of the encrypted token, a.k.a. Encrypt-then-MAC, is the most robust among the 3 choices [17,18]: Encrypt-and-MAC, MAC-then-encrypt, and Encrypt-then-MAC.

From Merchant to Bank: The merchant computes the hash of each of the actually purchased items $h(item_0||TransID||r_0)\ldots h(item_i||TransID||r_i)$ and passes them along with the encrypted transaction token to the bank.

The bank decrypts the token using its private key and then:

- checks the token integrity using the HMAC
- validates the customer's account number and PIN, ensuring that sufficient funds are available in her account,
- looks up the token's transaction ID in a database of previously redeemed tokens. It then verifies that none of the items to be purchased have already been bought using that token,
- compares the concierge ID or transaction PIN transmitted by the merchant to the one contained in the encrypted token,
- compares the actually purchased items as computed by the merchant $h(h(item_0||TransID)||r_0)\ldots h(h(item_i||TransID)||r_i)$ to those in the encrypted token,
- checks the additional options in the token,

then approves or rejects the transaction accordingly.

3.3   Specification language

So far we have assumed that the user can convey her shopping or restriction needs in an intuitive way to the bank. When it gets to the implementation, a *specification language* must be designed [19], similar to the ones used in supermarkets nowadays: groups (e.g. drinks), sub-groups (e.g. alcohol), sub-sub-groups, ..., down to the individual items (e.g. beer). This grouping should be further combined with "black list", "white list" that permit the user to specify which groups/items are allowed, and which are not. Using such a specification language, a company can give its employees, going on a business trip, some tokens for buying given items (e.g. food, drink), while restricting others (e.g. strong alcohols). Though essential to the deployment of Merx for large scale automatic usage, and since it is orthogonal to the security and privacy aspects, we keep this specification language out of scope of this paper.

3.4   A Revocation Protocol

The customer can contact the bank using any secure method (online, phone, in person) to revoke a given token. The customer will need to provide the unique transaction token ID or the entire token, as well as confirming her account number and PIN to prove that she created the token. The requirement to transmit her PIN to the bank can be eliminated through the use of a zero knowledge based key exchange protocol [20,21], but this is beyond the scope of our paper.

Should the customer wish to permit concierges to revoke tokens, such as in cases where the concierge loses a token that has not been locked with a transaction PIN, the customer would need to include a unique and random revocation number within the options field of the transaction token at time of token creation. This number would then be communicated to the concierge along with the encrypted token and shopping list, as well as instructions on how to contact the bank in case of loss.

4   System Performance

In this section we evaluate our scheme and its ability to withstand a number of different attackers with a variety of capabilities. We also evaluate the system's communication and processing overhead.

4.1   Adversarial Model

We consider a multi-role adversarial model that takes into consideration what the adversary is assumed to be able to do during an attack against the system.

1. A malicious concierge is able to save and later access transaction tokens and shopping lists. She can attempt to modify and reproduce the saved tokens and lists at a later date as well as attempt to use them with non-colluding merchants. In cases where the user discloses her identity to the concierge, that concierge may disclose the user's identity to others.
2. A malicious merchant is able to save and later view transaction tokens, shopping lists, concierge IDs and any other data given to it during previous transactions. It may later attempt to redeem them with a non-colluding bank.
3. A malicious bank is able to save and later view transaction tokens and any data given to it by merchants.
4. A malicious customer, willing to fraudulently repudiate his shopping bills.
5. A colluding concierge and merchant is the combination of adversaries (1) and (2). The concierge works with the merchant to try and defraud the customer or to evade the restraints imposed by the shopping list.
6. A colluding merchant and bank is the combination of adversaries (2) and (3). The merchant and bank work together to try to reveal the identity and full shopping list of the customer.
7. A colluding concierge and bank is the combination of adversaries (1) and (3). The concierge and bank work together to reveal the identity and full shopping list of the customer.

4.2   Security and Privacy Analysis

We now explore the options available to each adversary, and describe which sensitive information they know and can potentially reveal to those with whom they collude. This can also be seen visually in Figure 2.

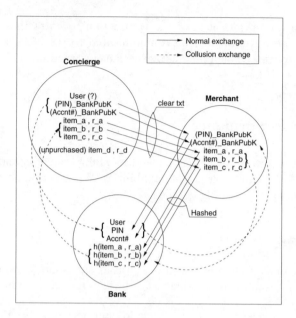

Fig. 2. A representation of the information that each potentially malicious party knows and what they can provide to those other entities with whom they collude. One can easily see the advantage over existing payment systems, for instance the one-time-use credit cards: using Merx the merchant does not know who the customer is.

A Malicious Concierge: This attacker has very few options. Any attempts at modifying, forging or replaying transaction tokens will be detected by the bank and rejected. If the customer sends the token to the concierge via an electronic medium, the concierge may never never learn the customer's identity. Furthermore, the concierge never learns the customer's account number and PIN, and thus, it is impossible to later create fraudulent tokens.

The size of the customer's anonymity set [22] increases as the number of other customers employing a single concierge (or a delivery service) increases. Customers who purchase uncommon items will reveal some information, enabling the linking of multiple transactions even though the customer's true identity remains unknown.

A Malicious Merchant: This adversarial scenario includes both corrupt merchants and situations involving an insider attack, where an employee of the merchant misuses or steals customer records. As the merchant never learns the customer's name or account information, any system breach or data loss incident involving the merchant's computer systems will not result in the release of identifiable customer data or billing information. The only link to the customer that the merchant has is the identity of the concierge. This link can be further weakened if the customer communicates with the concierge electronically.

A Malicious Bank: The bank is prohibited from learning the individual items that a customer purchases at each merchant. The bank is only able to learn how many total items are on a shopping list, how many items from the list have been purchased at each merchant, and the total transaction cost charged by each merchant.

Customers have their anonymity reduced when large shopping lists are broken up into smaller transactions. In situations where consumers wish to permit the purchase of a number of fixed and uniquely priced items from multiple merchants, it may be possible for the bank to learn which items the customer listed in their shopping list.

For example, this attack is possible when a concierge buys a single item from each of several merchants. While the bank does not know which items have been purchased, it does know how much each item costs, due to the the fact that each transaction was for a single item. Bank employees can later visit the merchant's store and attempt to find all items sold by the merchant for any particular price. This item identification risk can be mitigated through the purchase of variable price/quantity items (such as bulk weight food items), items from merchants that charge the same price for a large variety of different goods, or by requiring per-merchant transactions to consist of at least two or more items.

Repudiation Issues: Relying on shared PINs that are known to both the customer and the bank for authentication can lead to repudiation issues: the customer may try to dispute a given shopping bill by accusing the bank of forging it. This same problem exists under the existing banking system, and with the finger pointing that has occurred with "phantom withdrawals." That particular problem has been mostly solved through legal liability. In many countries, the burden is on the bank to prove that the charge was valid, not for the customer to prove that it was fraudulent [23].

Our scheme provides customers and banks with the same level of trust that they currently have using existing banking technologies (ATM, credit card charges without a signature, etc.). To avoid many repudiation issues, just as with 3KP [4], the bank could require that specific customers (e.g. who usually perform highly valuable transactions) sign transaction tokens with their private keys. This of course introduces the overhead of issueuing public/private key pairs for those customers. By assuming a level of mutual trust between the bank and the customer equal to the relationship that already exists with "traditional" bank accounts, we are able to keep the default authentication of Merx as PIN-based, and introduce key pairs for a fraction of customers, should they or the market demand it.

In addition to the repudiation issues between a customer and a bank, there is also the possibility of a dispute between the customer and merchant. In the case that a merchant sells a concierge a defective or poor quality item, the customer would not discover the problem until the concierge delivered the goods. This situation is in no way unique to our scheme, and is a major problem for cash-based transactions. This problem is beyond the scope of our scheme, as we focus on giving customers at least the same level of protection that they have with cash-based transactions.

A Colluding Concierge and Merchant: The bank does not learn the price charged for each item and instead relies on the merchant to enforce the maximum price specified for each item in the shopping list. Thus, in this collusion scenario, the merchant can also overcharge for individual items. This risk can be mitigated by requiring that merchants transmit the price of each item to the bank, but this will result in a loss of purchase privacy for the customer.

It is not possible to protect the privacy of the customer's shopping list from the bank, without at the same time enabling a colluding merchant and concierge to bypass the shopping list restrictions. This more advanced adversary is able to neutralize the enforcement of shopping lists. For example, the customer can list apples on her shopping list, yet the concierge can instead purchase oranges. The colluding merchant will provide the concierge with oranges but send the bank a transaction with the (hashed) apple item in the shopping list. The maximum total price specified in the transaction token will at least protect the customer from more egregious abuses.

A Colluding Merchant and Bank: This advanced adversary is able to neutralize the privacy protection associated with shopping lists. The merchant can reveal the complete shopping list to the bank, and thus permit the bank to create a full record of every item purchased by the customer at that merchant.

The bank is also able to share the customer's information with the merchant, and thus strip the customer of her anonymity. In such a situation, the merchant will know who the customer is, and the bank will know every item that the customer purchases from the colluding merchant.

A Colluding Concierge and Bank: This is a more extreme case of the previous adversary. Whereas a colluding merchant and bank are only able to violate the customer's privacy for that specific merchant, a colluding concierge and bank are able to do so for all transactions. Thus, the bank is able to create a complete list of every item purchased through the concierge by the customer.

If the customer has attempted to hide her identity from the concierge by transmitting the transaction tokens electronically, this collusion will strip the customer of her privacy. The bank can reveal the customer's identity to the concierge, while the concierge can reveal the complete list of purchased items to the bank.

A Law Enforcement Investigation: In situations where government agents or law enforcement officers are able to compel multiple actors to disclose transaction information, the customer's anonymity and transaction privacy are lost. For purposes of privacy analysis, a search warrant executed on the bank and a merchant is the same as the collusion scenario outlined above in section 4.2. Our system is not designed to protect the customer's purchase privacy against government investigations. Customers wishing that level of protection may want to stick with cash.

As we can see, Merx provides high levels of security and privacy against individual actors. The collusion between non-trusted parties leads to minor "controllable" effects. The only severe damages result from collusions involving the bank. However, such collusions are the least likely to occur in everyday life.

4.3   Communication and Processing Overhead

In this section we evaluate the additional costs, processing, and communication overhead our system requires from all parties. The main observation is that the delegation mechanism we propose, in its most basic form, requires no additional hardware. It is a simple software solution using off-the-shelf components that piggyback on the existing payment-network infrastructure.

For the numerical evaluation, we assume the customer uses a low-capacity mobile device (200MHz processor, 64MB RAM), whereas the merchant and the bank use an average speed server or desktop PC (Intel P4 2.8Ghz, 500MB RAM). We chose the SHA256 algorithm for all hashes, which we compute using the free OpenSSL library. GnuPG, an open-source implementation of Pretty Good Privacy was used for all encryption. We selected GnuPG's default algorithms of El Gamal with 2048 bit keys (public key encryption) and AES (symmetric encryption) as these provide sufficient security while being quick to compute on a mobile platform. While we have chosen these particular algorithms, the scheme is flexible, and alternative encryption/hashing technologies could easily be substituted.

The processing time results shown in Fig. 3 are averaged over 10 runs for each number of items. The confidence intervals are very small, therefore omitted from the figure.

The Customer: To use such a system, the customer must have access to either a mobile telephone or a computer. These devices do not necessarily need to be owned by the customer. In many cases, she merely needs to have temporary access to them. If the customer owns the device, the she can store her account number in it. If she is borrowing the device from someone else, she will need to find a way to input her account number. This can be done manually (e.g. by entering a 16+ digit number), or perhaps by reading a QR code printed onto the back of her bank card with a camera phone.

Figure 3 shows the processing time required to create a token, for a given number of items in the shopping list. We can observe that in spite of the low-processing power of the customer's device, the processing delay is still acceptable even for an exaggerated number of items. For low number of items, the processing delay remain below 10 s.

The total size of an encrypted transaction token for 10 items is approximately 1.6 KBytes, with an additional 1 KByte required for the shopping list. For a transaction involving 50 items, the token grows to nearly 3 KBytes while the

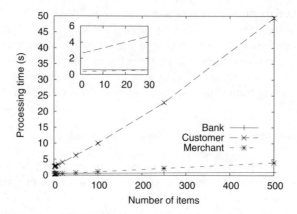

Fig. 3. Processing time for the customer, merchant and bank, with respect to the number of purchased items

shopping list grows to 4.5 KBytes, as the shopping lists are currently transmitted in plain text and are not compressed.

Depending on the level of personal interaction that the customer wishes to have with the concierge, the method of transmission and technical requirements will differ. A transaction token can be electronically transmitted using email, instant message, Bluetooth, IR, or MMS. The token, and its HMAC, can also be printed on to paper by representing them as a QR codes which can then be hand-delivered or faxed to the concierge.

With Bluetooth 2.0 transmission rates of 2.1 Mbit/s, it is clear that a user should be able transmit the token, its HMAC, and the shopping list to the concierge in under a second (plus the time required to setup and teardown the Bluetooth connection). If the user is not near to the concierge, the user can use MMS on her phone to transmit the token and shopping list. 3G cellular networks typically offer speeds of 144Kbit/s in a high-velocity moving environment, 384 Kbit/s in a low-velocity moving environment, and 2 Mbit/s in a stationary environment. Again, it takes less than a second for the token, its HMAC, and the shopping list to be transmitted.

The Concierge: If the token has been electronically transmitted to the concierge, she will either need to bring it to the merchant in electronic form, using a mobile phone or any other mobile computing device, or print it out onto paper. The technical requirements for the concierge's device will depend on the receiving equipment that the merchant has. There are no processing tasks to be performed by the concierge, as she merely relays the token and shopping list given to her by the customer. It is therefore possible for the concierge to simply receive paper printouts of the token and shopping list, which she can then hand-deliver to the merchant when she purchases items.

The Merchant: The merchant must have a means of reading in the transaction tokens. At the most basic and inter-operable level, the merchant will need to have the ability to read QR codes. To accept electronic tokens, the merchant will also need to support either MMS, Bluetooth or IR. All of these tasks can be accomplished with a camera-enabled smart phone. Complex integration with the merchant's existing computerized point-of-sale system will of course require additional hardware. The merchant will also need a way to transmit the encrypted transaction tokens, the HMACs, and hashes of the purchased items to the bank in order to validate the transaction. However, most merchants already have an electronic transmission system that enables them to process ATM and credit card transactions. The transaction token system can easily piggyback on the existing financial transaction transfer infrastructure, although the engineering task of this integration is beyond the scope of our work [24]. On the other hand, point-of-sales that already support mobile-phone payments, e.g. [25] widely deployed in Japan, would require simple software updates.

Smaller merchants may use a basic credit card machine with a 56Kbps modem, while the larger firms may use a sophisticated point of sale system connected to an ISDN line or even use a VPN over a broadband Internet connection. Even for these smaller merchants, the transmission time required to send a 1.6 KBytes transaction token for 10 items and a 1 KByte transaction request (listing the price of each item, as well as the hash of each item and associated random number) remains under 1 s. For the larger merchants with an even faster connection to a payment processor, the transmission time for the transaction token is negligible.

For a merchant to be able to process a Merx transaction, it must calculate a SHA256 hash for each $item_i, r_i$ pair before sending the list of hashes and the transaction token to the bank. Thus, in addition to transmission time analyzed above previously, we must also consider the time required to compute the item hashes. On the merchant's machine, a SHA256 hash takes approximately 10 ms. Therefore, even with 100 item hashes to calculate, the merchant will only introduce a 1 second delay to the retail checkout process.

Figure 3 shows that the time required for the merchant's server to process a token is approximately 4 s for 500 items. For a lower and more common number of items, the processing time is below 1 s.

The Bank: The bank already communicates with merchants during transactions over the existing financial network, so that credit card numbers can be verified. Merx additionally requires that the bank decrypts the transaction token, verify the contents and then transmit a message back to the merchant. In order to stop double spending and allow transactions to be broken up into multiple sub-transactions serviced by different merchants, the bank must keep track of and remember the contents of a transaction token for a significant time in the future.

Let us assume that the bank stores 100 Bytes of information per item purchased (which includes the item hash, the price paid, the customer's account number, and a time stamp), as well as an additional 100 Bytes for every transaction token that has been used at least once. Thus, the storage overhead for a transaction token with 100 purchased items is approximately 11 KByte. Assuming storage costs of $250 per GByte for a Fiber Channel RAID system ($7 per month for three years), the storage costs for a transaction token and 100 items is approximately 1/4 of a penny.

Figure 3 shows that the processing time for the bank increases very slowly with the number of items in the shopping list, however it remains less than 500 ms even for a transaction token with 500 items. Comparing the cumulative delays ($\approx 4s$ for transmission + processing) of the concierge, bank, and merchant, to the typical values of queuing delays at cash desks in [26], shows that the additional overhead introduced by Merx remains negligible.

Insider theft is a major threat to the financial service industry [27]. While customers can buy shredders, monitor their credit reports and take other pro-active steps to protect themselves against identity theft, there is little that they can do to stop a corrupt merchants (or their employees) from saving a copy of the customer's credit card information. Due to pro-consumer legislation, the banks are often responsible for this fraud. As a result, the banks often bear the financial consequences of merchant insider theft. In our scheme, the credit card or account details are stored in an encrypted token. As the merchant has no way of reading this information, there is no way for a corrupt employee to write down the user's account number for later use. By switching to Merx, banks should be able to significantly reduce their exposure to merchant insider theft.

5   Example Applications

Merx, as described in the previous sections, has various use cases such as:

- Delegated concierge service
- Corporate environments, where the employer delegates payments to her employees during business trips. Merx gives the company more control over the payments, while offering more flexibility to the employee. Moreover, the employer has the option of keeping her identity hidden to the merchant.
- Family situations where parents typically give money to their children (e.g. going on vacation), taking the risk of having it stolen, or simply used by the children for unwanted purchases

In addition to the above scenarios, Merx can be slightly modified to support other appealing applications such as ATM withdrawal delegation, or self-delegated travelers cheques.

5.1   ATM Withdrawal Delegation

PIN and password sharing is common amongst married couples and even some trusted friends [2]. Unfortunately, banking policies do not reflect the reality of the real world trust relationships. Often, financial rules stipulate that the banks will only be held responsible for fraud in cases where the customer has not shared their login information with anyone else. Thus, when users share their account authentication information with spouses or trusted friends, they lose any form of legal liability protection in cases of fraud, even when the fraud is later committed by complete strangers [2].

People in remote areas of the world often live and work very far from the nearest bank or ATM. Out of necessity, people must rely on their friends, family members or even neighbors for access to banking facilities. Typically, one person will travel to the nearest large town and take care of everyone else's business for them. This person will carry a large number of ATM cards, each with an accompanying PIN written down on a piece of paper [2].

This system requires a huge amount of trust, in that the trusted person could choose to draw down everyone else's accounts, and then leave the country. Users are not able to convey their intent (e.g. "Please allow Tom to withdraw 40 dollars from my account"), and instead must give complete control over their bank account to that trusted person.

While mobile-phone based e-banking would also provide a solution to this problem (in that customers could transfer money online to the account of the concierge, who would then withdraw it), this would require that each customer have access to online banking facilities. This is often not a practical requirement in remote parts of the world, and so our scheme is designed to work without access to the Internet. Users can be offline when they create transaction tokens.

We propose two adaptations of Merx to this problem. Both schemes require that the user wishing to delegate withdrawal have access to a mobile phone or computer. The first requires that the user have access to a printer or a Bluetooth enabled mobile phone and that the bank deploy a Bluetooth compatible ATM machine. The second solution does not require Bluetooth mobile support, can be used with a pen and paper and only requires that the bank deploy a software upgrade to enable the ATM machine to support long PINs.

The first solution works as follows:

Alice, who is staying at home, has asked her friend Bob to go to the ATM in the nearest large town, which is 8 hours away by bus. Using her mobile phone, Alice thus creates a transaction token, and its HMAC:

$$TransactionToken = (Acct\#, PIN, TimeStamp, Amount, ConciergeID,$$
$$TransactionPIN, MacKey, n)_{BankPubK}$$

Where n is a random nonce added to protect against dictionary attacks targeting the user's PIN. This token is then either transmitted to Bob's mobile phone via a Bluetooth connection or Alice prints the token in a computer-readable form, such as using QR codes.

If Bob tries to modify the transaction token in any way, it will be rejected by the bank. As he does not have Alice's PIN, he cannot create a valid token. Thus, the security of this scheme depends on Alice maintaining the privacy of her PIN, which is an existing requirement for the security of her bank account.

Furthermore, if Bob tries to reuse the same token twice, the bank will reject it. This of course requires that the bank must maintain a list of all redeemed tokens.

The second solution works as follows:

If Bob does not have a mobile phone, or the bank's ATM machine does not support Bluetooth, it is not possible to use the previously described scheme. We must then fall-back to a more limited protocol, which uses the existing infrastructure.

This scheme still requires that Alice have access a mobile phone or a computing device, but it does not need to support Bluetooth. Alice must, at some previous time, have established a long shared key ($LongPIN$) with the bank. This key must be suitably large, such that it is resistant to a dictionary attack.

If Alice is willing to type in her authentication details each time, it is possible for her to use someone else's phone to generate the token. This puts her at risk of PIN theft through keyboard sniffing and other attacks, and so it would be far safer for her to use her own device. However, in cases where users are willing to risk these additional threats, it is possible for a large group of people to share a single mobile phone to generate their delegated ATM withdrawal tokens.

Using her mobile phone, Alice then creates the transaction token:

$$TransactionToken = h(Acct\#||LongPIN||Timestamp||$$
$$Amount||BobID, TransactionPIN)$$

Alice can then write this hash down on a piece of paper, along with her account number, the timestamp, the transaction PIN and the amount to be withdrawn. We use SHA256 as our hash, which can be written as a 64 character string. This is short enough that it is reasonable to expect someone to type it into an ATM by hand.

5.2   Self-delegated Travelers Cheques

The delegated concierge scheme described before can be modified slightly to provide traveler cheque functionality. A user can either assign the ConciergeID to be her own ID, or to protect against cases where she loses her wallet and all other forms of identification, a password or one time PIN can be substituted for the ConciergeID field.

The transaction token can also specify loose requirements for the kinds of items or services that can be purchased. Examples of this can include a travelers cheque limited to one train ticket priced less than 100 dollars, a night in a 4 star or below hotel or a meal in a restaurant that cost less than 30 dollars.[6]

Such travelers cheques could be photocopied, allowing an individual to keep multiple copies on her person, should she be robbed or lose her wallet. A copy could be kept online by emailing it to herself. Likewise, business travelers could

---

[6] Again, the flexibility of such a system typically depends on the specification language used, as discussed in Section 3.3.

leave a copy with their secretaries back at the office, who could then fax them the transaction token upon demand.

Advantages Over Existing Travelers Cheques and money wiring

Travelers cheques are a stored payment medium, and not in any way a form of credit. In contrast with Merx, travelers Cheques have the following drawbacks:

- They cannot be photocopied, transmitted by fax or email.
- They must be paid up-front, therefore making the customer lost the interests.
- Travelers cheques are often used by customers in emergencies. However, due to the requirement that the customer purchase travelers cheques before they are used, it may be reasonable for someone to go into unforeseen debt, due to the circumstances of the situation.
- If lost, the issuing authority must be contacted to get them canceled and have new ones issued, therefore introducing undesirable delays.

As for the advantages over wiring money

- Banks typically charge a fairly significant commission or fee for a wire transfer.
- The two banks, at the sender's and recipient's locations, must be open for the money wiring to occur.
- Wiring money also requires the co-operation of someone on the other end of the transaction, which in emergency situations in foreign countries, can be rather difficult.

6 Conclusion

In this paper we present a secure and privacy preserving payment delegation system, Merx, for end-users with mobile devices not necessarily connected to the Internet. It allows users to delegate a third party that will purchase a specific list of items from a merchant, keeping the user's ID secret from the merchant, and the list of items secret from the bank, while securing the transactions from any fraudulent acts. The same mechanisms can be used to delegate money withdrawal from ATMs, for controlling children's expenses, or employees' expenses during business trips. When the user delegates himself for the transaction, the mechanism works as a secure travelers cheques solution. The user is required to use a computing device, which can be a shared one. The transactions can be performed using SMS, Bluetooth/IR, camera phones, or even using a pen and a paper. Finally, we evaluate the performance of our system at thwarting different levels of attack models, and its capacity and communication overhead. Merx can be gradually deployed since it can be used over existing payment network infrastructures.

References

1. The Near Field Communication (NFC) Forum (2007), http://www.nfc-forum.org
2. Singh, S., Cabraal, A., Demosthenous, C., Astbrink, G., Furlong, M.: Password sharing: implications for security design based on social practice. In: CHI 2007: Proceedings of the SIGCHI conference on Human factors in computing systems (2007)
3. Peirce, M.: Payment mechanisms designed for the Internet (2001), http://ntrg.cs.tcd.ie/mepeirce/Project/oninternet.html
4. Bellare, M., Garay, J., Hauser, R., Herzberg, A., Krawczyk, H., Steine, M., Tsudik, G., Waidner, M.: iKP – A family of secure electronic payment protocols. In: First USENIX Workshop on Electronic Commerce (1995)
5. Anderson, R.J., Manifavas, C., Sutherland, C.: Netcard - a practical electronic-cash system. In: Proceedings of the International Workshop on Security Protocols (1997)
6. Gabber, E., Silberschatz, A.: Agora: a minimal distributed protocol for electronic commerce. In: WOEC 1996: Proceedings of the 2nd conference on Proceedings of the Second USENIX Workshop on Electronic Commerce (1996)
7. Sirbu, M., Tygar, J.D.: Netbill: An internet commerce system optimized for network delivered services. In: COMPCON 1995: Proceedings of the 40th IEEE Computer Society International Conference (1995)
8. Rivest, R.L., Shamir, A.: Payword and micromint: Two simple micropayment schemes. In: Security Protocols Workshop (1996)
9. Glassman, S., Manasse, M., Abadi, M., Gauthier, P., Sobalvarro, P.: The millicent protocol for inexpensive electronic commerce. In: Proc. of the Fourth Internation World Wide Web Conference (WWW) (1995)
10. Herzberg, A., Yochai, H.: Mini-Pay: Charging per Click on the Web. In: Proc. of the Sixth World Wide Web Conference (WWW) (1997)
11. Paulson, L.C.: Verifying the SET Protocol: Overview. In: FASec. (2002)
12. Patil, V., Shyamasundar, R.K.: e-coupons: An efficient, secure and delegable micropayment system. Information Systems Frontiers Journal (2005)
13. Patil, V., Shyamasundar, R.: An efficient, secure and delegable micro-payment system. In: Proc. of IEEE International Conference on e-Technoloty, e-Commerce and e-Service (EEE) (2004)
14. Patil, V., Shyamasundar, R.: Towards a flexible access control mechanism for e-transactions. In: International Workshop on Electronic Government, and Commerce: Design, Modeling, Analysis and Security (EGCDMAS) (2004)
15. Patil, V., Shyamasundar, R.: ROADS: Role-based Authorization and Delegation System - Authentication, Authorization and Applications. In: Proc. of Int. Conf. on Computational & Experimental Engineering and Sciences (2003)
16. Ivatury, G., Pickens, M.: Mobile phone banking and low-income customers evidence from south africa. In: Consultative Group to Assist the Poor/The World Bank and United Nations Foundation (2006)
17. Bellare, M., Namprempre, C.: Authenticated encryption: Relations among notions and analysis of the generic composition paradigm. In: Okamoto, T. (ed.) ASIACRYPT 2000. LNCS, vol. 1976, pp. 531–545. Springer, Heidelberg (2000)
18. Okamoto, T. (ed.): ASIACRYPT 2000. LNCS, vol. 1976. Springer, Heidelberg (2000)
19. Blaze, M., Ioannidis, J., Keromytis, A.D.: Offline micropayments without trusted hardware. In: Syverson, P.F. (ed.) FC 2001. LNCS, vol. 2339, p. 21. Springer, Heidelberg (2002)

20. Jablon, D.P.: Strong password-only authenticated key exchange. SIGCOMM Comput. Commun. Rev. 26(5) (1996)
21. Bellovin, S.M., Merritt, M.: Encrypted key exchange: Password-based protocols secure against dictionary attacks. In: SP 1992: Proceedings of the 1992 IEEE Symposium on Security and Privacy (1992)
22. Pfitzmann, A., Hansen, M.: Anonymity, unlinkability, undetectability, unobservability, pseudonymity, and identity management - a consolidated proposal for terminology (2007)
23. Anderson, R.J.: Liability and computer security: Nine principles. In: Gollmann, D. (ed.) ESORICS 1994. LNCS, vol. 875. Springer, Heidelberg (1994)
24. International Organization for Standardization: ISO 8583: Financial transaction card originated messages – Interchange message specifications (2003)
25. http://www.nttdocomo.co.jp/english/service/osaifu/index.html
26. Noldus Information Technology: LineControl reduces waiting time in supermarkets: Labor analysts use The Observer to get a grip on work processes (2004), http://www.noldus.com/site/doc200401100
27. Sullivan, B.: Study: ID theft usually an inside job. MSNBC (2004), http://www.msnbc.msn.com/id/5015565

A Property-Dependent Agent Transfer Protocol

Eimear Gallery[1,*], Aarthi Nagarajan[2], and Vijay Varadharajan[3]

[1] Royal Holloway, University of London, Egham, Surrey, TW20 0EX, United Kingdom
e.m.gallery@rhul.ac.uk
[2] Macquarie University, NSW 2109, Australia
aarthi@ics.mq.edu.au
[3] Macquarie University, NSW 2109, Australia
vijay@ics.mq.edu.au

Abstract. This paper examines how a secure agent transfer protocol based upon TCG-defined mechanisms can be improved using property-based platform state information. In doing so, we demonstrate a practical implementation of property-based platform attestation using an enhanced version of the component property certificates defined in [16]. To illustrate our solution we provide examples of properties and component property certificates given a mobile aglet that is destined to execute on a group of devices, where the mobile aglet originator wishes to protect the confidentiality of the aglet code.

1 Introduction

A mobile agent, which is comprised of code, data and execution state, is defined as "an autonomous, reactive, goal-oriented, adaptive, persistent, socially aware software entity, which can actively migrate from host to host" [27]. Mobile agents have long been heralded as an important software paradigm in tackling problems such as bandwidth shortages, unreliable network connections, pre-defined and rigid system architectures, and network latency [13,18], which persist in the mobile environment due to the physical characteristics/constraints of the connections [26]. If, however, these persistent, autonomous programs are permitted to roam freely in a mobile network, interacting with systems and other agents to fulfil their predefined goals, the risk of a mobile host with malicious intent damaging a mobile agent or a malicious agent damaging a mobile host becomes a very real danger. While the topic of host protection has been widely discussed, see for example [4,9,12,17,19,29,30,39,40], a relative dearth of information exists on mobile agent protection. Recent research [3] suggests that the deployment of trusted computing technology in a mobile agent setting can solve many security issues intrinsic to mobile agent protection. However, the use of binary platform state information has proved to be problematic. In this paper we examine how a secure agent transfer protocol which leverages trusted computing functionality can be enhanced using property-based platform state information in order

---

* Research was sponsored by the Open Trusted Computing project of the European Commissions Framework 6 Programme.

L. Chen, C.J. Mitchell, and A. Martin (Eds.): Trust 2009, LNCS 5471, pp. 240–263, 2009.
© Springer-Verlag Berlin Heidelberg 2009

to provide mobile agent protection. In doing so, we extend and demonstrate a practical use of component property certificates, as defined in [16].

Sections 2, 3 and 4 review the necessary background material. In section 2 trusted computing concepts are explored. Section 3 highlights prior art relating to trusted computing and agent protection. In section 4 the concept of property-based attestation is introduced. The remainder of the paper describes a property-dependent agent transfer protocol. Section 5 identifies the security requirements that the protocol should satisfy and section 6 defines a key migration-based agent transfer protocol currently supported by the Trusted Computing Group (TCG) specification set. Following a discussion of why a TCG mechanism based protocol is not sufficient in this particular scenario, the assumptions upon which our protocol is based are outlined in section 7. Section 8 develops the concept of property-based state information and property certificates (with examples pertaining to the aglet environment). In section 9 a secure agent transfer protocol which leverages property-based platform state information is defined and analysed. We conclude in section 10.

2   Trusted Computing Fundamentals

A Trusted Platform (TP) is one that will behave in a particular manner for a specific purpose. The TCG's Trusted Platform Module (TPM) specifications [34,35,36] are central to the implementation of a trusted computing platform. These specifications describe a microcontroller with cryptographic coprocessor capabilities that provides a platform with a number of special purpose registers for recording platform state information; a means of reporting this state to remote entities; secure volatile and non-volatile memory; random number generation; a SHA-1 hashing engine; and asymmetric key generation, encryption and digital signature capabilities. The current documentation from the TCG also encompasses a vast set of specifications ranging from those relating to trusted personal computers [32], server systems [31], and to specifications for trusted networking [33]. The TCG Mobile Phone Working Group (MPWG) has recently published the TCG Mobile Trusted Module (MTM) specification [37,38] (namely, a TPM designed for a handheld mobile device) which enables the development of a Trusted Mobile Platform (TMP).

Trusted computing, as currently defined by the TCG, is built upon five fundamental concepts: *integrity measurement, authenticated boot, secure boot, platform attestation,* and *protected storage.*

- An integrity measurement is defined in [23] as the cryptographic digest or hash of a platform component (i.e., a piece of software executing on the platform).
- During an authenticated boot, a pre-defined set of platform components is reliably measured and the resulting integrity measurements condensed and reliably stored to form a set of platform integrity metrics.
- During a secure boot, a pre-defined set of platform components is reliably measured, the resulting measurements verified against their expected values,

and stored as above. A secure boot mechanism is required in a TMP, but is not mandated in other implementations.

- Platform attestation enables a T(M)P to reliably report information about its current state (namely, the integrity metrics reflecting (all or part of) the platform's software environment).
- Using its protected storage functionality a TPM/MTM can generate an unlimited number of asymmetric key pairs. For each of these pairs, private key use and mobility can be constrained. The notions of *binding*, the process of encrypting data so that only a particular TPM/MTM can decrypt it, and *sealing*, the process of encrypting data so that only a particular TPM/MTM can decrypt it when the TPM/MTM's host platform is in a particular state, are also of fundamental importance to trusted computing.

For a platform to be considered trusted, it must first obtain the following core credentials from an endorsement Certification Authority (CA), a platform CA, and one or more conformance CAs, respectively.

An endorsement credential: Each TPM is, and each MTM may be, associated with a unique asymmetric encryption key pair called an *Endorsement Key* (EK) pair. An endorsement credential binds the public component of this key pair to a TPM/MTM description and vouches that a TPM/MTM is genuine. The endorsement CA is typically the TPM/MTM manufacturer, with the binding taking the form of a digital signature created using a signing key of the manufacturer.

A platform credential: A platform credential asserts that a TPM/MTM has been correctly incorporated into a design conforming to the TCG specifications. The platform CA is typically the platform manufacturer. In order to create a platform credential, the platform CA must examine the endorsement credential, the conformance credentials relevant to the trusted platform, and the platform to be certified.

One or more conformance credentials: Conformance credentials vouch that a particular type of TPM/MTM and associated components (such as a RTM and the connection of the RTM and TPM to a motherboard) conform to the TCG specifications. Conformance CAs must be entities with sufficient credibility to evaluate platforms containing TPMs/MTMs, and are typically conformance testing facilities.

In order to address privacy concerns resulting from routine use of an EK, the TCG introduced the ability for a TPM/MTM to generate and use an arbitrary number of pseudonyms, in the form of *Attestation Identity Key* (AIK) pairs. In order for a relying party to have assurance that an AIK represents a trusted platform, a platform must obtain an AIK certificate from a mutually trusted third party. Two approaches to AIK certification have been proposed by the TCG. In the first approach, a trusted third party, referred to as a *Privacy-Certification Authority* (P-CA), verifies a trusted platform's core credential set and provides assurance that an AIK is bound to a genuine trusted platform in the form of an *AIK credential*. However, this approach has attracted a certain amount of criticism, as a P-CA is capable of linking all the AIK credentials it issues to a specific platform via the EK, putting the P-CA in a position where it is able to defeat the anonymity protection provided by the use of AIKs. The second approach, Direct Anonymous Attestation (DAA), was introduced to counteract this criticism. DAA requires a *DAA CA*, which can produce an anonymous *DAA credential* for a trusted platform, which in turn can be used by the platform to sign AIK credentials. Using this approach, trusted platforms can generate and use AIKs which cannot be easily linked to a particular EK by any third party. As privacy is not always of concern in a trusted mobile platform an MTM may be only be provisioned with a single certified AIK pair which attests that it is indeed genuine and is integrated into a trusted mobile platform.

The specification set produced by the TCG, however, is by no means the only work on trusted computing. Trusted computing also encompasses new processor designs [1,7,11] as well as Operating System (OS) support [22,23] which facilitate *software isolation*, i.e. the unhindered execution of software. For the interested reader, introductory texts on trusted computing include [2,15].

3   Trusted Computing and Mobile Agent Security

The use of trusted hardware as a method of protecting mobile agents can be traced back to Wilhelm, Staamann and Butty [41] who define a Trusted Processing Environment (TPE) to consist of a Computer Processing Unit (CPU), random access memory, read only memory, and non-volatile storage, all of which executes in a virtual machine. An agent executes within this isolated TPE, where it remains protected from observation by the host OS.

The use of trusted computing in agent systems has been proposed in [6,20,21,25]. [6,20,21] describe how non-mobile agents can be used in the preservation of user privacy. Recently, a trusted computing enhanced mobile agent platform called SMASH was proposed, [25]. In this system trusted computing is deployed to form a middleware-based instantiation of some aspects of Wilhelm, Staamann and Butty's proposal [41].

Most recently, in [3] Balfe and Gallery examined how trusted computing functionality could be used to protect sensitive agent information (be it code, data or state information) by demonstrating how an agent originator can extend their control over environments in which their agent will subsequently execute. In each approach described in [3], access to an agent is made provisional on the host platform's PCRs containing a particular set of binary integrity metrics, which is proved to be problematic. For example, an agent platform may leave itself open to attack from an incoming agent if its exact configuration (including all system vulnerabilities) is revealed. Privacy issues are also associated with such revelations. In conjunction with this, since a software component's binary changes every time a patch or update is applied, and as a mobile agent may potentially make numerous hops, it becomes next to impossible for an agent originator to choose a unique set of platform integrity metrics which reflect a platform state that meets his/her requirements and which all destination hosts satisfy, given updates, patches and the multiplicity of agent platform configurations/installations.

4   Property-Based Attestation

As an alternative to traditional binary integrity metric-based mechanisms, as described in section 2, the concept of property-based attestation and sealing has been introduced [10,24,28,42]. Using this approach, a platform's state is defined in terms of its security-related properties rather than a set of integrity metrics. In this way a platform's exact implementation details can be hidden, as can its vulnerabilities. In conjunction with this, properties of components do not change as often as software component binary integrity measurement values, thereby alleviating problems relating to patches and updates. Properties are also easier to understand, which can be helpful when writing meaningful policies. Three fundamental approaches to property-based attestation and sealing have been explored: delegation-based, the use of code control, and code analysis/property derivation [5].

Papers such as [24,28,42] describe a delegation-based approach, where a challenger platform or attestor is required to prove that a trusted third party has certified properties of its software state. The proof takes the form of property certificates, i.e. signed statements which describe the security properties of software components. Nagarajan, Varadharajan and Hitchens [16] refine this notion, and discuss certificates which describe course-grained platform properties, fine-grained properties of individual components, and mid-level properties of groups of components.

The property derivation approach of Halder, Chandra and Franz in [10] uses a language-based Trusted Virtual Machine (TVM) in order to facilitate property-based attestation. A TVM (such as the Java Virtual Machine) derives various properties of applications running within it on behalf of a remote party. For example, code analysis may be completed on the code by the TVM. In this scheme, software up to and including the TVM may be verified using binary attestation.

The TVM described above also employs code control/policy enforcement, whereby the code is under the control of the TVM, which monitors its execution. This approach is also adopted in [14], where SELinux and its associated policies are attested to, and the policies are enforced by the operating system.

5   Security Requirements

In order to provide comprehensive mobile agent protection, and so that a wide range of agent applications can be supported, the following requirements must be fulfilled by the property-dependent agent transfer protocol.

1. Destination host platform trust verification, so that the status of an agent host platform as a genuine TP and its security-properties can be verified.

2. Confidentiality of the agent code, data and state information in transit between and in storage on host platforms, so that unauthorised reading can be prevented.
3. Integrity protection of the agent code, data and state information in transit between and in storage on host platforms, so that any unauthorised alteration can be prevented, be it malicious or accidental.
4. Confidentiality and integrity protection of the agent code, data and state information during execution.
5. Availability of the required resources and services to an agent during execution.

6   A TCG Mechanism-Based Agent Transfer Protocol

The mobile agent architecture model upon which our protocol is based involves three parties: an agent originator platform (A_O); an agent host platform (A_H); and a trusted third party property certifier (TTP). A_O is the trusted (mobile) agent platform from which an agent (A) originates, whereas A_H represents the trusted (mobile) agent platform upon which incoming agents execute. Each trusted (mobile) agent platform is supported by a TCG compliant TPM or MTM (in the protocol description a TPM or MTM will be denoted by TM). In this model an agent originator does not need to have a long term relationship with the host platforms upon which its agent executes.

As shown in [3,8] there are a number of ways by which standard TCG functionality may be used to meet security requirements 1 — 5, as listed in section 5. All methods, however, utilise facets of the TCG protected storage functionality,

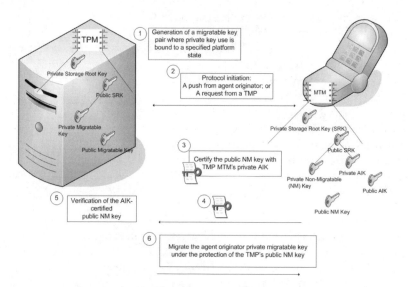

Fig. 1. TCG migration — Key exchange phase

as described in section 2. For this particular scenario involving multi-hop mobile agents, an approach founded upon TCG key migration is most appropriate. This approach essentially involves a key distribution phase and an agent transfer phase.

Figure 1 illustrates the key distribution phase of an approach based on TCG key migration. In this case each agent host possesses an AIK pair (which identifies it as a genuine TP). Each agent host platform's TM has also been used to generate a non-migratable key pair and to certify (sign) the public key from this pair using a private AIK. The agent originator generates a migratable key pair using his/her TM where private key use is bound to a specified host platform state. The public key from this key pair is used to protect the outgoing mobile agent. This key pair needs to be 'migrated' to all trusted (mobile) agent platforms which require agent access.

Prior to key pair migration a trusted (mobile) agent platform must forward its AIK-certified non-migratable public key to the agent originator for verification. Once this has been completed, and the agent originator has been convinced that he/she is communicating with a genuine TP, the agent originator key pair can be migrated under the protection of the public non-migratable trusted (mobile) agent platform TM public key. The key distribution phase described above may be completed while the agent is in transit or prior to its distribution. Once the key distribution phase has been completed, the mobile agent can be protected with the agent originator's public migratable key and distributed as shown in figure 2.

Problems, however, surround the use of TCG-defined platform state information (namely the PCR values) to restrict trusted (mobile) agent platform access to incoming executables. A mobile agent is designed to hop from host to

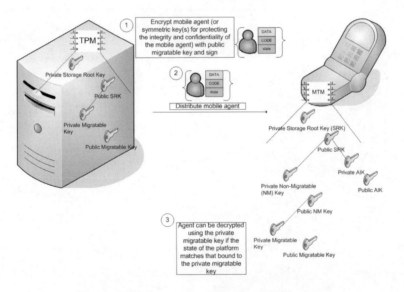

Fig. 2. TCG migration — Agent transfer phase

host. Given the huge number of possible platform configurations, and given the abundance of updates and patches, it is difficult if not impossible for an agent originator to choose one platform state to which the agent originator migratable private key (and therefore agent access) is bound. In order to overcome these problems we propose a property-based secure agent transfer protocol.

7 System Assumptions

We now examine how the secure agent transfer protocol based upon the TCG-defined mechanism described in the previous section can be improved using property-based platform state information. In doing so, we demonstrate a practical use case for property-based platform attestation using an enhanced version of the component property certificates defined in [16]. To illustrate our use case we provide examples of properties and component property certificates given a mobile aglet that is destined to execute on a group of devices, where the mobile aglet originator wishes to protect the confidentiality of the aglet code. The following pre-conditions need to be satisfied for use of the protocol described later in this paper.

1. It is assumed, for the purposes of illustration, that the agent originator and host platforms support an aglet system architecture. An aglet is a mobile Java agent that supports the concepts of autonomous execution and dynamic routing on its itinerary [13]. An aglet system architecture is comprised of an aglet runtime layer and a communication layer. The main elements in an aglet runtime layer's core framework include a *context*, i.e. the runtime environment in which an aglet executes, and a *security manager*. A *security manager* protects both the host and aglets from malicious entities. The security manager uses aglet permissions, message permissions, and a policy database, in which security policies for aglet contexts are stored. Privileges may be defined through the association of one of the following resource types with a set of permissions: local file system; network sockets; local windows; Java properties; system resources such as memory and CPUs; security information; contexts; aglets; and messages.

    Aglets leverage this runtime environment. An aglet originator may also define a set of aglet preferences for each aglet generated. The following methods can be restricted by the originator of an aglet: clone; deactivate; dispatch; retract; dispose; get AgentClassName/AgletContext/CodeBase/Identifier/ Itinerary/Message Manager/Property/Property Keys/Text; send Message; set Itinerary/Property/Text; subscribe/unsubscribe (all) messages [13]. Each aglet is represented by a *proxy*, which acts as a shield object that protects the aglet from malicious entities. The aglet proxy provides a common way of accessing the aglet behind it. When invoked, the proxy object consults a security manager, which in turn uses context and aglet policies to determine whether the caller is permitted to perform the method.
2. It is assumed that both the aglet originator platform and the aglet host platform are Trusted Aglet Platforms (TAPs) or indeed Trusted Mobile Aglet

Platforms (TMAPs). Therefore, a fundamental component in both the aglet originator platform and the aglet host platform is a TPM or, in the case of a TMAP, an MTM. One or more of these tamper evident modules, TM, is assumed to be bound either physically or cryptographically to each aglet originator and aglet host platform.

3. The aglet originator platform and the aglet host platform enable software isolation through the deployment of mechanisms described in section 2.

4. Both the aglet originator platform and the aglet host platform also incorporate a trusted computing extension which is capable of determining the properties of a particular system configuration given a set of property certificates and a list of entities trusted to issue property certificates, and of deciding whether a particular system configuration provides a specific property.

5. As a TMAP has more than one stakeholder, for example, the device manufacturer, network operator and potentially numerous service providers, all TMAPs contain a set of engines, namely constructs that can "manipulate data, provide evidence that they can be trusted to report the current state of the engine, and provide evidence about the current state of the engine" [38]. Upon start-up and reset of the TMAP device manufacturer engine, the software state of the engine is measured, verified and stored to the appropriate MTM PCRs (i.e. securely booted).

6. Upon the start-up and reset of the remaining TMAP engines, the software state of each is measured and stored to the appropriate MTM PCRs.

7. In the case of a TAP it is assumed upon platform start-up and reset that the software state of the platform is measured and stored to the TPM PCRs.

8. Each TAP or TMAP engine has at least one AIK pair.

9. The public signature verification key from the pair referred to in point 8 is certified by a P-CA trusted by both the agent originator and agent hosts.

10. The initial platform from which the mobile aglet originates, A_O, is considered trustworthy.

11. The agent originator platform possesses a signature key pair.

12. The public signature verification key from the pair referred to in point 11 is certified by a certification authority trusted by both the agent originator and agent hosts.

13. Every aglet host platform can acquire a set of software component property certificates to which the platform conforms from a trusted third party property certifier.

8   Required Properties

As described in [16], properties of computing platforms can be expressed using various levels of granularity. For the purpose of this paper we extend the concept of more granular component property certificates proposed in [16] for use in the delegation-based models described in [24,28]. Figure 3 illustrates a property granularity pyramid for use in defining properties of trusted platforms.

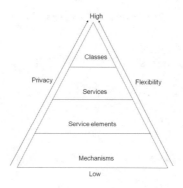

Fig. 3. Property granularity pyramid

At the top of the pyramid, properties are defined at a high level. Here, properties express an overall purpose or function. Properties at the lowest level of the pyramid are fine-grained. More generally, as we descend from the top of the pyramid, properties are expressed with an increasing focus on the implementation details. The pyramid is comprised of the following four levels (numbered 1–4).

- On top of the hierarchy are *classes*. A class is defined as a common intent regarding the services that belong to the class.
- A *service* addresses a class of security requirement.
- Services are provided using one or more *service elements*.
- A *mechanism* is used to implement a service element in a system.

Level 1 and 2 properties do not reveal platform implementation details and provide more privacy for the attesting party. However, there is less flexibility for expressing fine-grained access control policies based on these properties. On the other hand, properties at the lower levels of the pyramid provide greater flexibility for expressing policies although they may compromise the privacy of the attesting party. In the context of an agent environment, upper level properties allow an agent originator to specify host platform requirements without restricting an agent host platform to a specific configuration. To illustrate our solution we provide examples of component properties in the context of a mobile aglet, destined to execute on a group of T(M)APs, whose code the aglet originator wishes to confidentiality protect during execution [13].

'Aglet code confidentiality' is a class of security service, as shown in figure 4, which may be broken down into three core services — 'aglet code confidentiality during transmission', 'aglet code confidentiality during storage' and 'aglet code confidentiality during execution'. Confidentiality of aglet code in transit and while in storage on a host platform are provided through asymmetric encryption deployed in the secure transfer protocol described in section 9. In order to ensure confidentiality of aglet code during execution, a host on which the aglet executes must possess certificates which indicate that it provides a particular service and/or incorporates service elements/mechanisms which provide this particular

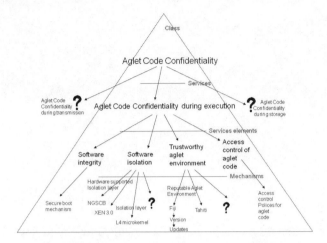

Fig. 4. Property granularity pyramid for aglet code confidentiality

```
grant
codeBase "http://some.host.com", owned by "RHUL" {
{
  // aglet protections
  protection com.ibm.aglet.security.AgletProtection
    "*", "dispatch,dispose,deactivate,activate,retract";
};
```

Fig. 5. Aglet code confidentiality

service. The service 'aglet code confidentiality during execution' may be provided by a number of service elements, namely, software integrity, software isolation, a trustworthy aglet environment and the implementation of aglet code access control policies, as shown in figure 4. A trustworthy aglet environment and a set of aglet access control policies ensure that the aglet is protected from other aglets executing in the context and indeed the host itself. Software isolation ensures that the aglet environment is executed in an isolated compartment such that malicious software executing in parallel cannot gain unauthorised access. Finally, software integrity implies that the software isolation mechanism can be verified as correct. A selection of mechanisms that provide these service elements include a secure boot mechanism, an up-to-date isolation layer, an up-to-date and reputable aglet environment and aglet access control policies (such as that shown in figure 5).

The sample policy statement, defined in figure 5, permits the host to dispatch, dispose, deactivate, activate and retract an aglet owned by 'RHUL' and originating from 'http://some.host.com' but does not at any stage permit aglet cloning. Properties describing a secure boot mechanism, an up-to-date isolation layer or an up-to-date and reputable aglet environment may include identification, version and update information for each of the components.

9   A Property-dependent Agent Transfer Protocol

In order to meet all requirements defined in section 5, and in order to provide an efficient solution given a multi-hop agent, we modify the protocol described in section 6 to incorporate the use of property-based platform state information. In this case, due to the modified T(M)P architecture assumed in section 7, we have TPM/MTM functionality as defined by the TCG and a TPM/MTM extension. This TM extension must enable the generation of a key pair where private key use is contingent on a platform fulfilling a specific set of properties. It must also support key use once a platform fulfills the set of properties to which private key use is bound. In order to do this the extension must be able to determine the properties of a particular system configuration given a set of PCR values, a set of property certificates and a list of entities trusted to issue property certificates.

9.1   Key Generation

In order to implement key generation a variant of the *TPM_CreateWrapKey* command functionality is required. Rather than specifying the state constraints to which private key use is bound in terms of PCR values (as is the case when defining the PCRInfo parameter of the keyInfo parameter input to the *TPM_CreateWrapKey* command) this new functionality inputs a new keyInfo parameter, for example propertyInfo, which allows state constraints to be specified as:

- the property/properties to which a platform must comply prior to private key use;
- the identity/identities of the third parties trusted to certify the properties specified; and
- the public key(s) of the root third party/parties trusted to certify the property/properties specified.

Private key use can be made dependent on a high level property, namely a level 2 property such as 'aglet code confidentiality during execution'. Alternatively, depending on the requirement of the agent originator, it may be dependent on a level 3 property such as 'software isolation' or indeed a level 4 property where a particular isolation layer in a set version with the required updates must be provided by a specified provider. An agent originator may even choose to 'mix and match' the properties required of an agent host platform.

9.2   Property Certificates

Each property certificate contains a validity period, component identifers, a set of properties to which the component complies, and an identifier for and a digital signature of a property certifier. When defining level 4 properties a property certificate will contain the integrity measurement (i.e. the hash) of a component in the 'Component Identifiers' field and the properties to which it complies in

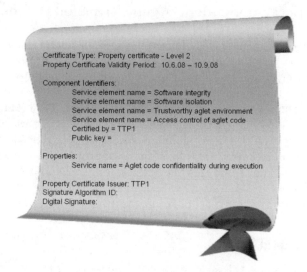

Fig. 6. Level 2 property certificate

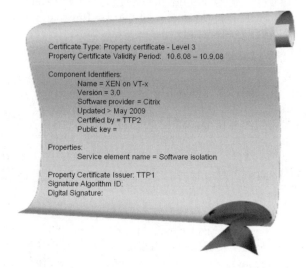

Fig. 7. Level 3 property certificate

the 'Properties' field. Given a level 2 or 3 property, however, the 'Component Identifiers' field may contain the integrity measurement of a component or a set of properties which identify a (set of) component(s). The 'Properties' field will list properties which the component(s) fulfill(s). Property certificates which define the level 2 property of 'aglet code confidentiality during execution', the level 3 property of 'software isolation', the level 4 properties of isolation layer 'name', 'version', 'software provider' and 'update status' may be defined as shown in figures 6, 7 and 8.

Fig. 8. Level 4 property certificate

Once the agent originator key pair has been communicated to each T(M)AP, the T(M)AP can decrypt and examine the properties to which private key use is bound and the root third parties trusted to certify the properties specified. Following this, the T(M)AP must acquire the required property certificates. This could involve a T(M)AP providing the specified TTP(s) with the required properties it must fulfill in return for all relevant property certificates.

If, for example, the key is bound to the level 4 property set $\{Name = XEN\ on\ VT - x,\ Version = 3.0,\ Software\ provider = Citrix,\ Updated > May\ 2009\ ||\ TTP2\}$ the agent host could request all certificates where the name is XEN on VT-x, the version is 3.0, the software provider is Citrix and the up-dated date is after May 2009 from TTP2, or, alternatively, it could send the measurement of its isolation layer in return for all certificates pertaining to this measurement. Once these certificates have been retrieved a chain can be con-structed from an integrity measurement representing a platform component to a root trusted third party-certified property/set of properties to which private key use is bound.

If, for example, the key is bound to the level 3 property set $\{Service\ element\ name = software\ isolation\ ||\ TTP1\}$ the agent host could initially request all certificates where the property field indicates that the service element name is software isolation from TTP1. Once it has received these it must examine the identifiers for components which fulfill the property 'software isolation', for example in the case of the Level 3 property certificate shown in figure 7, the 'Component Identifiers' are $\{Name = XEN\ on\ VT - x,\ Version = 3.0,\ Software\ provider = Citrix,\ Updated > May\ 2009\ ||\ TTP2\}$. It must then in turn request of TTP2 all certificates where the 'Properties' field in-dicates that the component's name is XEN on VT-x, the version is 3.0, the software provider is Citrix and the updated date is after May 2009. There is now sufficient information to build a chain representing a platform component to a root trusted third party-certified property/set of properties to which private key use is bound. Using this method provides two advantages in the mobile agent environment. Firstly, it adds a level of abstraction which allows a mobile agent originator to bind a key to a property which multiple platforms with different state configurations can fulfill. Secondly, it enables a mobile host platform to control the release of platform state information.

9.3   Property Mapping

Once the agent originator has generated and migrated an asymmetric key pair as described in sections 9.1 and 9.2, the agent originator can sign and encrypt any sensitive agent code, data, and state information (or indeed a symmetric key used to confidentiality and integrity protect an agent) using the agent originator public key, in the knowledge that this sensitive information can only be accessed by a destination host platform to which the agent originator key pair has been migrated and only when that platform fulfills the required security property/properties.

In order to use the private key the properties to which key use is bound must be compared to the properties which the host platform satisfies. A variant of the *TPM_Unbind* command functionality is required in this instance. Assuming we have a full set of TM PCRs, the corresponding stored measurement log (which names and lists the measurements of all components which have been reliably stored to the PCRs), and a set of property certificates, collected as described in the previous section, this command variant will result in the following actions.

- The {*Security properties, TTP ID, TTP public key*} sets to which private key use is bound are examined.
- The integrity of the stored measurement log is initially verified against the integrity metrics stored in the PCRs.
- Each integrity measurement is then compared against those held in all retrieved certificates.
- When a match is found between an integrity measurement and a level n property certificate, the properties of this component are compared against the component identifiers listed within the retrieved level $n - 1$ certificates.
- When a match is found, the public key of the TTP listed in the component identifiers field of the level $n - 1$ property certificate is used to verify the integrity of the level n property certificate.
- The property defined in the level $n - 1$ property certificate is then compared against the component identifers held in all retrieved level $n - 2$ property certificates.
- When a match is found the signature of the TTP who signed the level $n - 1$ property certificate is verified using a key belonging to the TTP identified in the level $n - 2$ certificate.

This process continues until a match is found between the security property from a {*Security properties, TTP ID, TTP public key*} set to which private key use is bound and one defined in a property certificate and the certificate can be verified using the public key associated with the TTP identified within the {*Security properties, TTP ID, TTP public key*} set. This process is repeated until all required properties have been fulfilled.

Suppose that the agent originator private key is bound to the level 3 property 'software isolation' and the identity and public key of the property certifier, TTP1. On receipt of the incoming aglet, the certificates shown in figure 7 and 8 are input into a T(M)AP trusted computing extension. The integrity of the stored measurement log is verified against the integrity metrics stored in the PCRs. The measurement of the platform's isolation layer is matched to the component identifiers held in the property certificate shown in figure 8. This measurement is mapped to a set of properties shown in figure 8 and these properties are in turn mapped to the service component property of 'software isolation' (to which private key use is bound) using the certificate shown in figure 7. The integrity of the level 4 property certificate is then verified using the public key of TTP2 listed in the level 3 certificate and the level 3 certificate is verified using the public key of TTP1 contained within the property set to which private key use is bound.

By design, once an aglet has executed, it is re-encrypted with the agent originator public key prior to its migration, or indeed re-protected in terms of confidentiality and integrity using its associated symmetric key(s) which is/are in turn protected using the agent originator public key. The protocol can be broken down into four phases: agent host key generation; agent originator key generation; key transfer; and mobile agent transfer.

9.4   Stage 1: Agent Host Key Generation

1. $A_H \rightarrow A_H\ TM$: *TPM_CreateWrapKey*. The *keyInfo* input parameter is used to request the generation of a non-migratable key.
2. $A_H\ TM$: Generates a non-migratable asymmetric key pair. A *TPM_Key* structure, which contains the public key P_{A_H} and the encrypted private key S_{A_H}, is output.
3. $A_H \rightarrow A_H\ TM$: *TPM_LoadKey2* — Request to load the *TPM_Key* generated in step 2.
4. $A_H\ TM$: Loads the *TPM_Key*.
5. $A_H\ TM \rightarrow A_H$: Outputs a handle to where the decrypted private key from the *TPM_Key* is loaded.
6. $A_H \rightarrow A_H\ TM$: *TPM_LoadKey2* — Request to load the *TPM_Key* structure, which contains the A_H attestation identity key pair as described in assumption 9.
7. $A_H\ TM$: Loads the *TPM_Key*.
8. $A_H\ TM \rightarrow A_H$: Outputs a handle to where the private AIK is loaded.
9. $A_H \rightarrow A_H\ TM$: *TPM_CertifyKey2*. The *keyHandle* and *certHandle* input parameters are used to specify the handles of the key to be certified (loaded in step 4) and the private attestation identity key to be used to certify the key (loaded in step 7).

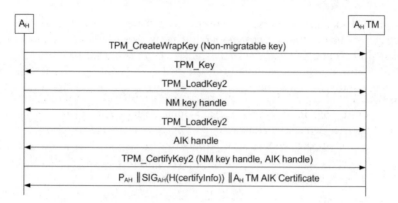

Fig. 9. Stage 1:Agent host key generation

10. $A_H\ TM$: Signs $H(certifyInfo)$ using the chosen private attestation identity key.

    The $certifyInfo$ structure describes the key-to-be-certified, including any authorisation data requirements, a digest of the public key-to-be-certified, 160 bits of external data, and a description of the platform configuration data required for the release and use of the certified key.

11. $A_H\ TM \rightarrow A_H : P_{A_H}\ ||\ SIG_{A_H}(H(certifyInfo))\ ||\ A_H\ TM\ AIK$
    $Certificate$

Following stage 1 of the protocol A_H is in possession of an AIK-certified non-migratable key pair, P_{A_H} and S_{A_H}. The protocol message flow is illustrated in figure 9.

9.5 Stage 2: Agent Originator Key Generation

1. A_O : Chooses the property/properties with which A_H must comply in order to gain access to the agent it wishes to protect, and the identities and public keys of the property certification authorities trusted to certify that a (set of) software component(s) provide(s) the property/properties specified, e.g. $\{Security\ properties,\ TTP\ ID,\ TTP\ public\ key\}$.

2. $A_O \rightarrow A_O\ TM : TPM\_CreateWrapKey$ variant. The $keyInfo$ input parameter is used to request the generation of a migratable key pair. The migration authorisation data for the new key is set to a value known only to A_O, so that the key pair can only be migrated by A_O. An agent host which has imported the key will not be able to migrate the key. In order to ensure that the private key from this key pair can only be used when the host platform conforms to a set of properties rather than a set of PCR values, the $pcrInfo$ parameter of $keyInfo$ must be changed. For example, a new $keyInfo$ input parameter called $propertyInfo$ could be defined to hold a parameter called $propertiesAtRelease$ which contains $\{Security\ properties,\ TTP\ ID,\ TTP\ public\ key\}$ sets.

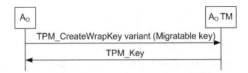

Fig. 10. Stage 2:Agent originator key generation

3. A_O TM : Generates an asymmetric migratable key pair, *TPM_Key*, which contains the public key, P_{A_O}, and the encrypted private key, S_{A_O}, where private key use is dependent on the host platform's conformance to a set of properties, and key pair migration is dependent on proof of knowledge of the migration authorisation data.

Following stage 2 A_O is in possession of a CA-certified signing key pair (as per assumptions 11 and 12) and a migratable key pair, P_{A_O} and S_{A_O}. The protocol message flow is illustrated in figure 9.

9.6   Stage 3: Agent Creation and Key Transfer

1. A_O : Creates a mobile agent, A.
2. A_O : Formulates the itinerary for A.
3. $A_O \rightarrow A_H$: Requests the certified public key generated in stage 1 for every A_H on A's itinerary.
4. $A_H \rightarrow A_O$: Transmits P_{A_H} $\|$ $SIG_{A_H}(H(certifyInfo))$ $\|$ A_H TM AIK *Certificate*.
5. A_O : Verifies A_H TM AIK *Certificate* for each A_H.
6. A_O : Verifies $SIG_{A_H}(H(certifyInfo))$ for each A_H using the public AIK of the A_H contained in its corresponding A_H TM AIK *Certificate*.
   Through verification of the AIK signature, $SIG_{A_H}(H(certifyInfo))$, the agent originator can verify whether or not the corresponding private key is stored within a genuine T(M)AP TM.
7. $A_O \rightarrow A_O$ TM : $TPM\_AuthorizeMigrationKey$.
   Using this command A_O can authorise each A_H public key under which the private key, S_{A_O}, will be migrated.
8. $A_O \rightarrow A_O$ TM : $TPM\_CreateMigrationBlob$.
   Using this command A_O indicates the key pair to be migrated and proves knowledge of the key's migration authorisation data.
9. A_O TM : Encrypts the migratable private key, S_{A_O}, with the A_H public key authorised in step 7, $E_{P_{A_H}}(S_{A_O})$.
10. A_O $TM \rightarrow A_O$: $E_{P_{A_H}}(S_{A_O})$.
11. $A_O \rightarrow A_H$: P_{A_O} $\|$ $E_{P_{A_H}}(S_{A_O})$.
12. $A_H \rightarrow A_H$ TM : $TPM\_ConvertMigrationBlob$.
    Using this command, $E_{P_{A_H}}(S_{A_O})$ is decrypted. Both S_{A_O} and P_{A_O} are then imported into the local A_H TM key hierarchy.
13. A_H : Examines {*Security properties, TTP ID, TTP public key*} sets to which private key use is bound.

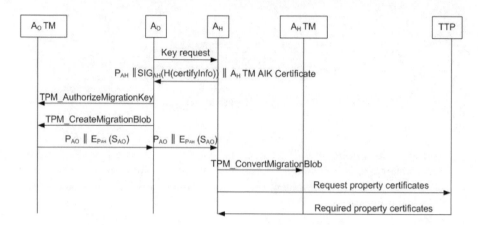

Fig. 11. Stage 3:Agent key transfer

14. $A_H \rightarrow TTP$: Requests the necessary property certificates from the specified third party property certifiers as described in section 9.3.
15. $TTP \rightarrow A_H$: The requested property certificates, for example those shown in figures 6, 7, 8.

Following stage 3, A_H is in possession of A_O's migratable key pair, where use of the private key S_{A_O} by A_H is dependent on the platform conforming to a set of A_O-defined security properties. The protocol message flow is illustrated in figure 11.

9.7   Stage 4: Mobile Agent Transfer

1. A_O : Signs A using its private signing key and encrypts the result using P_{A_O}, $E_{P_{A_O}}(A \parallel SIG_{A_O}(A))$.
   Alternatively, A_O may generate a symmetric key(s) in order to confidentiality and integrity-protect A and then sign and encrypt the symmetric key(s) as shown above.
2. $A_O \rightarrow A_H$: $E_{P_{A_O}}(A \parallel SIG_{A_O}(A))$.
3. $A_H \rightarrow A_H$ TM : $TPM\_LoadKey2$ — Request to load the private key, S_{A_O}, which has been migrated to each A_H in the agent's itinerary.
4. A_H TM : Loads the TPM_Key.
5. A_H $TM \rightarrow A_H$: Outputs a handle to where the private key, S_{A_O}, from the TPM_Key is loaded.
6. $A_H \rightarrow A_H$ TM : Variant of TPM_Unbind($E_{P_{A_O}}(A \parallel SIG_{A_O}(A))$). In order to use S_{A_O} the properties of A_H must conform to those to which S_{A_O} is bound.
7. A_H TM $Extension$: Examines the $\{Security\ properties, TTP\ ID,\ TTP\ public\ key\}$ sets to which S_{A_O} is bound.
8. $A_H \rightarrow TM$: $TPM\_PCRRead$
9. A_H $TM \rightarrow A_H$: $PCR\ Values$

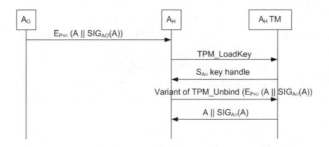

Fig. 12. Stage 4: Mobile agent transfer

10. A_H TM $Extension$: Verifies the stored measurement log entries (which name and contain the measurement of each platform component) against the PCR values to ensure their integrity.
11. A_H TM $Extension$: Attempts to build a chain from the properties to which S_{A_O} use is bound and the integrity measurements which reflect the platform's state as described in section 9.3.
12. A_H TM $Extension$:Verifies the property certificates within each chain.
13. A_H TM : Decrypts $E_{P_{A_O}}(A \parallel SIG_{A_O}(A))$ if all properties are fulfilled.
14. A_H : Verifies $SIG_{A_O}(A)$ using the public key certificate of A_O.
15. A_H : Executes A.
16. A_H : Re-encrypts the agent and the agent signature and forwards the agent.

The protocol message flow for stage 4 is illustrated in figure 12.

9.8   Security Remarks

In this protocol a mobile agent (or indeed a symmetric key used to confidentiality and integrity protect the agent) is signed and encrypted such that it can only be decrypted and executed upon a host platform which has retrieved the required private key and which satisfies certain security properties. In this way:

1. A platform is verified as trusted prior to the migration of the agent originator key pair through the validation of the A_H TM AIK $Certificate$ and $SIG_{A_H}(H(certifyInfo))$ as shown in steps 5 and 6 in stage 3. The security properties of a host's software environment are verified as trusted prior to key use (i.e. agent decryption).
2. The confidentiality of the aglet code, data and/or state information is protected in transit between and in storage on a host platform through the use of asymmetric encryption using the public agent originator key P_{A_O}.
   (a) *Secure encryption/decryption key pair generation:* The migratable key pair (which is used to protect the confidentiality of the agent) is generated securely within the TPM or MTM of the mobile agent originator.
   (b) *Secure encryption/decryption key pair transmission:* As stated above, the migratable key pair is initially generated within the agent originator TPM/MTM and must then be securely transmitted to each mobile host.

In order to do this, the agent originator takes an AIK-certified public non-migratable key from a mobile host, and verifies that it is from a non-migratable key pair and has indeed been generated within a TPM/MTM. The private key from the agent originator key pair is then encrypted using the public key from the mobile host's non-migratable key pair and migrated to the mobile host in conjunction with the corresponding public key.

(c) *Confidentiality-protected agent transmission, storage and access control:* The mobile agent is then encrypted using the agent originator public key. The agent remains encrypted while in transit to and in storage on the mobile host, until its use. Because the corresponding private key is known only to TPM/MTMs to which it has been migrated and can only be used on the platform when it fulfills particular properties, an attacker cannot compromise the confidentiality of the agent in transit or in storage.

3. The integrity of the aglet code, data and/or state information is protected in transit between and in storage on host platforms through the use of a digital signature $SIG_{A_O}(A)$.

   (a) *Secure signature/verification key pair generation:* The signature key pair is generated securely by the mobile agent originator. The TPM/MTM may be used for key pair generation and private key storage to enhance the security of its protection.

   (b) *Secure verification key transmission:* Is is assumed that the agent originator public signature verification key is certified by a trusted certification authority.

   (c) *Integrity-protected agent transmission and storage:* The mobile agent is digitally signed by the mobile agent originator. This signature can be verified by an agent host prior to agent execution to verify that the agent has not been accidentally or maliciously modified.

4. Binding the use of S_{A_O} to a set of properties as described in stage 2 steps 1–3 allows A_O to ensure A is protected as required when executing and also that the required services are available. Properties can be chosen such that the confidentiality and/or integrity of agent code, data and state is protected, for example.

10   Conclusions and Future Work

This paper explains how trusted computing technologies can be extended to protect mobile agents from attack. We outline the shortcomings of previous solutions [3] that focus on the use of binary integrity measurements to allow an agent originator to extend their control over subsequent environments in which their agents will execute. Instead we examine how a TCG mechanism-based secure agent transfer protocol can be enhanced to incorporate the use of property-based state information. We extend the work completed on property component certificates in [16] through the definition of a property granularity pyramid and provide examples of properties (and property certificates) that can be used in the context of a mobile agent environment. If this solution is to succeed, however, further work must be completed in the area of property derivation/definition and certification. We are currently refining the property granularity pyramid defined in this paper and investigating its application.

Acknowledgements

We wish to acknowledge the valuable contributions provided by Sigi Guergens, Chris Mitchell and the anonymous TRUST2009 referees, which have significantly improved the paper.

References

1. Alves, T., Felton, D.: TrustZone: Integrated Hardware and Software Security. White paper, ARM (July 2004)
2. Balacheff, B., Chen, L., Pearson, S., Plaquin, D., Proudler, G.: Trusted Computing Platforms: TCPA Technology in Context. Prentice Hall, Upper Saddle River (2003)
3. Balfe, S., Gallery, E.: Mobile Agents and the Deus Ex Machina. In: Proceedings of the 2007 IEEE International Symposium on Ubisafe Computing (UBISAFE 2007), May 21–23, pp. 486–492. IEEE Computer Society, Los Alamitos (2007)
4. Berkovits, S., Guttman, J.D., Swarup, V.: Authentication for Mobile Agents. In: Vigna, G. (ed.) Mobile Agents and Security. LNCS, vol. 1419, pp. 114–136. Springer, Heidelberg (1998)
5. Chen, L., Landerfermann, R., Rohe, H.L.M., Sadeghi, A.R., Stuble, C.: A Protocol for Property-Based Attestation. In: Proceedings of the 1st ACM Workshop on Scalable Trusted Computing, Fairfax, Virginia, USA, November 3, 2006, pp. 7–16. ACM, New York (2006)
6. Crane, S.: Privacy Preserving Trust Agents. Technical Report HPL-2004-197, HP Labs, Bristol, UK (November 11, 2004)
7. Ekberg, J.-E., Asokan, N., Kostiainen, K., Eronen, P.: OnBoard Credentials Platform Design and Implementation. Technical Report NRC-TR-2008-001, Nokia Research Center, Helsinki, Finland (January 2008)
8. Gallery, E., Tomlinson, A.: Secure Delivery of Conditional Access Applications to Mobile Receivers. In: Mitchell, C.J. (ed.) Trusted Computing. IEE Professional Applications of Computing Series 6, ch. 7, pp. 195–238. The Institute of Electrical Engineers (IEE), London (2005)
9. Gray, R.S., Kotz, D., Cybenko, G., Rus, D.: D'Agents: Security in Multiple-Language, Mobile Agent System. In: Vigna, G. (ed.) Mobile Agents and Security. LNCS, vol. 1419, pp. 154–187. Springer, Heidelberg (1998)
10. Haldar, V., Chandra, D., Franz, M.: Semantic Remote Attestation – A Virtual Machine Directed Approach to Trusted Computing. In: Proceedings of the 3rd Conference on Virtual Machine Research And Technology Symposium, San Jose, California, USA, May 6–7, 2004, pp. 29–41. USENIX Association, Berkeley (2004)
11. Intel. LaGrande Technology Architectural Overview. Technical Report 252491-001, Intel Corporation (September 2003)

12. Johnston, W., Mudumbai, S., Thompson, M.: Authorization and Attribute Certificates for Widely Distributed Access Control. In: Proceedings of the IEEE 7th International Workshops on Enabling Technologies: Infrastructure for Collaborative Enterprises (WETICE 1998), Palo Alto, California, USA, June 17–19, 1998, pp. 340–345. IEEE Computer Society, Washington (1998)
13. Lange, D.B., Oshima, M.: Programming and Deploying Java Mobile Agents with Aglets. Addison Wesley Longman, Inc., Reading (1998)
14. Marchesini, J., Smith, S., Wild, O., Stabiner, J., Barsamian, A.: Open-source Applications of TCPA Hardware. In: ACSAC 2004, pp. 294–303. IEEE Computer Society, Washington (2004)
15. Mitchell, C. (ed.): Trusted Computing. IEE Professional Applications of Computing Series 6. The Institute of Electrical Engineers (IEE), London (2005)
16. Nagarajan, A., Varadharajan, V., Hitchens, M.: Trust Management for Trusted Computing Platforms in Web Services. In: Proceedings of the 2nd ACM Workshop on Scalable Trusted Computing, Alexandria, Virginia, USA, November 2, 2007, pp. 58–62. ACM, New York (2007)
17. Necula, G.C., Lee, P.: Safe, Untrusted Agents Using Proof-Carrying Code. In: Vigna, G. (ed.) Mobile Agents and Security. LNCS, vol. 1419, pp. 61–91. Springer, Heidelberg (1998)
18. Nwana, H.S., Ndumu, D.T.: An Introduction to Agent Technology. In: Nwana, H.S., Azarmi, N. (eds.) Software Agents and Soft Computing: Towards Enhancing Machine Intelligence. LNCS, vol. 1198, pp. 3–26. Springer, Heidelberg (1997)
19. Ousterhout, J.K., Levy, J.Y., Welch, B.B.: The Safe-Tcl Security Model. In: Vigna, G. (ed.) Mobile Agents and Security. LNCS, vol. 1419, pp. 217–235. Springer, Heidelberg (1998)
20. Pearson, S.: Trusted Agents that Enhance User Privacy by Self-Profiling. Technical Report HPL-2002-196, HP Labs, Bristol, UK (July 15, 2002)
21. Pearson, S.: How Trusted Computers can Enhance for Privacy Preserving Mobile Applications. In: Proceedings of the 1st International IEEE WoWMoM Workshop on Trust, Security and Privacy for Ubiquitous Computing (WOWMOM 2005), Taormina, Sicily, Italy, June 13–16, 2005, pp. 609–613. IEEE Computer Society, Washington (2005)
22. Peinado, M., Chen, Y., England, P., Manferdelli, J.L.: NGSCB: A Trusted Open System. In: Wang, H., Pieprzyk, J., Varadharajan, V. (eds.) ACISP 2004. LNCS, vol. 3108, pp. 86–97. Springer, Heidelberg (2004)
23. Peinado, M., England, P., Chen, Y.: An Overview of NGSCB. In: Mitchell, C.J. (ed.) Trusted Computing. IEE Professional Applications of Computing Series 6, ch. 7, pp. 115–141. The Institute of Electrical Engineers (IEE), London.(2005)
24. Poritz, J., Schunter, M., van Herreweghen, E., Waidner, M.: Property Attestation – Scalable and Privacy-friendly Security Assessment for Peer Computers. Research Report RZ 3548, IBM Research GmbH, Zurich Research Laboratory, Switzerland (October 2004)
25. Pridgen, A., Julien, C.: A Secure Modular Mobile Agent System. In: Proceedings of the 2006 International Workshop on Software Engineering for Large-Scale Multi-Agent Systems (SELMAS 2006), Shanghai, China, May 22–23, pp. 67–74. ACM Press, New York (2006)
26. Reinicke, M., Strasser, M.: Decentralized Management of Persistent Bandwidth Provision for Mobile Devices in Cellular Radio Networks. In: Sprague, R.H. (ed.) Proceedings of the 37th Annual Hawaii International Conference on System Sciences (HICSS 2004), Big Island, Hawaii, January 5-8. IEEE Computer Society, Los Alamitos (2004)

27. Rothermel, K., Schwehm, M.: Mobile Agents. In: Kent, A., Williams, J.G. (eds.) Encyclopedia for Computer Science and Technology, vol. 40, pp. 155–176. M. Dekker Inc., New York (1999)
28. Sadeghi, A.R., Stuble, C.: Property-based Attestation for Computing Platforms: Caring about Properties, not Mechanisms. In: Proceedings of the 2004 Workshop on New Security Paradigms (NSPW 2004), Nova Scotia, Canada, September 20-23, pp. 67–77. ACM, New York (2004)
29. Sekar, R., Ranalrishnan, C.R., Ramakrishnan, I.V., Smolka, S.A.: Model Carrying Code (MCC): A New Paradigm for Mobile Code Security. In: Proceedings of the New Security Paradigms Workshop (NSPW 2001), Cloudcroft, New Mexico, USA, September 10–13, pp. 23–30. ACM Press, New York (2001)
30. Tardo, J., Valente, L.: Mobile Agent Security and Telescript. In: Proceedings of the 41st International IEEE Computer Society International Conference: Technologies for the Information Superhighway (COMPCON 1996), Santa Clara, California, USA, February 25–28, pp. 58–63. IEEE Computer Society Press, Los Alamitos (1996)
31. TCG. TCG Generic Server Specification. TCG specification Version 1.0 Revision 0.8, The Trusted Computing Group (TCG), Portland, Oregon, USA (March 2005)
32. TCG. TCG PC Client Specific Implementation Specification For Conventional BIOS. TCG specification Version 1.2 Final, The Trusted Computing Group (TCG), Portland, Oregon, USA (July 2005)
33. TCG. TCG Trusted Network Connect TNC Architecture for Interoperability. TCG specification Version 1.1 Revision 2, The Trusted Computing Group (TCG), Portland, Oregon, USA (May 2006)
34. TCG. TPM Main, Part 1: Design Principles. TCG Specification Version 1.2 Revision 94, The Trusted Computing Group (TCG), Portland, Oregon, USA (March 2006)
35. TCG. TPM Main, Part 2: TPM Data Structures. TCG Specification Version 1.2 Revision 94, The Trusted Computing Group (TCG), Portland, Oregon, USA (March 2006)
36. TCG. TPM Main, Part 3: Commands. TCG Specification Version 1.2 Revision 94, The Trusted Computing Group (TCG), Portland, Oregon, USA (March 2006)
37. TCG MPWG. The TCG Mobile Reference Architecture. TCG specification version 1 revision 1, The Trusted Computing Group (TCG), Portland, Oregon, USA (2007)
38. TCG MPWG. The TCG Mobile Trusted Module Specification. TCG specification version 1 revision 1, The Trusted Computing Group (TCG), Portland, Oregon, USA (September 2007)
39. Varadharajan, V.: Security Enhanced Mobile Agents. In: Proceedings of the 7th ACM Conference on Computer and Communications Security, Athens, Greece, November 1–4, pp. 200–209. ACM, New York (2000)
40. Vigna, G.: Cryptographic Traces for Mobile Agents. In: Vigna, G. (ed.) Mobile Agents and Security. LNCS, vol. 1419, pp. 137–153. Springer, Heidelberg (1998)
41. Wilhelm, U.G., Staamann, S., Butty, L.: Introducing Trusted Third Parties to the Mobile Agent Paradigm. In: Vitek, J., Jensen, C. (eds.) Secure Internet Programming. LNCS, vol. 1603, pp. 469–489. Springer, Heidelberg (1999)
42. Yoshihama, S., Ebringer, T., Nakamura, M., Munetoh, S., Maruyama, H.: WS-Attestation: Effecient and Fine-Grained Remote Attestation on Web Services. In: Proceedings of the IEEE International Conference on Web Services (ICWS 2005), Orlando, Florida, USA, July 11-15, pp. 743–750. IEEE Computer Society Press, Washington (2005)

Author Index

Printing: Mercedes-Druck, Berlin
Binding: Stein+Lehmann, Berlin